TYR

Myth—Culture—Tradition

TYR

Myth—Culture—Tradition

Edited by
Joshua Buckley, Collin Cleary,
and Michael Moynihan

1

Arcana Europa

TYR: Myth—Culture—Traditon
Volume 1, 2002
Second Printing: 2008
Arcana Europa Reprint Edition: 2019

Typeset by Michael Moynihan at the Dominion Press.

Contributors: Alain de Benoist, Stephen Edred Flowers, Aaron Garland, Joscelyn Godwin, Elizabeth Griffin, Annabel Lee, Nigel Pennick, Steve Pollington, Alby Stone, Þeedrich, William Wallace, and Markus Wolff.

Special thanks to Annabel Lee, Stephen O'Malley, Markus Wolff, Jim Banner, and Kevin Slaughter.

Note: The reader may notice occasional stylistic inconsistencies between articles, as we have retained conventional British spellings and punctuation at the request of some contributors. *The text of this third reprint edition has not been modified from the original, which first appeared seventeen years ago. Therefore, readers are strongly advised to contact the advertisers for updated information regarding products and services.*

©2002, 2008 Ultra Publishing. ©2019 Arcana Europa Media, LLC. All rights reserved. Copyrights for individual articles rest with the respective contributors. No part of this journal may be reproduced, transmitted, or utilized in any form or by any means without the express written permission of the publishers and/or authors, with the exception of brief quotations embodied in literary articles or reviews. To contact the publishers or authors, write to the address below.

ISSN: 1538-9413
ISBN (Æ Reprint Edition): 978-0-9997245-6-9

Arcana Europa
P.O. Box 6115
North Augusta, SC 29861

www.arcanaeuropamedia.com

Email: info@arcanaeuropamedia.com

Contents

Editorial Preface..7

The Idea of Integral Culture:
A Model for a Revolt Against the Modern World
by Stephen Edred Flowers..11

Knowing the Gods
by Collin Cleary..23

Priests, Warriors, and Cultivators:
An Interview with Georges Dumézil
by Alain de Benoist..41

From Lore-Giver to Law-Giver: The Tale of Woden
by Steve Pollington...51

Indo-European Trifunctional Elements
in Celtic Foundation Myths
by Alby Stone...59

Divine Traces in the *Nibelungenlied*,
or Whose Heart Beats in Hagen's Chest?
by Michael Moynihan..73

The Goddess Zisa
by Nigel Pennick...107

The Dark Side of the Mountain
by Annabel Lee...111

On the Spiritual Arts and Crafts
by Nigel Pennick...119

Julius Evola: A Philosopher for the Age of the Titans
by Joscelyn Godwin...127

Hermann Löns: An Introduction to His Life and Work
by Markus Wolff......143

The Easter Fire
by Hermann Löns......156

The Saxon Songwriter: An Interview with Fire + Ice's Ian Read
by Joshua Buckley......159

"Son of man, can these bones come to life?"
Review Essay: *The Prisoner*
by Collin Cleary......167

Reviews: Books......191

Reviews: Music......251

About the Editors......275

About the Contributors......276

The editors wish to dedicate this first volume of *TYR* to the Taylor family: Robert, Karen, Mary, Thor, and Randolph, whose spirited example has always been a source of strength.

> *O why are ye abiding till the sun is sunk in night*
> *And the forest trees are ruddy with the battle-kindled light?*
> *O rest not yet, ye Wolfings, lest void be your resting-place,*
> *And into lands that ye know not the Wolf must turn his face . . .*
>
> —William Morris, 1888

Editorial Preface

The dominant theme in most of the art and literature produced during the first half of the 20th century was alienation. Authors spoke of the "age of anxiety." They decried the materialist reign of "quantity over quality," the absence of any meaningful spiritual values, the breakdown in the relationship between the sexes, environmental devastation, the mechanization and over-specialization of urban life, and the imperialism of corporate mono-culture, with its vulgar "values" of progress and efficiency.

What has become of these critics of the "modern condition"? Many have died off, others have given up complaining and have decided to remain silent. Modernity may be the reign of Nietzsche's *Last Man*, but at least when men like Pound, Eliot, Lawrence, and Heidegger were alive the Last Man was made aware that something was wrong with him. His enjoyment of his material comforts was tempered by a nagging sense that something was missing from modern life. Today, the Last Man is arrogant and shameless in his materialism. He flaunts his shallowness and spiritual poverty. Should any doubts be raised about modern values, the Last Man quickly responds that values are "relative." If something can be good for us merely because we believe it to be, then we are saved the trouble of doing any serious thinking about our lives and our values.

Today, critics of modernity have been thoroughly marginalized. They are kooks and cranks. When it was discovered that a young American named John Walker was fighting for the Taliban, media pundits wondered aloud how anyone could possibly prefer life in Afghanistan to life in San Francisco. Anyone who could voluntarily turn his back on sport-utility vehicles, cellular phones, MTV, and Oprah must be crazy. When Ted Kaczynski's articulate and well-reasoned anti-modern *Unabomber Manifesto* came to light, it was greeted as further proof of his insanity.

But the anxiety and alienation continue, despite the state of denial in which most people exist. How else can we explain why, by the end of the last century, anti-depressants came to be the largest pharmaceutical growth industry? How else are we to explain the fortunes made every year by psychotherapists and "self-help" gurus? How else are we to explain the phenomenon of "school shootings," in which intelligent, alienated teenagers (more clear-sighted, in their own way, than their parents) have shown their contempt for the society offered them by departing it in a blaze of gunfire? Hungering after values, they found none—or were given the hall pass and sent off to the school psychologist.

Environmentalism is the only high-profile, "mainstream" contemporary school of thought which might plausibly be termed anti-modern. One strand within the environmental movement which has recently gained momentum has been bioregionalism. According to Earth First! founder Dave Foreman, the central tenet of bioregionalism is that human culture, politics, and economics should be based on organic regional ecosystems—what he calls "living in place." The advocates of bioregionalism insist that their approach is not anthropocentric, but it is obvious that the theory has profound implications for human society. For human beings to overcome the alienation and uprootedness of modern life, however, it will take more than just re-establishing a harmonious relationship with Spaceship Earth.

Enter neo-paganism. This movement, which has come to prominence since the 1960s, advocates a kind of *spiritual regionalism* as a complement to bioregionalism. In many respects, of course, the pagan "scene" has been a pawn to the worst excesses of modernism and post-modernism: subjectivism, relativism, and a confused syncretism that borrows from a hodge-podge of different traditions without ever committing itself to one. Nevertheless, the broad resurgence of interest in paganism is an encouraging development, and cause for (guarded) optimism.

Stephen Edred Flowers, one of the most informed and thoughtful writers on neo-pagan topics, has suggested that this budding romance with pre-Christian spirituality might more accurately be described as a longing for *integral culture*. (Flowers develops this concept elsewhere in this issue.) Briefly stated, an integral culture is one in which spirituality, culture, and politics form a seamless whole. The small, ethnically and culturally homogenous tribal societies that flourished before Christianity were societies in which every aspect of life was integrated into a holistic system. Modern tribal ("primitive") societies are also integral cultures. American Indians have long been at pains to explain why virtually any concession to the dominant Western culture, no matter how seemingly trivial, has had such devastating consequences for their people. To compromise one aspect of the tribal tradition—spiritual, cultural, or political—is to compromise the entire system.

Of course, our tradition is not the American Indian tradition, but the European tradition. We make no apologies for this. Like the bioregionalist, the proponent of European integral culture is interested in "living in place" in an organic, homogeneous human community, as well as in an organic, regional ecosystem.

Our ideals are simple:

1. *Resacralization of the world versus materialism.*

2. *Folk/traditional culture versus mass culture.*

3. *Natural social hierarchy (based, perhaps, on Dumézil's "three functions") versus an artificial hierarchy based on wealth.*

4. *The tribal community versus the nation-state.*

5. *Stewardship of the earth versus the "maximization of resources."*

6. *A harmonious relationship between men and women versus the "war between the sexes."*

7. *Handicrafts and artisanship versus industrial mass-production.*

Nevertheless, we are not revolutionaries or politicians. We do not vote or participate in the political process. We offer no panacea for the modern condition. Nor can we be certain that any "solution" is even possible.

Yet there are reasons not to despair.

Paradoxically, perhaps, one of the advantages of living in the modern period is the tremendous number of options available to us should we choose to follow an anti-modern "script" within our own lives. Although these freedoms are increasingly imperiled as the Machine strives to consolidate its power, they remain for those with the strength to take advantage of them. To some extent, one can inoculate oneself from the popular culture. It is still possible to live a life in accord with tradition. It is still possible to practice spiritual discipline, and to be an honorable human being—to be a whole man or woman in a world of automata. These may be the only truly revolutionary options left.

In the pages of *TYR* we will examine the European (or *Indo-European*) tradition and the different perspectives of those groups and individuals who have championed that tradition. We will articulate a critique of modernity informed by the idea of integral culture. And we will chart the emergence of the contemporary heathen "counter-culture" now taking shape in Europe and North America. Join us.

—The Editors, spring 2002.

The Idea of Integral Culture:
A Model for a Revolt Against the Modern World

Stephen Edred Flowers

I. Introduction

Our culture is sick. It has been undergoing a process of disintegration for a number of centuries now. Its various constituent parts have progressively been scattered and disconnected from their natural or organic moorings. Such disintegration can only be rectified, healed, as it were, by integration, or reintegration.

The word "culture" has somewhat irritated me over the years. People seem to use it in a vague and ambiguous way. When I began teaching world literature in translation at the University of Texas in the fall of 1984 I undertook a more detailed study of the term "culture," with the intention of using what I found in my lectures. What resulted was the discovery of the "culture grid." Culture is made up of a minimum of four different categories, each of which is essential to the whole idea of culture, and none of which can be ignored when trying to describe a culture in its entirety. These four categories are: ethnic culture, ethical culture, material culture, and linguistic culture. In most previous discussions of these cultural categories, the emphasis has been laid on the existence of the four categories, and the necessity of each to a description of the whole.

This emphasis was good as far as it went, but it was rather static. In fact, what occurs in dynamic cultures is that the categories of culture are all constantly interacting with one another. There is a constant ebb and flow and interweaving of the categories, each of which serves to reinforce the others.

Our first task is to identify the constituent parts of culture, i.e., of the complete map of human experience and action. Then there follows the imperative to develop each of the categories intensely and to the best of one's ability. Finally it becomes necessary to complete the circle by reintegrating the component parts into an organic and vital whole in which the individual will stand as a culturally authentic man. More importantly, the process of "completing the circle" serves to reinvigorate the culture itself.

This dynamic process is achieved by a conscious effort to integrate the cultural categories and thus reconstruct an integral culture. This must first be done on an individual basis before it can be transferred to a collective level. Cultural reintegration begins within.

At the conclusion of this article it will become apparent that if one is able to agree that the ideal culture is an integral one, and that individuals are really only truly free within the context of an integral culture, then a whole series of personal and collective imperatives follow. These imperatives generally run counter to the trends of modern life, which tends to disintegrate culture in favor of the apparent interests of the isolated individual. This individual, separated from his culture, then becomes an easy target for promoters of various transitory interests. These interests could involve a political notion, or a new consumer product, or any one of a million other things. The disintegrated, atomized individual, cut out of his organic cultural context is relatively more susceptible to these suggestions than someone firmly rooted in a set of objective and conscious cultural values. Real cultural values of this kind cannot, however, be manufactured artificially. They must grow from deep historical soil.

II. Culture

In order to develop more fully the idea of integral culture, a more global understanding of the categories of culture must be attained. The so-called culture grid appears in the illustration below. This grid shows the four cultural categories arranged in a way that suggests more meaning than the mere listing of them can convey. The two on the left side of the diagram are primarily material in nature, while the two on the right side are mainly symbolic. While the two in the top tier might be considered to be primary, the two in the bottom tier are secondary.

CULTURE

ETHNIC Corporal vehicle	ETHICAL Ideology: religious, political, economic, etc.
MATERIAL Manufactured objects	LINGUISTIC Language and symbolic codes

All categories of culture involve contact between two or more humans. *Ethnic culture* is rooted in the sexual connection between a man and a woman which leads to the production of children. The product of this union is the bodily vehicle for culture to manifest itself in the material world. Without this reproductive activity—the literal *incarnation* (embodiment) of culture—obviously no culture is possible. The body itself, in the form of DNA, is thought by many to encode certain cultural patterns, and it is also true that cultural data absorbed by the developing human (especially during the first few years of life) actually results in permanent physical changes in the brain. (See Brad Shore's *Culture in Mind*, Oxford, 1996.) The link that living individuals have with their ancestors is not only a symbolic one. It is also physical. The entirety of the bodies of our ancestors constitutes a sort of cultural hyper-body for us. *Ethnic culture* is embodied culture.

At the other end of an apparent spectrum is *ethical culture*. The ethos of a culture is its symbolism or ideology. This is the part of culture that most interests us, as we are usually most fascinated by the ideas of our own culture and others. This is the part of culture that contains structures, patterns, and myths (or meta-narratives) made up of symbolic ideas. The words "ethnic" and "ethical" are chosen here, although other terms might have been used, to demonstrate the archaic link between biology and ideas. To the ancient Greeks the *ethnos* or tribe was determined by the gods to whom one sacrificed, and hence from whom one got one's values. Greeks were those who sacrificed to the Greek gods, spoke Greek and perpetuated the Greek *ethnos* biologically. A similar pattern of belief can be detected in other Indo-European branches of the tradition.

Symbolic, or ethical, culture is entirely invisible and supersensible. We know about it through its manifestations in the other three branches of culture: ethnic, material, and linguistic.

The symbolic culture is most perfectly encoded in the *linguistic culture*. This amounts largely to the language code spoken and understood by the members of a given culture. But the linguistic code, its phonology, morphology, syntax, and semantics also constitute a complex semiotic code by which members of the culture understand the world and express themselves to other parts of the world. Without such communication between humans, and meta-communication between humans and other parts of the cosmos (e.g., gods and/or nature), humans would be impotent in the world.

Material culture is easily seen. It is made up of everything a culture produces, i.e., all of the physical objects made by members of that culture. This could be a flint arrowhead, or a skyscraper. These are the objects fashioned by the human hand after having been imagined in the human heart. In other words these objects are *artificial*, i.e., "made by craft of man." It is often the case that all we know of an archaic culture is summed up in the objects it left behind. But from these objects we can often reconstruct the culture's values. If modern culture were to be evaluated by its material culture alone, I am not sure what the archaeologists of the future would make of it. They would certainly find it titanic, but perhaps also sterile and empty.

One thing that should be obvious is that these four components of culture are not discreet and isolated categories. Rather they are four poles of manifestation which belong to a larger whole. Each category interacts with the other three in a lively discourse. Linguistic culture crosses the material in the form of writing, inscriptions, books, computer software, etc. Symbolic culture not only provides forms for the production of material objects (such as temples and sculptures) but also usually determines the nature of the physical reproduction of human bodies in the form of laws and customs surrounding marriage and child bearing and rearing. (The current general chaos and breakdown in these customs is just as much a statement on this topic as are the most traditional customs found in former times or in other cultures.) The four basic categories of culture intersect and influence each other, and no one of them can exist without the other three. Changes in one will inevitably lead to alterations in the other parts. Vitality in one will help invigorate the others, while weakness in one will just as naturally result in the spread of this weakness to the rest of the whole. In our current state of cultural fragmentation, this sense of the integrated nature of culture has been lost. The root cause of this fragmentation should also be apparent. One of the most effective ways in which to revolt against the modern world is to undertake the (re)integration of culture, to realize a personal and cultural *synthesis*—or "bringing together"—of the various categories of culture.

In order to undertake this revolt, one must begin with one's self. The synthesis of the cultural categories within should be a *harmonious one*. That is, although humans are in a practical sense free to "mix and match" cultural elements, only fools would seri-

ILLUSTRATION BY FIDUS (HUGO HÖPPENER, 1868–1948).

ously suppose that they themselves were wise enough to design such a synthesis before they were virtually finished products of culture and character. It would be like asking a child to design its life when it was eight years old! In such a case we would not wonder at why such a person would be very unhappy at twenty years of age. One's individual cultural synthesis theoretically exists *in potentia*. It is the work of the individual to realize this, to make it real, to actualize the potential.

This pre-existing cultural synthesis, to which we strive to return on a higher octave, can only have its roots in a time when an integrated whole was in evidence. This is why individuals interested in cultural authenticity so often yearn for pagan or archaic times. It is not so much a longing for "paganism" per se, as it is a longing for the *wholeness* and integral nature of the self and culture which is possible in such societies.

On a personal, individual, level it is the task of the practitioner of integral culture to discover and then to harmonize the contents of his body, brain (mind), tongue (language) and his deeds or daily actions. Each part of life takes its cue from another integral part of that multidimensional life. The body contains a code which bears the essential story of all of one's ancestors. One's cultural myths articulate these, and these myths are re-encoded in actual tales expressed in often archaic languages. These codes bear the blueprint for inner action which can lead the individual back to an integrated state of being. This is how they functioned in former times, and this is how they can function today. Merely reading and thinking about these patterns is usually not enough. Other techniques designed to imprint the codes on the conscious mind must be experienced. High levels of repeated, concentrated, ordered and intense thought must be experienced. This is not the place to enter into these techniques.

An essential part of the process of culturally re-integrating the personality involves conscious interaction with others belonging to that culture. Culture is, in the final analysis, always about inter-human *contact*. Isolated individual experience is a form of mysticism, but not a manifestation of integrated cultural activity. One must determine for oneself how one can best contribute to the task of cultural integration, or allow it to be determined by others. Some will provide strong bodies for the future, others will create institutions that will re-invigorate and carry culture along, others will teach the lore and languages of the culture, others will shape and craft the artistic and practical tools that bear the culture materially. Some noble souls will be able to contribute in more than one of these areas. But all of these realms are necessary; no one is really more important than the others. They must all be seen to work together as a whole.

It might be noted that all of the ideas of culture seem to be somehow rooted in the "past." In order to understand the idea of the "past," the idea of *history* itself must be examined.

III. A "History" of Ideas

Depending on how it is understood, the concept of "history" can either be irrelevant or essential to the idea of integral culture. If by history one means an objective string of events progressing from the distant past to the present moment and endowed with cosmic meaning and significance, then "history" can be dismissed as "bunk." History never has been, nor will it ever be, some sort of scientific pursuit limited to the "hard facts." History is what it says it is: a *story*. All stories are narratives. To have any meaning at all they have to have certain characteristics of morality, tension, and most especially certain "plots" which are inherently interesting to the listener or reader. These latter characteristics show just how much "history" is really only mythology recast in a secularized mode. There is nothing wrong with this, aside from the deceptions that might be fostered if people were to believe otherwise—which of course most people do. This is due to the fact that the *myth*, or meta-narrative, of the modern world within which most people live today has as one of its mainstays the idea of an "objective history." (This is a meta-narrative inherited from Judeo-Christianity, which was the first ideology to sacralize mundane historical events and endow them with cosmic significance.) On the other hand, if by history we mean a synthetic view of myths, structures and ideas as well as various events viewed over time, then "history" is fundamental to culture.

Mircea Eliade never tired of pointing out that myth seeks to destroy history. That is, myth is eternally true and recurrent, due to its inherent structural characteristics. History, as commonly understood, however, was supposed to be provisionally true, inevitably open to various interpretations, and fundamentally chronological and progressive. Myth is eternally true, whereas history is often a celebration of the absurd. French thinker and critic Alain de Benoist, and others, have pointed out that the past, present and future are not, in reality, a linear progression, but rather three entirely different *dimensions* of human existence. Other ideas, such as those of Oswald Spengler, emphasize the "morphology of history" and see cultures as organic subjects of "history" bound by cyclical laws of birth, life, and death.

Although it is most certainly a meta-narrative, or myth, in itself, it is nevertheless useful to review the ordinary historian's idea of the progression of epochs in the history of European ideas.

The time prior to the advent of Christianity is lumped by historians into a period they call "ancient." They don't know what to do with it in the larger sense, as there is no one overriding myth or general theory in terms of which it can be understood. The Indo-Europeans (and all their cultural branches) had their own set of values, the Egyptians theirs, the Chinese theirs, and so on. An intelligible plurality reigned and ethnic labels sufficed to differentiate cultures in a more general sense as well: We can speak of Germanic people, religion, art objects, and language as a more or less coherent and integrated whole. The same goes for the Greeks, or Romans, or any of the other branches of the Indo-European tree. Of course, it is equally true of all other "ancient" cultures. We confront a curious situation, however, when we examine cultures of continuous authenticity: be they found in Japan, China, India, or elsewhere. Certain cultures suffered no major breaks between their archaic pasts and their present states. However, the majority of cultures have endured major disruptions in symbolic continuity.

This disruption is identified at the point the ruling paradigm shifts from the particular and culturally authentic one to a more generalized (international) one. This generalized paradigm is most often characterized by *monotheism*, e.g., Christianity or Islam. With the advent of this paradigm in a culture, no matter how partial and imperfect the advent was, it is said that the culture has entered into a new phase. In Europe this phase subsequently came to be called the "medieval" period, or the "Middle Ages." Anything in the *middle* comes between two things. In this case these two are the "ancient" and the "modern." The Middle Ages were dominated by the myth of faith as institutionalized in the Church. This is not the place to discuss the merits of this myth. It is only important here to realize that the various plural and nationally determined mythologies were at least partially replaced by a single and international one. Although much is often made of the transition between the medieval and the modern period, the differences between medieval and modern mythologies are not nearly as great as those between the ancient and either the medieval or modern.

Modernity merely replaced one monolithic myth with another. Instead of faith and the Church being the highest arbiters of the truth, reason and science took the helm. Often medieval "religious" values were merely secularized and repackaged "political" models. The Church promised the salvation of all of humanity through faith, whereas science promised the same sort of universal perfection through the progressive application of reason. Those who criticize the monotheosis of both the medievalist and the modernist, those who see malevolent foolishness in the promises of both faith and reason—as embodied in the ideologies of the Middle Ages and the "progress" of modernity—can be called "postmodernists." It should be noted that the term "postmodernism" has generally been hijacked by campus Marxists and crypto-Marxists to further their own agendas (which are usually related to their own career advancement at universities, now the last bastions of the Marxist faithful). For this reason it is difficult to use the term without invoking alongside it a whole host of "politically correct" fables.

IV. The Idea of Integral Culture

In the context of the modern meta-narrative the most effective revolt would be one which challenged the modernistic atomization—the splitting up of all integrated units into their smallest parts for the sake of homogenizing them politically and/or economically—by promoting a reintegration of cultural elements or categories in a harmonious and authentic whole. From what has been said perhaps a good idea of how this can be done has already been understood. However, in conclusion, I would like to be more specific.

There are certain pathways or paths of action toward integral culture. These are not alternatives or options but rather things which must be, to one degree or another, integrated in one's life. The first is tradition, the other personal authenticity, and the third cultural action.

Tradition is that which has been handed down from time immemorial along various pathways: genetic, mythic, linguistic and material. The subject, i.e., *doer*, of this kind of action must discover the tradition, myth and school to which he or she belongs. This is not a "choice" in the sense of being something that is entirely arbitrary. It is a *realization* of a truth. Once this authentic choice has been made, which can just as easily be seen as an "election" by some aspect of that tradition, one can never go back or waver from the implications of that realization.

The reason for this is that it is a matter of personal authenticity. Modern people seem to think that they can choose to become something which they are not in reality, e.g., an Amerindian shaman, or a Kabbalistic mystic. But one can never truly become that except in one's own imagination (and perhaps in the imaginations of others). In truth, we can only, to paraphrase Fichte, *become who we are*. Within that realm of possibilities is an infinite number of directions, but the tradition is a fixed one. The modern world makes the path of discovery of an authentic tradition almost impossible. Yet a few have persevered, in hopes that someday the door will be opened for the many. One must simply ask oneself: "Of what can I be a 'first class' exemplar?" Can I be a first class Amerindian shaman? No, an *Amerindian* can be that. Can I be a first class Kabbalist? No, an *orthodox Jew* can be that. The positive answer to this question can be many things. But in one's own heart, if the honesty of that answer is complete, the authentic awakening will be unmistakable and irrevocable in life. The true path will be opened, but it will be far from accomplished.

The third component in the path toward integral culture involves interactions with others. One must participate actively with others within the same school or tradition, with others who have similarly discovered their authentic path. Being taught by others, teaching others, creating in cooperation with others, and in general interacting in any and all ways possible with others from the same tradition forms the quintessential laboratory not only for broad cultural action, but inner personal work as well.

This approach to individual development necessarily takes more into account than one's momentary and transitory desires. It views the individual in his or her true context, as a being which exists in many dimensions, past, present and future simultaneously. The individual has a *history*, in the sense that the individual only exists as a part of a stream of culture which cannot be understood apart from its constituent events and structures. The reconstruction of culture on the model of a healthy, integrated view of society could not help but have a beneficial effect on interpersonal relations, and hence on all aspects of culture.

The deep and subtle malaise of the modern world has its roots in disintegration and promotes it at every turn. Such rootlessness is marketed under noble terms like "freedom" and "individual rights." But once the tree has been uprooted and killed by the onslaught of progressive modernism, and by the time those living in the tree have realized what has happened in the name of "individual freedom," it is already too late. The eternal good of the whole has been sacrificed to the ephemeral appetites of the individual. How then can the individual mount a revolt against this modern world? Cultural disintegration is countered by cultural re-integration. The return pathways to this level of being are marked with the signs of tradition, authenticity, and action. Without these no effective revolt is possible.

Sic semper tyrannis!

Extraordinary Nordic Music

Welcome to the most exciting music movement on the planet. Scores of young musicians from Sweden, Finland, Norway, Denmark and Sámiland are taking the music and instruments of their ancestors and bringing new ideas, arrangements, influences & instrumentation to an often lost art.

NorthSide

Värttinä *Live In Helsinki*   NSD6066

From Finland, Värttinä have become well known around the globe for their stunning female vocals and progressive arrangements. Their first-ever live album features some of their audience's favorite pieces over the past decade, including early classics rearranged for extra punch. The dynamic acoustic and vocal gymnastics of this 10-piece group shine through. **Enhanced CD includes a video!**

Väsen *Live At Nordic Roots*   NSD6065

Sweden's "fab four" Väsen are in their element on stage, breathing fire into their already complex instrumental compositions for nyckelharpa, viola, acoustic guitar & percussion. While their studio albums are masterpieces, carefully balanced and planned, on this live concert recording made at the 2000 Nordic Roots Festival, you can hear the humor and joy that are integral parts of Väsen.

Aly Bain & Ale Möller *Fully Rigged*   NSD6064

Celtic meets Nordic in this new recording by master musicians from both sides of the North Sea. **Aly Bain** is one of the best-known fiddlers in the Celtic tradition as a founding member of Boys of the Lough. **Ale Möller**, from Sweden, is a leader in the Nordic roots revival. Master of many instruments, he is an important element in the music of Frifot and the Nordan Project.

Since we began in 1997, we have sold over 100,000 of our **Nordic Roots** sampler CDs. There are 3 discs in the series, each selling for $5 each — that's **cheaper than food!** If you are new to this music, we suggest you start here, to get a little taste of everything on the Nordic scene. Find these CDs at your local music retailer...you can also order direct from us online or call toll-free.

www.noside.com • 1-866-HEARFUL

Knowing the Gods

Collin Cleary

1. A False Knowing

There are those today who wish to return humanity (or a portion of humanity) to an older, pre-Christian faith. Almost all of these religious radicals hold that the gods exist, but that human beings have become somehow "closed" to them. The most common explanation for this "closedness" is the development of the intellect: man's big brain has shut him off from an experience of the divine. This explanation is dangerous, for it leads to anti-intellectualism (see, for example, the works of Jack London, D. H. Lawrence, and others). It is a theory that erroneously brands all use of reason as "rationalism," then posits that the only cure is the polar opposite error, irrationalism.

If one asks the proponents of this view what openness to the gods consists in, one is usually told that it means openness to certain natural "forces" which are recognized or intuited by human beings in the form of "archetypes." One finds something like this view, for example, in Julius Evola:

> Before the high and snowy peaks, the silence of the woods, the flowing of the rivers, mysterious caves, and so on, traditional man did not have poetic and subjective impressions typical of a [modern] romantic soul, but rather real sensations—even though at times confused— of the supernatural, of the powers *(numina)* that permeated those places; these sensations were translated into various images (spirits and gods of the elements, waterfalls, woods, and so on) often determined by the imagination, yet not arbitrarily and subjectively, but according to a necessary process. . . . [The power of imagination in traditional man] was so disposed as to be able to perceive and translate into plastic forms subtler impressions of the environment, which nonetheless were not arbitrary and subjective.[1]

Certain forces of nature are simply perceived by man *as* Thor, or *as* Indra, in the same way that a certain molecular configuration of the surface of objects is perceived *as* red, and another *as* green. Red is not "subjective" in the sense that it is "invented" by the subject. I have no choice when I open my eyes but to experience a cardinal's wings as red. But "red" would not exist without eyes capable of registering light waves refracted off of those wings, and a brain capable of processing the data in a certain manner. (The intrinsic structure of the object would exist with or without a perceiver, but the sense datum of "red" would not.) Thus, red is not subjective in the strong sense—but in a weaker sense it clearly is subjective, since without perceivers redness would not exist.

Let us apply this reasoning to the experience of the gods. The forces in nature registered by imagination (according to set processes) would exist with or without a subject. But the registration of those processes as sensuously-given "gods" would not. *Ergo, without human beings there would be no gods.* This conclusion was drawn by the German philosopher G. W. F. Hegel in the nineteenth century. His follower Ludwig Feuerbach took it one further, logical step and declared that Man is God. Feuerbach's contemporary Karl Marx then took the final step of declaring that if this is the case we may dispense with talking about God altogether.

The theory of "openness to the gods" outlined above is part and parcel of the modern perspective, which is rationalist, reductionist, and man-centered. It takes the experience of the gods as something to be "explained" rationally. It analyzes it as an "imaginative intuition" of natural forces, processed according to laws which are presumably physiological. It reduces the experience of the divine to a neural epiphenomenon. And it thereby implicitly declares that without human brains "gods" would exist no more than would "red." If the proponents of this theory are even partially correct in thinking that modern rationalism has eradicated man's openness to the gods, how in heaven's name do they think their theory could help to restore it?

2. Openness to Being

Restoration of this primal openness must begin with abandoning all attempts to explain "what" the gods are. All such attempts are implicitly atheistic. They assume that the gods must *really* be something else. Via analysis or reduction or dream interpretation or what have you, the gods are "explained" as being something other than the gods, as what they are not. We must abandon all talk of archetypes and Innate Releasing Mechanisms, of Bicameral Minds and the powers of mushrooms—if we wish to again open ourselves to the gods. Openness must be openness to the gods . . . and nothing else.

This openness must be an openness to a universe in which such things as the gods may exist as a brute fact, inexplicable to the analytical mind. This is not "irrationalism." It is not irrational to believe that some things cannot be analyzed, reduced, or explained, if, indeed, they cannot. True rationality and enlightenment must consist not only in recognizing facts as facts, but in recognizing that ultimately there may be no answer to why they are, or why they are the way they are.[2]

Am I suggesting that we should believe in the gods on a naive literal level? For instance, am I suggesting that we should believe that Valhalla is an actual, physical place, or that Thor's hammer is an actual, physical object? Of course not. I do not mean to deny that there are "levels" of understanding in religion. But what we must realize is that if we are to again come into possession of Tradition, of the mindset of our ancestors, we cannot *begin* at the highest level. This is not what our ancestors did. They began their individual lives as children, believing in the literal reality of the gods, and then (in the case of some) they penetrated deeper into this reality. In other words, you cannot begin with the *Upanishads*. You must begin with the *Vedas*. We do this first through achieving an openness to the divine *as such*, eschewing all pre-conceived notions or theories about what the gods "really are." We must reconnect with Tradition in the same way a child learns its native language: not through conscious intention or rote memorization, but through a kind of naive and non-reflective openness, and through total immersion.

But openness to the divine begins with a much more fundamental openness: an openness simply to the being of things. To be open to the being of beings means *to let beings be*, as Heidegger put it. It is to let beings show us what they are, instead of forcing some essence or some meaning onto them. This openness is fundamentally at odds with modernity, as I shall discuss shortly. There is no magic formula, no twelve-step program for reactivating this open-

THOR BY FRANZ VON STUCK (1863–1928).

ing. Fortunately, openness to the being of things is not an achievement per se, but the natural standpoint of mankind. It is closedness that has been "achieved." The way may be cleared for re-opening, then, by unlearning closedness. This unlearning must begin with a ruthless critique of the ideology and standpoint of post-Christian modernity.

3. Will

An old Scandinavian legend from Christian times tells how when the gods ceased being worshiped in the Northlands, the dwarves abandoned that country, hiring a ferryman to take them across the river one night and away from the land of men. On reaching the other side, the ferryman was informed that the dwarves "were leaving the country for ever in consequence of the unbelief of the people."[3]

This tale tells of closedness from its other side: when we cease to believe in them, the gods depart; they close themselves off from us. But in truth, the action of closing is performed by man. We close ourselves to the gods. The gods *do* nothing (nor should we expect them to, for they are gods). Human beings have a remarkable capacity for closing themselves off to the truth. Human nature is actual only in the relationship to the supernatural, but this relationship is a channel that must be kept open.

Human nature, as actual living in the presence of what is "higher" (the supernatural, the divine, the transcendent, the ideal) exists in a constant tension between twin impulses: the impulse to open to the higher, and the impulse to close to it. One is the impulse to reach out to something greater than ourselves, letting it direct us and (literally) inspire us. The other is the impulse to close to this and to raise oneself above all else. For lack of a better word, I will refer to this latter tendency as *Will*. Both tendencies—openness and Will—are present in all men. They explain the greatness of men, as well as their evil.

Will is an impulse to "close off" from the not-self. It is a shutting-off that is at the same time an elevation and exalting of the self to absolute status. Will manifests itself in its most basic form as a lashing out against whatever frustrates the self's desires. In human life, this begins in infancy merely as *screaming*, but once the organism has attained a certain strength and dexterity, it graduates to acts of destruction directed at the frustrating other. It devours or destroys that which opposes it. In consistently removing or rebelling against the other which limits its desires, the organism wills the principle that it exist without limit. This is why Will is an exalting of the self to absolute status. The (unrealizable) *telos* of Will would be a condition in which the organism would exist unopposed—and this could only be, of course, if the organism were the only thing in existence. The lashing-out of Will is also a shutting to the other, for to seek the annihilation of otherness is to deny it ultimate reality.

Based on this description, it can easily be seen that all organisms, not just man, exhibit Will. Only man, however, can complement Will with the openness to the higher. Also, it is clear that all men *begin* life purely as an embodiment of Will, and growth and maturation involve a tempering of Will.

If pure will—the absolute shutting-off to all otherness, including the divine—is the nature of *evil*, then human beings begin life as purely evil. Infants are noisy, messy, wrathful little bundles of pure evil. The infant recognizes nothing higher than himself. He wails and beats his fists against the world as soon as his desires are frustrated. The parents are "loved" only as conduits for the satisfaction of his desires (and even after birth, the psychic boundary between the infant and the mother remains blurry—it is the father who is the problematic other). What we call "selfishness" is just Will, and this is why we regard it as evil.

Throughout the course of a human life, Will comes to manifest itself in different and more refined forms. In its higher forms, Will manifests itself not in destruction but in (1) the transformation of the given world according to human designs, and (2) the yearning to penetrate and master the world through the instrument of the human mind—through exploration, analysis, dissection, categorization, observation, and theory. In its most refined form, Will becomes what might be called a "Titanic Humanism": a seeking to make man the measure, to exalt man as the be-all and end-all of existence, to bend all things to human desires. It is no accident that all the grand schemes and contrivances of modernity (the technological mastery of nature, the global marketplace, socialism, universal health care, etc.) have as their end exactly what the infant seeks: the satisfaction of desires, and the maintenance of comfort and security. The modern age is the Age of Will, the age of Titanic Humanism. Modernity is unique in human history in that at no other time has Will so thoroughly triumphed over openness.

This description may make it seem that much of what we consider to be human is to be attributed to Will. This leads to troubling questions. For example, if scientific curiosity is a manifestation of Will, does that make science "evil"? The answer is a qualified *no*. Only an unbounded and unchecked Will is evil—and so only an unbounded and unchecked scientific curiosity would be evil. Will is natural and necessary to human nature. Like anything else, however, it must be held within the bonds of a limit. Human nature happens in the tension between Will and openness, between closing and opening. We open to receive truth—to receive the *logos*, to receive the will of the gods—then we take possession of such truth as our own and project it on the world, transforming the world, propagating the truth we have won from openness to the trans-human. In acting thus man fulfills his role as *steward* of the divine creation: assisting nature in achieving perfection. Will becomes destructive only when it becomes completely disconnected from the trans-human. There is then, in the properly-human being, an oscillation between opening out to receive truth, and closing and taking that truth in, making the truth one's own, and willing that this should be the truth for all.

If human beings begin in Will, how did man ever become open to the trans-human? Children are forced to open by a power stronger than themselves which puts them in awe: their parents, teachers, and (formerly) clergy. If ancient man was more open, it was because he was put in awe by his surroundings, by nature, by the hardships of existence. Modern man is insulated from the awe-full by (1) technology, which allows him to manipulate the natural world and thus to avoid confronting the natural in its pure form, (2) by impregnable dwellings which shelter him from nature, (3) by cities, which create a whole human world apart from nature, and (4) by science, the story we tell about nature, which leaves us with the impression that its mysteries have been fully penetrated and cancelled.

It is through being awestruck by the power and sublimity of nature that man is forced into openness to the being of that which he did not create. This openness to the being of the natural world facilitates openness to the *supernatural world*, the world of spirits and of Ideas, which also precedes and surpasses the being of man. In closing oneself to the first, one gradually becomes closed to the second. Post-Christian man has shut himself to the natural world, and this has led to his being shut off from his own nature—for the uniqueness of man among the animals consists precisely in his openness to the higher. It has also led to his becoming shut off from other men—as city life makes so plain. Without an openness to the transhuman—beginning in an openness to nature—we are shut off from a knowledge of the good. Hence the notorious "inhumanity" of civilized, urban humans.

4. The Age of Will

As mentioned earlier, it is in the modern period that Will has been loosed from its bonds and has, perhaps, irreparably torn us away from the gods. The form taken by Will in the modern period is the ideal of humanism, which is the man-centered, scientific, materialist, rationalist project of transforming the world and human beings in order to progress towards a state in which all resistance to desire is cancelled, and all frustrations are ameliorated.

The modern humanist project, as an expression of infantile Will, is an attempt to cancel the otherness of nature. This is expressed quite nicely in the opening passages of Ayn Rand's *The Fountainhead*:

> He looked at the granite. To be cut, he thought, and made into walls. He looked at a tree. To be split and made into rafters. He looked at a streak of rust on the stone and thought of iron ore under the ground. To be melted and to emerge as girders against the sky. These rocks, he thought, are here for me; waiting for the drill, the dynamite and my voice; waiting to be split, ripped, pounded, reborn; waiting for the shape my hands will give them.[4]

When man looks at nature only as matter onto which he can impose a form of his devising, then he declares, in effect, that nature has no form, no being of its own. To cancel the otherness of nature is to abolish the distinction between us and it. The modern accepts no limitations on his ability to penetrate and control. His is simultaneously a Titanic will toward divine omnipotence—and toward a state of infantile autism in which there is no boundary between subject and object.

This dual will of modern man was perfectly expressed by Hegel (who heartily approved of it). Hegel wrote that the aim of his lectures on the *Philosophy of Nature* was "to convey an image of nature, in order to subdue this Proteus: to find in this externality only the mirror of ourselves, to see in nature a free reflection of spirit."[5] "An out-and-out other simply does not exist for Spirit [i.e., for mankind]," Hegel says.[6] And: "what seems to happen outside of [the self], to be an activity directed against it, is really its own doing, and substance shows itself to be essentially subject."[7] Hegel argues—correctly—that when modern man transforms the world according to his will, when he seeks to cancel the otherness of the other, he is moved by a desire to absolutize himself, to remove that which resists and frustrates his will or his mind. In other words, *to be left totally alone.* Thus, we can see that humanism = nihilism (a conclusion Hegel himself did not draw).

As I have said, this mentality not only cuts us off from the being of beings, and from the gods, but from ourselves. As Jakob Böhme said, "Nothing can be revealed to itself without opposition: For if there is nothing that opposes it, then it always goes out of itself and never returns to itself again. If it does not return into itself, as into that from which it originated, then it knows nothing of its origin."[8] Without an other that opposes and resists the self, against which the self discovers its boundaries, no self-knowledge is possible. Is it any surprise, then, that so many modern people need to "find themselves"? When we take the world of human ideas, constructions, aspirations, projects, prejudices, contrivances, and conveniences as the only world, and cut ourselves off from the being of the world we did not create, should it surprise us if we find ourselves experiencing a feeling of "unreality"? When everything is open to our will, open to change and revision and fine-tuning, when everything can be "new and improved" including ourselves, is it any wonder that modern people seem simply to . . . drift?

And when we are "left alone" with ourselves in the universe, when the universe is no longer other at all, and the self has become absolute, what then? For Hegel, history is ended, and human beings find themselves at their zenith. Hegel thought that for man to learn his true nature was for him to achieve self-actualization. It would lead to an experience of exaltation.

The truth is rather different, as we have discovered since this mighty Prometheus was struck down by cholera in 1831. The truth is closer to what Nietzsche's "Madman" tells us in *The Gay Science*. The Madman comes to the marketplace in the wee hours with a lantern, telling the people that they have killed God:

> *We have killed him*—you and I. All of us are his murderers. But how have we done this? How were we able to drink up the sea? Who gave us the sponge to wipe away the entire horizon? What did we do when we unchained this earth from its sun? Whither is it moving now? Whither are we moving now? Away from all suns? Are we not plunging continually? Backward, sideward, forward, in all directions? Is there any up or down left? Are we not straying as through an infinite nothing? Do we not feel the breath of empty space? Has it not become colder?[9]

The modern humanist project of the penetration, mastery, and control of nature is the sponge that has wiped away the entire horizon. It has refused to allow beings to be anything other than what we want them to be, and so they have hidden themselves from us—and the gods have hidden themselves from us. Nietzsche's reference to the sun calls to mind the sun of Plato's *Republic*, which represents the "Idea of the Good," the ultimate source of all, the highest ideal, the being of beings. We have "unchained this earth from its sun," Nietzsche says. We have disconnected ourselves from the ideal, from Tradition. There is no "up or down" left because there is nothing objective left with which we can orient ourselves in this universe. Having lost this sun, it has become colder.

But Nietzsche's "death of God" was no mere accident, brought about when people stopped going to church. Given the logic of Christian monotheism, God had to die—and to give way to the new god of humanism, which Freud called "our God *Logos*."[10]

5. Modernism and Monotheism

As soon as man admits that there are limits to his powers to penetrate and transform, a space is made for the gods in human life. As I have said, however, the whole drift of modern thought is toward the cancellation of all limits on man, and thus the exaltation of man to the status of Supreme Being. But as soon as it is admitted that there are limits to what we may change and—especially—that there is an ineluctable hiddenness to things, then Will is checked, and openness opens again, just a bit.

To admit limits is to grant the world being. It is to admit that there are certain inescapable and unchangeable *eidetic* realities—the natures of things, the patterns and principles of order—which are brute, unalterable facts. The recognition that the world is simply one way and not another is the recognition of a brute facticity which must be, to all reflective persons, an inexplicable mystery.

It is not monotheism that is suggested here, but polytheism. The world is a Bacchanalian revel of forms, a multiverse of beings and powers. It is the gods who account for and embody the chief features of this world. And the gods are, at least in some sense, *in the world*, like the things or powers they govern.

Monotheism is moved not by openness to being, but by Will in its guise as "philosophy." Monotheism essentially seeks to go *behind the phenomena*, and beyond the gods, and asks, "but what *accounts for* these brute facts? It is no explanation simply to chalk these things up to gods. What explains these 'gods'?" In a sense, monotheists have a point. There is no genuine metaphysical explanation in polytheism. There is no answer to the question "why is there something rather than nothing?"[11] But polytheists essentially believe that there can be no answer to this question, and that none is needed. Existence needs no explanation—or justification—outside itself.

The "explanation" of the world provided by monotheism is vacuous: behind the gods, there lies . . . GOD. This may seem a peculiar way to describe the transition from polytheism to monotheism, but this is in fact exactly how it occurs. Through one agency or another, one God becomes supreme. Others become less important, until their worship finally dies out, or is actively killed.

GOD is a supreme deity, existing outside the world, who created everything in the world. The schoolboy question, "If everything needs a maker, who made God?" forces the monotheist toward more and more abstruse and philosophical and remote descriptions of this God. In the hands of Christian theologians like St. Thomas Aquinas, God essentially becomes a kind of "principle" which we must *think* if we are to think the world. For Aquinas, God is "existing" itself . . . and so He becomes indistinguishable from that brute facticity He was intended to explain. In short, He becomes . . . a mystery!

Meanwhile, what has become of man's relationship to nature? Monotheism sucks all the mystery out of nature and injects it into God, who is the "explanation" for nature. While polytheism, through the worship of many gods, affirms the life and mystery of the world in all its complexity, monotheism declares the world to be a mere artifact, the product of God's making, and thus about as living and mysterious as a thumb tack. The transition from polytheism to monotheism is the "de-godding" of the different aspects of the world.

Monotheists therefore progressively cede the complexity of creation to the natural scientist. And what happens to their God as a result of this? The natural scientist need make no reference to God in any of his investigations of nature. The entire material world is understandable by science, on its own terms. Eventually, scientists and others realize that this is the case and God essentially becomes a *deus otiosus*. God becomes a dispensable "hypothesis" that does no work in explaining the world. In steps the scientist to take God's place.

The scientist recognizes that the world exhibits an intelligible order, but without God to underwrite creation, the natures of things no longer seem so "fixed." John Locke founded his doctrine of individual rights (life, liberty, and property) on the idea that man's nature is created by God. Remove belief in God and the status of man's nature—and his rights—becomes highly questionable. Less than two-hundred years later the followers of Marx (e.g., Trotsky) explicitly declared their intention to change human nature through "scientific socialism." The result to the supposed "rights" of men is well-known.

Thus, in the absence of God (or the gods) the scientists come to believe that they can radically, infinitely alter what they study. Since there is no God, there is no reason to believe in the soul, or in any non-physical reality. Human beings are therefore simply a highly complex form of meat, which can be studied and manipulated using the same methods we use to study and manipulate other meat.

Since there is no non-physical reality, there are no objective or eternal ideals. Truth is "posited" by human beings.[12] This must mean, then, that moral idealism is a delusion. Men who exhibit the quality Plato called "spiritedness," men who are ready to fight for ideals, are simply sick or deluded. This position was explicitly put forward in the twentieth-century by the so-called Frankfurt School of sociology.[13] Modern "humanism"—modern science and psychology—considers a person "normal" if their concerns do not rise above the level of what Plato called "appetite": concern with the satisfaction of desires, and the maintenance or attainment of security and comfort. Hence the almost complete disappearance of terms like "honor" and "nobility" and "self-sacrifice" from modern discourse.[14]

Here again, we see Will manifested: the closing off to anything "higher" than the self, and the setting up of personal desire-fulfillment as the end of existence. But human beings cannot live entirely without ideals, and so a new ideal is created: the achievement of a society in which desires are satisfied, in which physical security, comfort and health are realized. Having cut themselves off from any higher aspiration, scientists rush to place themselves in the service of this ideal.

And so, to come back to the beginning, what is the ultimate result of monotheism? Atheism, the violation of nature, the destruction of ideals, the destruction of morals, the barbarization of men, the eradication of human dignity, and the general debasement of human life (what is called "materialism").

6. The Achievement of Openness

Openness may be achieved only by the cancellation of what closes us. Thus we must critique all of our modern ideas, intellectual tendencies, and ways of living in the world, and thoroughly know their lineage. Such a radical critique is itself a feature of modernity, but here we may be able to use one of the weapons of modernity against it. We may be able to use the shovel with which we have dug ourselves into this hole as a pick with which to climb out of it. We must begin by recognizing that no matter how critical we may be of modernity, we ourselves are products of it. It is useless to rail against "people today" if our goal is a recovery of a more authentic way of being. Our critique must begin with ourselves.

We see the modern in ourselves when—with all good intentions—we attempt to "explain" what the gods are, or to "explain" the experience of the gods. Such efforts at explanation are bound up with the modern tendency to insist that everything be explicable. But the gods are precisely that outer edge of the real beyond which explanation cannot go. They define the boundaries of the real, only *within which* explanation is possible. Our ancestors who believed in the gods had no "explanation" for their experience of them. *To think in terms of explaining the experience of the gods is to already have adopted a critical distance from that experience.*

We must also abandon all efforts to explain what might be called "the place of religion in human life." In other words, we must banish from our thinking all propositions which begin "Religion is important because . . ."; or, "For our ancestors, religion served to . . ."; or, "The function of religion is to . . ." Such an attitude is not religious, it is a reflective, critical attitude toward religion.

But how else, it might be asked, can we moderns find a way back into religion except by figuring out what religion *does*, or what it provided our ancestors? The problem with this approach is that it assumes that religion is merely one of the many things human beings do or engage in, along with, for example, making war, and writing poetry, and building dwellings, and starting a family. In short, it assumes that religion is an *attribute* of human beings. In fact, it is their *essence*.

Religion *is* human nature. I do not mean by this that it is "natural" for human beings to be religious. I mean that human nature *just is* religion. What distinguishes human beings from other creatures is that they are more than just Will, they are also openness—openness to that which is "higher." If this state of openness or living in openness is religion, then human nature is religion. In short, the being of man is constituted in and through his relation to the divine. There is no such thing as "human nature" to which religion must be related. There is no such thing as a human being who can be human with or without religion. One is only truly human through openness, through relatedness to the divine.[15] This is the ultimate reason why—as alluded to earlier—modernity, the Age of Will, cuts us off not only from nature but from our own nature. Modernity is the Will-full destruction of human nature. Modern man, Nietzsche's "Last Man," is no man at all, but wholly inhuman.

Human nature is openness toward being, and toward divine being. But to be open is possible only if there is, in effect, a space within the human being; only if the human being is not, in some sense, whole or complete. Human nature is a vector, a towardness, a relationship. A relationship requires two terms, which must ever remain distinct from one another if the relationship is to persist. The directedness of the human being toward the divine can never be satisfied, in the sense that one can never have or reach or comprehend the divine. But some objects, in the yearning for them, can improve and elevate one. Man's incompleteness is never overcome, but through it he is raised up. Other objects, of course, only make the incompleteness and emptiness intolerable. The tragedy of modern man is that he has become turned away from his proper object. He is still incomplete, but his yearning, his need, have become turned toward objects which can never improve or satisfy him.

At this point, an objection might occur to some. Isn't this description of openness to the divine as an incompleteness and a "yearning" a rather Christianized, monotheist treatment? This does not seem to describe the religious experience of, for example, the Norse or the Greeks. Yearning is, admittedly, an inadequate term for a very difficult concept. But one finds the sort of thing I am talking about in Greek descriptions of the "awe" with which men regard the divine (see especially Homer). The "yearning" I have described is not really a desire to become a god or, certainly, to physically possess a god. Rather, to describe it from the other end, it is a "pull" exerted by the divine on the human. What the divine provides is a frame of reference, an order, a structure to existence, which *fascinates*—and the nature of the fascination is not reducible just to these terms. Human nature just is this directedness toward, pulling toward, or fascination with the divine.

Will destroys religion in two, related ways. The first is the way I have already described: man can spurn the beloved, declare that he has no need of Him. "I can stand alone. I don't need you," man declares. This is modern rationalism and scientism. The second way is to try and devise some special method of bridging the gap between human and divine, without denying the reality of the divine. This way is called mysticism. Mystics think that they are raising themselves to at-one-ment with the divine. They fail to see that this process could equally well be described from the other end: as the lowering of God to the level of man. The divinization of man and the anthropomorphization of God are the same. The rise of mysticism has always signalled the corruption or degeneration of a religion. The *Upanishads* were the undoing of the *Vedas*—the destruction of the religion of the warrior, and the exalting of the priest as supreme even over the gods. The result of this Titanic humanism for India requires no comment.

7. Conclusion, with Some Practical Suggestions

In sum, the recovery of openness to the divine must begin with an unlearning of closedness. It must begin with a thoroughgoing, radical critique of the modern way of being, especially as it shows up in oneself. Openness to the gods presupposes a more basic openness simply to the being of things, and principally to the being of things humans did not create. It is through this openness that openness to the gods happened for our ancestors. Thus, it is through such an openness that we might know the gods again.

I mentioned earlier that modern man cuts himself off from the being of nature through four basic things: (1) technology (which manipulates what is), (2) self-contained, self-sufficient and impregnable dwellings, (3) cities (whole "human worlds"), and (4) science (the story of how we have supposedly cancelled the hiddenness of nature). A reasonable formula for beginning to recover openness would thus be to:

1. Eliminate technology as much as possible from one's life. To live as simply as possible. To eliminate technologically created "needs" (which are really unnecessary wants). To live from nature directly (e.g., to grow or to kill one's own food).

2. To leave one's dwelling and encounter nature directly, as much as possible.

3. To live in such a way that nature can be encountered directly simply by stepping outside of one's dwelling; i.e., not to live in a city.

4. To develop a healthy skepticism about the claims of science. (An excellent place to begin would be with a critical examination of the theory of evolution, which rests on a very shaky foundation, and which enjoys the status of a religion-substitute among scientists.)

Through such a physical and mental separation from modernity, it is hoped that a meditation may begin, and that this meditation will lead to a rediscovery of that space within us which is the pre-condition of openness. In an oscillation between, on the one hand, self-examination and critique of modernity and Will, and, on the other hand, an encounter with being, openness becomes possible again.

A familiarity with the polytheistic traditions of our ancestors would also be helpful, as a kind of roadmap to guide us in understanding that which will enter in, once we are open.

Notes:

1. Julius Evola, *Revolt Against the Modern World*, trans. Guido Stucco (Rochester, Vermont: Inner Traditions, 1995), pp. 150–151. Evola would, of course, reject my use of the term "archetype," as he was a strong critic of Jung.
2. This is not the same thing as claiming that the universe is "absurd," meaningless, or purposeless. Such "existentialism" only comes about when human beings reject the meaning and purpose that are readily apparent to them and look for *some other*. This search always fails.
3. H. A. Guerber, *Myths of the Norsemen*, (Mineola, N.Y.: Dover, 1992 [first published: George G. Harrap & Company, London, 1909]), p. 243.
4. Ayn Rand, *The Fountainhead* (New York: Bobbs Merrill, 1968), p. 4.
5. G. W. F. Hegel, *Philosophy of Nature*, trans. J. M. Petry, 3 vols. (London: Allen and Unwin, 1970), vol. 3, p. 213.
6. G. W. F. Hegel, *Hegel's Philosophy of Subjective Spirit*, trans. J. M. Petry, 3 vols. (Dordrecht: Reidel, 1978), vol. 1, p. 5.
7. G. W. F. Hegel, Hegel's *Phenomenology of Spirit*, trans. A. V. Miller (Oxford: Oxford Univ. Press, 1977), p. 28
8. Jakob Böhme, *Der Weg zu Christo*, Sixth Book, "Von Göttlicher Beschaulichkeit," in *Sämtliche Schriften*, vol. 4, Chap. 1, § 8.
9. *The Portable Nietzsche*, ed. and trans. Walter Kaufmann (New York: Viking, 1968), pp. 95–96. It must be added that Nietzsche's answer to the modern predicament is a more radical dose of humanism. Speaking of the murder of God, he writes, "Must not we ourselves become gods simply to seem worthy of it?" Nietzsche's belief is that the ideals we have abandoned are empty ideals, and that "God" never really existed at all. Having discovered this, we must "invent" new ideals. Nietzsche's "overmen" have the strength to do this—and to test their mettle by doing battle over these ideals. But is it psychologically realistic to think that anyone could fight and die for ideals he has simply "made up," and does not honestly believe to be objectively true?
10. See Sigmund Freud, *The Future of an Illusion*, trans. James Strachey (New York: W. W. Norton, 1961). By *Logos* Freud means simply logic or reason. He does not mean "the *logos*" in Heraclitus's sense of the term—a use of *logos* I alluded to earlier.
11. Polytheist creation myths never literally begin with *nothing*.

12. Eventually, of course, in the hands of thinkers like Nietzsche, this logical consequence of scientific humanism is turned as a weapon on science itself.

13. Actually, it is implicit in the works of the founder of modern political theory, Thomas Hobbes.

14. "Courage" is a term one still encounters, but it is rarely applied to the man who risks his life in service to an ideal. It is applied to people desperately hanging onto life in the face of a debilitating, terminal disease, or to homosexuals coming out of the closet, or to Supreme Court justices who have made a leftward turn in their old age.

15. It goes without saying, I hope, that when I refer to "religion" I mean it in its true sense as an uncorrupted openness to the divine. I do not mean just anything that goes by the name of religion, and I am certainly not upholding today's "religious people" as exemplars of humanity.

Priests, Warriors, and Cultivators: Alain de Benoist's Interview with Georges Dumézil

Alain de Benoist

By far the most popular American writer on comparative mythology has been Joseph Campbell. Campbell's books have been read and re-read by an entire generation hungry for spiritual values. But Campbell's psychological approach to mythology—derived largely from the works of Carl Jung and Erich Neumann—is only part of the picture.

One problem with the psychological approach—at least when considered in isolation from other perspectives—is the degree to which local distinctions become blurred in the quest for perennial, universally applicable "types." For Georges Dumézil, it was fundamental that myths be understood in their cultural and historical contexts. The most profitable approach to comparative mythology, then, involves studying the myths of culturally and historically related peoples. Thus, Dumézil's exclusive focus on the Indo-Europeans.

Just as linguistic scholars had begun to piece together a proto-Indo-European language by identifying common traits in the individual Indo-European languages, so Dumézil began piecing together a proto-Indo-European religion. The most striking thing that he discovered was the structural similarity between the different Indo-European pantheons. This three-tiered, hierarchic assignment of "functions" (sovereignty-physical force-fecundity) was also replicated within the social sphere. Proto-Indo-European society consisted of three corresponding "castes": priests, warriors, and herder-cultivators. Although it might be objected that a similar pattern is characteristic of many traditional civilizations, the difference lies in the extent to which this three-tiered arrangement was reinforced in almost every facet of culture. This has led Dumézil to posit "tripartition" as *the* Indo-European ideology.

The interview that follows first appeared in 1978 in the French periodical *Le Figaro Dimanche*. The interviewer, Alain de Benoist, is largely regarded as the founder of the French *Nouvelle*

Droite, or "New Right." Equally disdainful of "conservatism, liberalism, socialism, and Marxism," Benoist's critique of modern society (he has called his approach "the *Gramscism* of the Right") has been influenced by the works of Carl Schmitt and Julius Evola. As one commentator puts it: "this *New* Right is anti-capitalist, anti-American, pagan, and places a higher value on culture and identity than it does on economics." Although Dumézil was consistently reticent about his own philosophical commitments, the Nouvelle Droite has appropriated the Indo-European ideology as a common basis for European culture.

After a long and fruitful career, Georges Dumézil died in 1986.

(Introduction by Joshua Buckley)

The comparative mythology of the nineteenth century believed in a universal distribution, in all cultures, of the same values and the same social functions. You are one of those who has shown that this is not the case, and quite the contrary, societies, according to time and place, are differentiated by eidetic structures, of which they are simultaneously product and exemplar. In the course of your work you have, for example, isolated the seminal elements of an Indo-European "ideology," characterizing the culture from which the majority of historical European civilizations originate. How do you define the term "ideology"?

In a manner that is not entirely that of common usage: the constellation of world-views, the global understanding of the universe and the forces that direct and maintain it, as it manifests in religion, philosophy, poetry, language, social rapports, etc.

The core element of this "Indo-European ideology" is something you have designated as functional *tripartition*. It was in 1938, in your study on "the pre-history of the High flamines" (a theme which you had taken up again nine years ago in your article "Roman Ideas"), that you had first recognized its importance . . .

The reality of the tripartite structure of the Indo-European ideology as it relates to human society first came to me when I was struck by the similarities between a religious notion, the pre-Capitoline trinity of the ancient Romans (Jupiter, Mars, Quirinus), and a social notion, the division of Indian society into three Aryan classes (varna): the Brahmans (priests), the Rajanyas (kings) or Kshatriyas (warriors), and the Vaicyas (farmers-herders). This correlation led me to ask if it could be generalized. That has now shown itself to be the case.

It would be useful to reiterate the elements that constitute this tripartition.

It is a triple structure, characterized by (in a real or figurative sense) three essential functions: one part, magical and juridical sovereignty, another part, the force and might of the warrior, and finally fecundity and fertility (vegetable, animal, and human). The comparison of the oldest Indo-Iranian, German, Celtic, and Italian documents enables one to affirm that the Indo-Europeans had conceived of human or divine relationships based on the separation and hierarchization of these three functions. Among the Indo-European peoples, it was not only the Indians and Iranians (before the Zoroastrian reformation), but also the Celts who exemplified this. First, there was their Druidic class (that is to say the "most wise"); then the military aristocracy (the sole land-holders, corresponding to the Irish *flaith*, in the proper sense of power—exact semantic equivalent of the Sanskrit *ksatriya*, the essence of the warrior's function); and finally the animal husbandmen, the Irish *bô airig*. Other peoples limited themselves to projecting this tripartite system onto the domains of theology or of "history."

The first function covers two aspects. On one side, it consists of the mysterious administration, the "magic" of the universe, the general ordering of the cosmos. This is a "disquieting" aspect, terrifying from certain perspectives. The other aspect is more reassuring, more oriented to the human world. It is the "juridical" part of the sovereign function. In India, this duality, characteristic of the first function, is illustrated by the contrast between Varuna, the magician-king, mysterious and terrifying, and Mithra, the god of contracts and honest, orderly, and regulated affairs. With the Germans, one finds the same opposition between Óðinn-Wotan, who is similarly a master of magic and of runes, and Týr.

From Rome to Ireland

Does the case of ancient Rome present any noteworthy exceptions?

In Rome, Jupiter seems to have subsumed the entire role of sovereignty very quickly, to the detriment of the development of the divinity that corresponded to Tyr or Mithra, Dius Fidus (the guarantor of *fides*, that is to say good faith). In fact, the first of these high priests—of those three supreme priests, accountable only to the singular authority of the *rex sacrorum*—would not call himself *flamen Jovius* or *Jovialis* (the keeper of the flame of Jupiter), as one might expect, but *flamine Dialis:* flamine of Dius Fidus.

And the second and third functions?

Represented in Rome by the god Mars, by Thor for the Germanic peoples, by Indra (Vâyu) for the Aryans, and undoubtedly by Heracles in Greece. The second function, as I have said, carries the trait of physical force in all its manifestations, from energy, to heroism, to courage. In Indra as in Thor, one finds all the necessities and the movements that produce the power and procure the victory of those insatiable champions, whose weapon is the thunderbolt, divinities that vanquish demons and save the universe.

The third function is the generative function. It is the domain of the healers, of youth, of luxury, of fecundity, of prosperity; also the domain of the healing gods, the patron deities of goods, of opulence—and also of the "people," as opposed to the small number of warriors and kings. As divinities of this third function, we must mention the Norse gods of the Germanic peoples (Njörð, Frey, Freyja), the Quirinus of the Romans (*Vofionus* in the Umbrian trinity), and the Indo-Iranian Nåsatya twins which, in India, are the Açvin.

This tripartite theology, around which multitudes of other givens are organized, is found in the roots of Iranian, Scandinavian, and Latin cultures. Moreover, the major factor that leads the ancient god of the Celts, the Tuatha dé Danann, to victory over the formori "demons" at the second battle of Mag Tuireadh, is the formation of a fundamental trinity, where one first finds Lug and Dagda, then Ogme, and finally the healer Dian Cecht and the blacksmith Goibniu. In every case, these groups are found operating within the same parameters and are indicative of the same originating structure.

Just the same, it seems odd that this structure is so meticulously hierarchical . . .

The Indo-European vision of a smoothly functioning world required an "organization" in which the representatives of the first function commanded, the second fought for and defended the community, and the third (the greatest number of them) worked and were productive. In their eyes, it was in this hierarchy that one found the harmony necessary to the proper functioning of the cosmos, as well as that of the society. It's an Indo-European version of the "social contract."

If one reviews the Indo-European mythologies, one finds that this harmony between the three classes was arrived at, not without effort, but over the course of a "foundational war" culminating precisely with a contractual compromise. One finds, for instance, the war between the Æsir and the Vanir in the Germanic peoples, the war of the proto-Romans and the Sabines in the version of the Roman historians, the difficulties of incorporating, for the Indo-Iranians, the Nåsatya into the community of the gods, etc. It seems that they saw a special affinity between the first and second functions, as against the third, correct?

Emile Benveniste has, since 1937, established the etymological relation of the Roman noun *juvenes* and the Indo-European notions of "vital force" and of "eternity" (Vedic *åyu*, Greek *aion*). From a certain perspective, the relationship between the representatives of the first two functions could in effect cover over an opposition between two generations, which had probably played an important role in the Indo-European expansion. These two classes, contrary to the third, are affiliated with more "masculine" notions (Indo-European society has at all times been a patriarchal society). Consequentially there is most likely a rapport between the function of the warrior, the clamorous entourage who encircle the gods of this second function (the Indian battalion of Marut, for example), and the *Männerbünde*, those Indo-European "men's societies" that researchers like Otto Höfler and Stig Wikander investigated in the 1930s.

The Germanic, Indo-Iranian, Latin and, in a certain sense, the Celtic peoples have been the focus of Indo-European studies. But what then of the Greeks, who you devoted your first works to?

I am still very attached to them! But the truth is that the Indo-European people seem to have lost the essential characteristics of their religious ideology more quickly than the others. While the Greek language has preserved a great many archaic expressions, its religion was greatly transformed. The critical apparatus of a culture, if mobilized early on, modifies even that which it attempts to preserve.

Is it not true that several "Dumézilian" researchers—such as Lucien Gerschel, Francis Vian, Michel Lejune, Atsuhiko Yoshida, Udo M. Strutynski—have brought to light numerous Hellenistic examples that stem from a trifunctional analysis?

There are effectively a certain number, from the apologue of Cresus at Solon's up until the social tripartition instituted by Plato in his *Republic*. The origin of the Trojan war contains an evident tripartite character, since Paris, in giving the apple must choose between Hera, who offers him power, and Aphrodite, the most beautiful of women.
    Nevertheless, those are isolated events and, on the whole, it doesn't seem possible to see many Greek myths as conforming to the systems of the Indo-Europeans.

There is also the classical objection to consider, according to which the tripartition has no specifically Indo-European characteristics, but would correspond instead to forms that are common to all social structures . . .

That's an objection that I hear often, but it only rests on a superficial observation of reality. This mode of observation confuses the social structures with mental or ideological structures. To call attention to the presence of more or less identical social roles in different cultures is one thing. To reflect on this difference as a means of fabricating an intellectual structure and establishing a classifying and categorizing mentality is another. What constitutes the originality of the Indo-Europeans is that they created the philosophical and ideological backbone of their entire worldview. Indo-European tripartition is found in the most diverse domains. Benveniste has brought to light the functional value of the "trinity of calamities." For my part, I studied the "three sins" constituting the traditional fatalities of the warrior for the Indo-Europeans. There are also ritual formulas of tripartite eulogies, medical and judicial triumvirates, tripartite episodes of the great epic poems, etc.

Even in the symbolism of colors, one finds this distinction. With the Indo-Iranians, for example, the functional social groups are designated by colors, of which the distribution is equally attested to elsewhere: white for the priests, red for the warriors, black (or dark blue) for the farmer-herders. "Black, white, red is his path" the *Rig-Veda* says with respect to Agni, the most trifunctional of gods.

Neither with the Egyptians before their contact with the Hittites, nor with the Hebrews, nor with the Siberians, the Finno-Ugric or the Chinese, does one find this same ideological tripartition. In Antiquity, only the Indo-Europeans had made this philosophical distinction and, since it can be found in the speculations or in the literary productions of so many peoples of this family and amongst them alone, the most economical explanation is to admit that the distinction is anterior to the dispersion of these peoples, and that it is the work of thinkers of which the Brahmans, Druids, and Roman sacerdotal colleges are, in part, the inheritors.

The Three States

This evidently poses the problem of survivals. Independently of those that could be preserved in legends and popular folklore, one observes in the Middle Ages the appearance of a tripartite structure, that one might think is drawn directly from the Indo-European model, and that, according to certain authors (Jacques Le Goffe, J. H. Grisward), exhibits a certain ideal schematic. I refer to the distinction between clerics, "those who pray" *(oratores),* **the barons, "those who fight"** *(bellatores),* **and the peasants, "those who work"** *(laboratores).* **What should one think about the medieval system of the "three states," upon which the** *ancien régime* **was built?**

It's an absolutely fascinating problem, on which several working hypotheses have been founded. The hypothesis of a coincidence seems to exclude these theories. This resurgence of the three functions was most likely an attempt to establish a relationship with the ancient system of the Celtic islanders, notably the Irish, who, even though Christianized, had preserved the old social tripartition. This then progressed across Great Britain and then to the continent, where it was to be generalized. It was elsewhere with the Anglo-Saxons, in the north of France, that one sees its early manifestations.

Another important issue is the way in which myth and history become "mixed up" among the Indo-Europeans. The Roman example in this regard is particularly telling.

The Romans have always had a "historicizing" disposition. They incorporated mythic facts into their history. It has always been less in their theology than in the "history" of their origins that the Romans preserved the functional tripartition. In their annals, in the accounts of their first sovereigns, the Romans, who had all but forgotten everything about their gods, present figures and themes which display a correspondence with Indo-European mythology, notably Indian, and with archaic theology itself. The chronological succession of Romulus and Numa Poppillus, the two founders of Rome, followed by the exclusively warrior-king Tullus Hostilius, and finally by Ancus Marclus, corresponds to the hierarchical pantheons of the Germanic and Indo-Iranian people (Varuna and Mithra, followed by Indra and the Nåsatya).

You have also noted the story of the one-eyed and the one-handed.

One finds in effect, especially in the Germanic peoples, a blind god, Óðinn, and a one-armed god, Týr. However, these two divinities possess qualities that have a rapport with their infirmities. The all-seeing Óðinn has only one eye: it is for this reason that he sees what others cannot. Similarly, the god Týr, the guarantor of contracts voluntarily sacrificed his right hand as a guarantee for a false oath. I have shown that in Rome these "exceptional mutilations" have been transposed onto a historic register, and that one finds the correlations of Óðinn and Týr in the legendary personalities of Horatius Cocles, the one-eyed, who strikes down his enemies with a single gaze, and of Marcus Scaevola, who, in order to uphold a false declaration, sacrificed his right hand.

In the past century, works on the Indo-Europeans have increased. The development of linguistics has broken through the "wall" of writing. Progress in the field of comparative mythology is considered as comparable to that in archeology and ethnology. The existence of an epic literature, of a poetry, of a highly elaborate theology no longer seems to be in doubt as far as the origins of the Indo-European community is concerned. But in France, Indo-European studies, contrary to what is going on in Germany or the Anglo-Saxon countries, have reached only the smallest number of students and researchers. What do you think of this predicament?

It's a question of time. Only a short time ago professors of Greek and Latin did not take into account that these two languages were closely related to Sanskrit. The situation has improved since then. There is certainly still plenty of room for progress. But this shouldn't stop us from approaching our work with the right attitude.

(Translated by William Wallace)

Suggested Reading

Books About Dumézil:

C. Scott Littleton, *The New Comparative Mythology* (Berkeley and Los Angeles: Univ. of California Press, 1982).
Jaan Puhvel, *Comparative Mythology* (Baltimore: Johns Hopkins, 1987).

Selected Works by Dumézil Available in English:

The Destiny of the Warrior (Chicago: Univ. of Chicago Press, 1970).

Archaic Roman Religion, 2 vols., (Chicago, Univ. of Chicago Press, 1970).
From Myth to Fiction (Chicago, Univ. of Chicago Press, 1973).
The Destiny of a King (Chicago, Univ. of Chicago Press, 1973).
Gods of the Ancient Northmen (Berkeley and Los Angeles: Univ. of California Press, 1973).

Books About Benoist:

Tomislav Sunic, *Against Democracy and Equality* (New York: Peter Lang, 1990).

A number of Benoist's essays have appeared in translation in the journal *Telos* (431 East 12th Street, New York, NY 10009). "Nazism and Communism: Evil Twins?" may be viewed at the *Telos* website: www.angelfire.com/biz/telospress/telosintro.html

From Lore-Giver to Law-Giver: The Tale of Woden

Steve Pollington

In Norse mythology as it has come down to us in the works of Snorri Sturluson and the verse on which he based his accounts, the high god of the pre-Christian Scandinavian religion was Óðinn—chief of the gods, father of the Æsir clan. He is the god of magic, of knowledge, of death, the special favourite of kings and warriors whose ideal characteristics he embodies: resourcefulness, cunning and guile. He travels among men wearing his broad-brimmed hat and copious cloak to hide his missing eye, pledged at the Well of Mimir in exchange for more secrets.

This Icelandic image dates from the 13th century. To what extent does this version of the High God match the evidence for him from earlier and elsewhere? What, indeed, is the origin of Óðinn?

The earliest references to Germanic folk beliefs—found in P. Cornelius Tacitus's quasi-ethnographic work *Germania*—do not name the gods and other beings forming the object of worship among the Germanic folk of his day, the 1st century AD. Instead, the Roman writer interprets native Germanic deities in terms of Roman gods. It is generally assumed that when he says of the Germans that they worship Mercury, that this refers to the pre-Óðinn figure whose name is reconstructed as *Woðenaz. What they believed about this figure, what his myths said of him and how he interacted with men are the subject of many studies.

It seems fairly safe to assume that this pre-Óðinn took part in an early version of the creation myth. This assumption is based on the evidence from Norse. In the Norse cycle of stories, Óðinn is everywhere, he is the prime mover in many of the tales and the leader of the gods. He is seldom shown in the passive role of a monarch aloof from his court. Due to his involvement in most of the tales that have come down to us, it could be argued that he originally had no part in the creation and has been slotted in by convention, or has even replaced one of the more shadowy figures from the mythic cycle. Yet one factor weighs heavily in his favour: in the myth he is said to act with his brothers Vili and Ve. The three brothers' names are mediaeval Icelandic, of course, but projecting these names back to the time of Tacitus, undoing all the phonetic changes that have intervened, we find that in the original myth they were called *Woðenaz, *Wiliz and *Weihaz—all alliterating on "w-". This is the kind of detail that a later storyteller would be likely to edit out—to harmonise all three by changing the lesser brothers' names into more transparent ones also beginning with a vowel. The fact that the tradition stuck (and that the Viking Age storytellers would probably not have invented such an incongruous detail) argues for some antiquity to this factor. So Óðinn's place in the creation myth seems to go back at least to the time when his name still began with "W-"; this can be roughly dated to about the 8th century for Danish but it is much harder to be so precise for the West Norse (Norwegian) regions from which the original Icelandic dialects came. It is nonetheless safe to say that in broad terms the association of the three divine names must go back beyond the 8th century.

In German dialects the name appears as Votan, Uotan and in English as Woden. While there is no vast body of tales attached to him in either the surviving continental German or English tradition, there are enough scraps to demonstrate that his name was more than an obscure curio from a forgotten age. Early (Old High) German, for example, when adopting the seven-day week from the Roman calendar, refused to designate the fourth day by this god's name, and rather took over the innocuous term "midweek" (modern *Mittwoch*) than continue the association with Uotan. In England, where the process of religious conversion was more accommodating to native sensibilities, the day retained the name *Wodnesdæg* "Wednesday." As with the traditions of ritual feasting and runic writing, which were adopted by the early English church, the old ways were continued under a new guise.

What does Woðenaz mean? The form of the word **woðenaz* is interesting in itself. It can be roughly translated as "master of excitement," based on the word **woþaz* which has a range of meanings connected to inspiration, incantation, initiation into sacred mysteries. In OE there are two related forms. The first cognate *woþ* is "singing" and "music" but a *woþbora* (bearer of *woþ*) is a "prophet" or "soothsayer." The implication is that *woþ* relates to chanting and inspired mental activity, to ecstatic travelling, to the realms of the dream-warrior and shaman. The other cognate is the adjective *wod* which means "angry, enraged" or better "insensed." The derived verb *wedan* means "become angry, lose control of one's senses, become deranged" and here again there is an element of the highly excited or agitated mental state which seems to attend the shaman-figure. During his spirit-journey he may first become intoxicated or convulsed, then lie in a torpid state while his soul travels forth. *Woðenaz is then the master and bringer of these mental conditions, the god who enters the shaman's mind and takes control of him spiritually and physically.

The term *woðenaz then indicates one who is imbued with this quality, who personifies and represents these practices. Many societies have a god or gods whose area of interest lies in the world of spirit travel; it is not clear that this is what Mercury represented to the Romans, but there are nevertheless points of contact between that god and the Germanic *woðenaz. One is the connection of the god to secret knowledge and to writing; another is the adoption of his cult by the military. In the case of Mercury this was most noticeable in Gaul where the Gallo-Roman military authorities fostered the god's worship.

In a recent study of the rise of the Germanic warband and its cult, Enright suggested that all attributes of Óðinn—including his single eye, his hat, his spear, his military background, his supernatural associations, his prophetic female companions—are directly attributable to the cult fostered by the Batavian governor Julius Civilis in an attempt to unite the Rhenish Germanic tribes into a cohesive military force to drive out the Roman imperial authorities. His model, suggests Enright, was the Gallic Mercury cult adopted by Celtic warbands of the late La Tène culture who were responsible for the introduction of new fashions in armour and weapons to the lower Rhine. Working from the list of Odinic by-names found in the Norse tales, he selects specific terms, such as *Grimr* "masked one," and relates them to aspects of Civilis's life and campaign. Civilis himself deliberately evoked the affection, bordering on religious awe, which the Rhineland Celts had for an earlier local figure, Sertorius, who was one-eyed and a skilful military leader. Enright's book is a fascinating examination of the warband and its leadership, but his conclusion seems to run way outside the evidence.

The English evidence for Woden is not great. From OE literature there come a handful of references, almost all in genealogies of royal lines where the name appears as a "glorious ancestor"

ODIN (WODEN), ILLUSTRATION FROM A GERMAN CALENDAR, CIRCA EARLY 1900S.

alongside many other names from the distant past. One medical manuscript preserves a charm in which the god is mentioned in his fight with the serpent (the apotropaic power of the god invoked against the powers of disease and misfortune). A gnomic verse refers to him: *woden worhte weos* "Woden made idols" in contradistinction to Christ who wrought marvels.

Iconographic evidence is perhaps more plentiful although identification is less certain: the metal image-bearing plates from the Sutton Hoo helmet and other treasures, the Gilton buckle and many other pagan period finds bear small figures which could plausibly be identified with the god. None of them appears to be one-eyed, which may be significant in itself. The notion that Odin had always been one-eyed has been challenged (Stone, 2001). While this is a clear feature of the Icelandic tales, where his eye is said to have been pledged to Mimir in return for knowledge, it is not so evident elsewhere. Saxo's references in his *Gesta Danorum* are not helpful as he represents Othinus as a human king who, by his great cunning and wisdom, was posthumously revered as a god by his people. He is described in generally favourable terms, is handsome and no mention is made of a missing eye. It is worth stressing that Snorri is ambivalent also: he differentiates between a one-eyed sorcerer Odin who is grim and war-minded, and a handsome, kingly Odin who is the leader of the gods. It may be that Odin was not at all times and in all circumstances a one-eyed figure after all.

The earliest pictorial references which could be interpreted as one-eyed are the bracteates of Denmark, southern Scandinavia and England. These small gold or electrum pendant disks were produced for unknown purposes during the 5th and 6th centuries; many have been recovered from apparently votive contexts. They often bear Style I animal art, but a significant proportion feature small scenes of presumably cultic or religious significance.

One large group with many variants shows a human head in profile above a quadruped, which is often depicted with a trailing foot. This has been read as an early reference to the myth alluded to in the First Merseburg Charm where Uodan chants spells to heal his horse's wrenched tendons. Versions of this tale were collected by folklorists in England in the 19th century, and on this basis it has been assumed once to have been a very common myth invoked during medical procedures (Pollington, 2000). However, there is more than one area of weakness in the identification of this figure with Woden. First, the head shown in profile often has a prominent eye, but there is no way to determine whether the artist intended to represent the subject as one-eyed. There are no known figures with a "blank" where the eye should be, and an artist wishing to stress the lack of an eye would have had to show the face frontally. Secondly, the animal shown beneath the head is often equine but in many cases it has a small U-shaped device between the ears and a pendant triangle beneath the chin; this suggests a goat (horned and with a beard) rather than a horse. There is no known association between Odin and the goat, but there is a Norse tale in which the god Þorr heals the leg of his goat after it has been accidentally maimed by a farmer's son. The bracteate heads are not strongly linked to what we know of Þorr, it must be said: they are not bearded and there is no suggestion of the hammer, Mjöllnir, which is the god's symbol and weapon. However, the iconography of the bracteate does often display the swastika or hooked cross which has been seen as the symbolic representation of the god's hammer.

The prominent eye of the bracteate figures is, then, not necessarily indicative of Odin but could it denote Þorr? There are a couple of references which stress Þorr's eyes. One is a runic text: *gliaugir uiu r[u]n[o]r* "[I of the] glaring-eyes hallow [the] runes" on the Dannenburg bracteate. Another is the story of Þorr's cross-dressing escapade recounted in the *Þrymskviða* verse where the god travels in disguise to reclaim his hammer from the giant Þrym, who wishes to wed Freyja. Þorr dresses up in bridal gown and veil, and when the giant lifts the head-dress to snatch a kiss from his intended, he is dismayed at the fierce, glaring gaze emanating from his bride-to-be. This "glaring eyes" motif is not accidental: some of the hammer amulets found in Scandinavian contexts feature a prominent pair of eyes on the shaft, suggesting that his fierce gaze was a strong feature of the god's cult.

The earliest representations of a one-eyed god in Scandinavian contexts date from the end of the Viking period, from the 11th century and after. Even here, there is room for debate: for instance, the 13th century carved head from the church at Hegge, Norway, depicts a figure with one eye and a lolling tongue. The right "eye" is present as a slit, rather than an empty socket, which may be equally taken to show a face with one eye closed.

Conclusion

The rise of Odin to his position at the head of the Norse pantheon in Snorri's mediaeval collection of stories and poems may have been a comparatively recent event—probably dating from Viking times. However, the English manuscript evidence tells a different tale. Here, Woden stands at the head of all but one kingly genealogy. (The only exception is the East Saxon royal house, which traced its line from Seaxneat, a figure known from Old Saxon records as Saxnot and believed to be the tribal god of the Saxon folk.) These English genealogies appear to be genuine tradition from the 7th century, although they might be earlier. Their form is largely fixed by the 8th century and developments after that date mainly involve tracing Woden back to some biblical forebear; in other words, the part between the known historical figures and Woden was "fixed" and the only place left to add names was at the front end, before Woden, in the mythical past.

It seems probable, then, that there was a connection between Woden and kingship itself. This is dealt with by both Kershaw and Enright. The original *Woðenaz figure was a lore-giver, a tutor, a shamanic guide, a mentor to the young men of the tribe who underwent a sustained period of initiation living wild in the woods in a group known as a *koryos. Sometime around the 2nd–1st century BC this institution was transformed from a rite of social integration into a purely or mainly military institution; its leader likewise developed from "fount of wisdom" to "leader of warriors" and the presiding deity retained his role as god of magic but added important new skills in the giving of military victories. The original *koryos "social grouping of young men awaiting initiation" became the Germanic *xarjaz "group of young warriors." Germanic kingship in the Roman period drew on this model for its inspiration, and the god of the warband became the god of the rulers and the social élite.

Woden's rise in status, then, mirrors the increased prominence of the youthful bands of warriors and their leaders, who were able to transform the political map of Europe between the 1st and the 8th centuries, moulding ancient, imperial, Roman-dominated territories into more self-sufficient and inwardly focussed groupings. While political leaders often sought to expand and increase the territory under their sway, the contrary trend towards keeping land units manageable and political institutions useful and relevant checked this. The history of Europe since the fall of Roman power demonstrates clearly that this is a circle never to be squared.

References:

Enright, Michael J. *The Lady with the Mead Cup* (Dublin: Four Courts Press, 1996).

Gordon, E. V. *Introduction to Old Norse* (Oxford: Oxford Univ. Press, 1962).

Kershaw, Kris. *Odin: The One-Eyed God* (Washington, D.C.: Journal of Indo-European Studies, 2000).

Pollington, Stephen. *Leechcraft: Early English Charms, Plantlore and Healing* (Hockwold-cum-Wilton: Anglo-Saxon Books, 2000).

Stone, Alby. "Odin's Lost Eye" in *3rd Stone* (issue 41, 2001).

Indo-European Trifunctional Elements in Celtic Foundation Myths

Alby Stone

The Indo-European Ideology among the Celts

Indo-European myths of national or tribal origins tend also to be societal myths. That is, they explain not only how a people came into being but also how and why the social structure is the way it is. Georges Dumézil has shown that traditional Indo-European societies were organised according to three strata that encompass the full range of human activity. Dumézil called the three strata *fonctions*, "functions," a sociological term modified for his own purpose. In Dumézil's usage, a function refers to one of the three social strata, plus its divine representations and attributes, and their associated behaviours and qualities—but it has a more fundamental meaning, denoting "the principles in terms of which these phenomena are defined" (Littleton 1982: 5). This is stressed by his equation of "three modes of activity" with "three social functions" (Dumézil 1938) and the apparent synonymy of the terms "activity" and "function" elsewhere in his work (Belier 1991: 29). The functions are usually ranked hierarchically:

1. Qualities associated with religion, ritual, magic, knowledge, speech, poetry, rule, governance, and law. It is the "head" of the social body, with characteristics relating to the human head. This function is embodied by the idea of priests (but in later tradition incorporating or in tandem with kingship)

2. Qualities associated with physical force, courage, strength, protection and aggression—the "arms" of the social body, with characteristics relating to the arms and upper torso. Warriors embody this stratum.

3. Qualities associated with food production and consumption, fertility, love and sex, beauty, pleasure, and wealth. This function is analogous to the "belly" and "genitals" of the social body, whose character relates to those parts of the human body. This also includes the legs, as this function supports the other two. The

third function is mainly represented by farmers (but also by herders, merchants and artisans).

This tripartite pattern does not refer solely to social stratification. As Lincoln (1986) has shown, society follows the template of the human body, as does the cosmos. The social activities encapsulated here are found in virtually all human groups—the significance of the Indo-European version is that it was ritualised, codified in myth. It permeates Indo-European tradition. This pattern, which Dumézil called the *idéologie tripartie* (I prefer to use the term "trifunctionalism"), is clearly indicated in the type of myth to be discussed here.

Textual evidence for a trifunctional ideology among the Celts goes back as far as the first century BCE. In *De Bello Gallicum* 6.13 Julius Caesar tells us that the Gauls were divided into *druides*, *equites* and *plebes*—druids (priests), horsemen ("knights") and commoners. Caesar does not record a Gaulish tradition of their origins, except to say that they believe themselves descended from "Dis Pater"—a name that could, within the flexible framework of the *interpretatio Romana*, signify any one of many Celtic deities. We also have the Gaulish divine triad described by the first-century Roman poet Lucan in *Pharsalia* 1.441–6. Lucan describes human sacrifices made to three gods, Teutates, Esus (or Aesus) and Taranis. Puhvel (1987: 168–72) makes a strong case for these as a functional triad: Esus "(the) lord"; Taranis "thunder"; and Teutates "(god of) the people/tribe." There is even some archaeological evidence in favour of Lucan's triad. Esus is depicted on the Gallo-Roman altar found in 1711 at the cathedral of Notre Dame in Paris, along with two other gods named as Jovis (Jupiter) and Volcanus. Jupiter would naturally translate as the thunder god Taranis, as he does in other inscriptions. Volcanus is better known to us as the divine smith Vulcan. But before he acquired attributes of the Greek deity Hephaistos, Volcanus was a very different god indeed, associated with the protection of grain from fire. Dumézil (1970a: 320–1) locates him firmly as a god of the third function.

It seems that the Gauls had a ritually tripartite society and perhaps a group of gods who each represented one of its strata. In Ireland, according to various Old Irish laws and other texts, there were three social groups who were considered *aire*, freemen: the *druí* (druids); the *flaith*, the aristocracy, those who exercised authority (a word related to German *gewalt*, "force"); and the *bó-aire*, "cattle-freemen" (Rees and Rees 1961: 111). These clearly correspond to the Gaulish social structure, and are evidently closely related to the *arya* castes of ancient India.

The Gaulish social tripartition was sufficiently pronounced for Caesar to remark upon it, while the early Irish thought their own version important enough to enshrine in law. Presumably a similar division existed among the ancient Britons, although nothing of the kind is mentioned in Classical sources. Nor is there any clear evidence of it in the archaeological record. But it would seem likely if only because a trifunctional division existed among their near-neighbours and fellow Celtic-speakers. We do know that there were druids in Britain, along with chieftains, kings and queens, warriors, farmers, herders, and artisans. Unfortunately, Roman sources are not informative with regard to British social organisation or religious ideology, and medieval Welsh literature is inevitably post-Roman. It is doubtful whether the historical Celts had a common pantheon—one view is that they had clusters of gods specific to different tribes, and archaeology tends to support this idea, up to a point (Webster 1989). This means that we should not look to either medieval Ireland or ancient Gaul as a definitive measure of the situation in Britain in Roman or pre-Roman times.

However, there is some evidence from Welsh literature to support the idea that the trifunctional ideology was known to the British. For instance, in the *Mabinogion* story *Math vab Mathonwy*, Lleu Llaw Gyffes is given three "destinies" by his mother—that he shall not have a name unless she names him, that he shall not bear arms unless they are given by her, and that he shall not have a wife of any race on earth. These are surely a trifunctional set: name (knowledge of identity), weapons, and wife (sexuality). In the same story, Lleu's rival Gronw Pebyr commits three acts against Leu—adultery with Lleu's wife, cowardly murder and usurpation—that agree with a mythic theme found in several Indo-European traditions, in which an exemplar of the warrior function commits a sin against each of the functions in turn and is thus destroyed or neutralised (Dumézil 1970b; Lloyd-Morgan 1988; Stone 1996). Furthermore, Markey (1982) has identified the three daughters of King Lear—in Geoffrey of Monmouth's collation of older texts into the coherent narrative presented in his *Historia*—as representatives of the three functions.

There are other examples of trifunctionalism from Irish literature. For example, there is the story of Lugaid Riab nDerg ("Lugaid of the red stripes") who was conceived when his mother slept with her three brothers on the same night, so that he had three fathers. He was born with red stripes around his neck and waist: his head resembled that of his father Nár ("noble"); his arms and chest resembled Bres ("combat"); and from the waist down he resembled Clothru ("washtub" or "trough"). Each of Lugaid's fathers clearly belongs to one of the three functions, and it is no surprise that he went on to become a king (Lincoln 1986: 158-62). A king must embody the social totality: Lugaid was born with the necessary attributes, unlike Lleu Llaw Gyffes, who had to earn them. The Irish and Welsh had traditions of trifunctional kingship, while Irish and Gaulish societies were organised along trifunctional lines. The Gauls also seem to have had a divine functional triad, and similar groups have been discerned in Irish myth (Rees and Rees 1961: 142). This is enough to suggest that trifunctionalism was part of the common heritage of Celtic-speakers, as the idea of the Indo-European tripartite ideology would predict.

The Indo-European Trifunctional Foundation Myth

In some traditions the tripartition is said to derive from the emanations of a primordial being sacrificed so that the cosmos can be made from his body parts. In the *Rig Veda* of ancient India, for example, the three *arya* castes—*Brāhmanas, Ksatriyas* and *Vaiśyas*—are born from the dismembered body of Purusa. In other Indo-European groups the myth of social origins involves three descendants of a divine or heroic ancestor, and the populations representing the functions are propagated through the normal biological process. The consequence is the same, however: a land is populated (or repopulated; or a nation founded) in such a way that usually three brothers, sons of the same father, are the fathers of the three elements of the population that make up the social and ethnic totality.

The ancestral figure is sometimes a primordial being—whether man, giant or god—but is more usually the first person to inhabit the particular region associated with a particular people. Hence the myth is generally associated with themes of kingship, and the main characters are often kings and the sons of kings. In accordance with Indo-European cosmology, the three sons represent the social totality, the entire nation. They do so by each embodying one of the three functions.

In the fifth century BCE Herodotus (*The Histories* 4.5–6) recorded what he claimed was the Scythian story of their own origins. The story goes that Scythia was uninhabited until the birth of Targitaos, the son of Zeus by the river Borysthenes (the Dnieper). Targitaos had three sons of his own: Lipoxaïs, Arpoxaïs and Kolaxaïs. Four golden treasures fell from the sky, a plough, a yoke, a battle-axe, and a cup. Lipoxaïs and Arpoxaïs each tried to take these objects, but when they tried the treasures caught fire. When Kolaxaïs, the youngest brother, made the attempt the fires went out, and he was able to take the objects. The brothers took this as a sign, and made Kolaxaïs their ruler. From him descended the Paralatai, the tribe of Royal Scythians; the descendants of Lipoxaïs were the Aukhatai, while from Arpoxaïs came the Katiaroi and Traspies.

There is every indication that this is an authentic Scythian myth. Certainly the names of these so-called tribes are Hellenised forms of Iranian words that clearly indicate Indo-European social strata (Puhvel 1987: 113–4). The Aukhatai ("mighty") are the warriors, while the "tribal" names Traspies and Katiaroi respectively signify horses and cattle-pastures. Herodotus acknowledged the Paralatai ("foremost") as the "Royal Scythians." Kolaxaïs's possession of all the treasures signifies that he embodies the social totality, a prerequisite of Indo-European kingship (Lincoln 1986: 158). The fact that there are four objects does not mean that this tale deviates from the tripartite pattern of Indo-European cosmology. The third function—that of food-production, consumption and fertility—is often divided; and in any case the plough and yoke ought properly to be seen as a united pair, linked as they are in agricultural practice.

The mythic pattern persisted among Iranian-speakers. As late as the tenth century CE the Persian poet Ferdowsi was retelling tales that had their origins in the distant past, long before Zoroastrianism and Islam came to his people. His epic poem *Shāh Nāma* contains a number of old myths, updated, stitched together with genuinely historical material and presented as a history of the Persian kings. *Shāh Nāma* 4.7–8 tells how Feridun (a version of the much older Iranian dragon-slayer Thraētaona, whose myth is told in Avestan texts), disguised as a dragon, tests his three sons. The eldest flees; the middle son draws his bow and prepares to attack; and the youngest tells the dragon to be gone before it meets its doom. From their actions Feridun gives them their names and divines their respective natures. The eldest is Salm, of whom Feridun says "May the whole world resound with your prosperity because you chose safety from the dragon's mouth"—a pun on *kam*, which can mean both mouth and prosperity. The middle son is Tur "a brave lion." The youngest son is Iraj, "a man of sense" with "an alert mind." When Feridun divides the world among his sons, it is the first-function representative Iraj who is given Feridun's throne and the choicest realm, Iran itself.

A parallel myth is attributed to the Germans about six hundred years later. In *Germania* 2 Tacitus reports that the Germans venerate Tuisto, a god born from the earth. Tuisto had a son named Mannus, "the beginning of their people." Mannus had three sons: from these were descended the three branches of Germans, the Istaevones, Herminones, and Ingaevones. This corresponds in part to archaic Indo-European creation mythology, which begins with a pair of twins—"Man" and "Twin." *Tuisto* means "two-fold," and is equivalent to the Norse primal giant Ymir, whose name means "twin." *Mannus* is "man," and ought properly to be Tuisto's twin—he has become displaced in this case. The Ingaevones are named for Ing or Yngvi, another name for Freyr the Norse god of peace, prosperity and fertility. The Herminones and Istaevones are problematic. The name Herminones is certainly related to the Old Saxon name Irmin ("great, mighty"). This is cognate with Old Norse Jörmunnr, a name for Óðinn, the divine sorcerer-king. But the name Jörmunnr is also applied to the belligerent thunder-god Þórr, who clearly reflects the second, warrior function. The name Istaevones is obscure, but it may be derived from a word meaning "strong," which implies the second function. These problems aside, the *Germania* account does appear to fall into a definite trifunctional pattern found elsewhere in Germanic myth and religion. For instance, the "tribal" names parallel the divine triad later venerated at Uppsala, which according to Adam of Bremen's eleventh-century *Gesta Hammaburgensis Ecclesiae Pontificum* comprised Freyr, Óðinn and Þórr.

Nearly a thousand years after Tacitus the Icelandic poem *Rígspula* recounts the story of how Heimdallr (calling himself Rígr as he travelled among mortals) sired the social classes through his sons Þræll, Karl and Jarl. These sons have names that reflect their social status. Þræll ("slave") corresponds to the non-*arya* caste of India, who as slaves and subject peoples were not recognised as properly belonging to the social body. The third function son is clear enough: Karl, in accordance with the meaning of his name, is a farmer. The second function is represented by Jarl ("noble")—the poem associates him with warfare and weapons. The first function is represented by Jarl's son Konr unger, "young son," whose name is a play on *konungr* "king" and comes to be called Rígr like his grandfather. Konr is a rune-master and magician as well as his father's heir—this demonstrates the close connection between kingship and magic in the first function. The presence of the non-Germanic name Rígr has given rise to speculation that *Rígspula* was based on a now-lost Celtic myth or folktale. The linguistic aspect of that argument is still a matter of debate, but even if the supposition that the name Rígr was borrowed from a Celtic source is correct there is still ample evidence that the trifunctional founders are not only Germanic, but quintessentially Indo-European.

The Greek hero Deukalion's children fall into this pattern. *Ehoiai* 3–4 describes the offspring of Deukalion—Hellen, Pandora and Thuia in that particular version of the Deukalion myth—in terms that leave their trifunctional nature in little doubt, though there are displacements. Hellen is said to be the "war-loving king"; Pandora, impregnated by Zeus, gives birth to Graecus, described as "staunch in battle." Thuia, also impregnated by Zeus, bears two sons: Magnes and Macedon, who are characterised as "rejoicing in horses"—compare these with the Dioskuroi and Aśvins, the equestrian representatives of the third function in Greece and India. While the trifunctional pattern is fractured, with functional figures displaced to a subsequent generation, just as in *Rígspula*, it is still discernible: the ethnic population, stratified according to function, descends from three children of a founding father.

The Trifunctional Foundation Myth in Celtic Tradition

Interestingly, the early Germanic foundation myth recorded by Tacitus was later incorporated into British and Irish histories. Around seven hundred years after Tacitus, chapter 17 of the *Historia Brittonum* tells us that Noah's son Japheth was an ancestor of a man named Alanus, "first man to come to Europe." This Alanus had three sons: Hessitio, Armenon and Negue. Hessitio was ancestor of the Franks, Latins, Albans and British; Armenon gave rise to the Goths, Walagoths, Gepids, Burgundians and Langobards; and Negue was progenitor of the Bavarians, Vandals, Saxons and Thuringians. These peoples, we are told, are subdivided throughout Europe. Three centuries later an almost identical account is given in manuscripts of the *Lebor Gabála Érenn*, the "Book of the Taking of Ireland" or "Book of Invasions" as it is more popularly known. Alainus (the name occurs as the manuscript variant Elanius) is once again a descendant of Japheth, and his three sons are Armen, Negua and Isicón (or: Armenon, Neugio and Hisican). These three are ancestors of a list of peoples that corresponds exactly to that given in the *Historia Brittonum*. When we compare the father and his three sons from each of these accounts, it is immediately clear that they are one and the same family and are derived from *Germania*. *Alanus* (and so *Alainus/Elanius*) is evidently a misreading of *Mannus*. Hessitio and *Hisican/Isicon* are derived from the ethnic name *Istaevones* (which also occurs as *Iscaevones* in a manuscript of *Germania*). *Armenon* and *Armen* are from *Herminones*. *Neugiu/Ngua* and *Negue* are from *Ingvaeones* (or the variant *Ingaevones*). Both histories have ignored the mythical side of the *Germania* story and have worked the Germanic primogenitors into the Biblical account of the descent of populations after the Flood.

Littleton and Malcor (1997) cite the name Alainius as evidence that the *Lebor Gabála Érenn* records a genuine tradition of an Alan (Scythian) element reaching Ireland. Yet the context clearly signals that the name is probably a copyist's misreading of *Mannus* in a manuscript of *Germania* or a second-hand quotation from Tacitus. In fact the Irish text has the same patchwork look as the *Historia Brittonum*. They are both cobbled together from a variety of disparate sources and each is broadly typical of medieval attempts to reconcile classical histories and native genealogies with those of the Bible. The *Historia Brittonum* is thought to be derivative of an earlier version or predecessor of the *Lebor Gabála Érenn*. The latter gives Alainius's father the name Dói, which could perhaps be a shortened variant of *Tuisto*—but in *Historia Brittonum* 18 the name is Fetebir. Tacitus might or might not have been the immediate source of the Irish reference. But it does not seem likely that either Tacitus or the *Lebor Gabála Érenn* was a direct source for this particular component of the *Historia Brittonum*.

But the Celtic traditions did not rely wholly on Tacitus for trifunctional foundation myths. The tripartite pattern is clearly replicated in chapter 48 of the *Historia Brittonum*, in a section taken from a life of Saint Germanus. Guorthigirnus (i.e., Vortigern) had three sons: Guorthemir (i.e., Vortimer: from *vortamorix* "great king"); Categirn ("battle-prince"); and Pascent (from the Latin name Pascentius, perhaps from *pasco*, "to feed; fatten; support", "to feast"). A fourth son, Faustus (Latin: "lucky, prosperous"), was born of an incestuous relationship between Guorthigirnus and his daughter. Each name refers directly to one of the three functions of Indo-European cosmology—priesthood/sovereignty; war; food production, prosperity/fertility.

According to most versions of the *Lebor Gabála Érenn*, the first abortive invasion of Ireland was that of Partholón, which endured for some time but was exterminated by plague. Partholón's sons were: "the lordly being" Slánga; the "sword-wielding" Láiglinne; and "the very manly" Rudraige. Slánga and Láiglinne are obviously described in terms that accord with the first and second functions of Indo-European cosmology. Rudraige's manliness may refer to martial prowess, but rather suggests good looks and sexual virility, which are third function attributes. However, it is possible that the functional attributes have been wrongly allocated. *Slánga* is a variant of the name Sláine "health," suggesting the third function—in the *Metrical Dindshenchas* 4.300 he is called the first physician in Ireland. The name Rudraige means "red king" and so belongs to the first function. This wave of settlers endured for some time but was exterminated by plague.

These examples of trifunctional foundation mythology are unambiguous, but there are a number of others where the Indo-European functions are not readily apparent. For the most part all that remains is the motif of the settling ruler and his three sons, or of three founding fathers who are only notionally related. For instance, in the first rescension of the *Lebor Gabála Érenn*, before the arrival of Partholón an attempted settlement of Ireland was led by Cesair "daughter of Bith son of Noah" who reached Ireland just before the Flood with three ships, two of which sank. The surviving ship bore fifty maidens and three men, who divided the women between them. The men were Cesair's father Bith, son of Noah; Ladru the steersman; and Fintan son of Bóchra. However, everyone except Fintan—who lingered on as a shape-shifting observer of Irish history—perished just before the Flood and Ireland remained empty for many years. Some of the names—such as *Bith* "world," and *Fintan* "white" son of *Bóchra* "ocean"—hint at a more primal cosmic structure, the actual physical world rather than the ideological one expressed by the three functions. The names of these men do not reflect a trifunctional pattern, nor do they have any obvious functional attributes. But there is a hint that their settlement of Ireland may have been undone in functional terms. Ladru died of an excess of women, while Fintan was overwhelmed by the Flood when he fled the remaining women and went on a "journey of weakness." These would seem to be third and second function failings—lechery, and cowardice followed by loss of strength.

Later in the *Lebor Gabála Érenn* it is said that Ireland was first divided into three parts by the Dagda's grandsons, who became the kings of the Tuatha Dé Danann. They are Mac Cuill, Mac Cécht and Mac Gréne. Their names reflect the "gods" to whom they are each said to venerate—the hazel, the plough and the sun. O'Rahilly (1946: 66) asserts that these three are manifestations of the Irish sun god, but there is more than a suggestion of the three functions in their names. The epithet *mac* "son of" does not indicate a biological relationship with gods associated with the hazel, plough and sun. The three are sons of Cermait Milbél and their real names are Sethor, Tethor and Cethor. Mac Cuill, Mac Cécht and Mac Gréne are nicknames and are probably derived from things with which they were commonly linked. In Irish tradition the hazel is associated with wisdom, a first function trait, while the plough self-evidently symbolises the third function. Mac Cécht seems to be a hypostasis of Dian Cécht, who is the physician of the Tuatha Dé Danann, a third function figure. But Mac Gréne sits oddly among his siblings: the sun is not a second function attribute.

The second book of Geoffrey of Monmouth's *Historia Regum Brittonum* (c. 1136) may also preserve a later memory of the trifunctional foundation myth. Geoffrey, who claimed to be retelling stories he found in a book written in the British language, tells how a group of Trojans led by Brutus came to Britain and displaced the race of giants who then inhabited the island. Brutus had three sons, Locrinus, Kamber and Albanactus. When Brutus died they divided Britain between them, each giving his name to the part he ruled. Locrinus had Loegria (England); Kamber took charge of Kambria (Wales); and Albanactus controlled Albany (Scotland). A fourth region, Cornwall, had already been given by Brutus to his comrade Corineus, after whom it was named. This division obviously reflects the political situation at the time

Geoffrey was writing, after the unification of England and the Norman Conquest. It does not accord with the historical reality of pre-English kingdoms in Celtic Britain. Geoffrey seems partly to have followed a tradition in which Celtic founders were expected to institute a three-fold division. However, he was constrained by the fact that twelfth-century Britain had four principal parts that were not based on traditional ethnic or cosmological divisions but were rather an accident of history. Like the followers of Cesair, the personal names and attributes of Brutus's sons do not follow the trifunctional formula. Instead, they are back-formations from the names of the four nations of Britain acknowledged in Geoffrey's day. It would have been simpler for Geoffrey to make Corineus a fourth son of Brutus. The obvious reason for not doing so is that tradition dictated that the founding father should have three sons.

Only *Lebor Gabála Érenn* and the *Historia Brittonum* contain unambiguous trifunctional foundation myths with a wholly Celtic setting. This sparse haul, and the presence of early Germanic material in these two key texts, might be enough to cast doubt on the existence of such a mythic theme among the ancient Celts. But there are strong reasons for accepting their authenticity.

In the first place, it must be remembered that no Celtic myths or legends were recorded prior to the earliest written texts of Ireland and Wales. Classical scholars have left us a few fragments of lore here and there, and divine names and some iconography is preserved on artefacts of the Roman era from Britain, Gaul and elsewhere—but there are no complete myths that date from before the Christianisation of the British Isles. We really have very little idea of how the Celts saw their gods and told their myths before the new religion came. Even the earliest myths and legends were committed to writing by the clergy, and often show traces of having been tidied up to accord with the medieval Christian worldview. Both *Lebor Gabála Érenn* and the *Historia Brittonum* have been rationalised. They each tell a story of how kings and leaders, descended from Noah, spread through Europe with their offspring and followers. Each incorporates genealogical and historical material that came from Roman historians, and—because it had come to be accepted as historical fact—had to be accommodated. In a sense, the Irish and Welsh had their early history written for them—and little of it was actually Celtic, in content or in origin. It was the story of Noah and the post-Deluge diaspora, the story of Greeks, Trojans and Romans, and it had to agree with the ethnographies and histories of Roman scholars. In the circumstances it is remarkable that we still have the stories of Partholón and Guorthigirnus at all. But still there are sure signs of loss and amendment. *Partholón* is an Old Irish rendering of the Biblical name Bartholomew and does not have a Celtic origin. And the nation he founds is short-lived. The story of Guorthigirnus as we have it is about the founding of a royal line rather than an ethnic or tribal group. Yet otherwise each fits the ancient trifunctional pattern.

References:

Wouter W. Belier (1991), *Decayed Gods: Origin and Development of Georges Dumézil's "Idéologie Tripartie."* Leiden: E. J. Brill.

Georges Dumézil (1938), "La préhistoire des flamines majeurs." *Revue de l'Histoire des Religions* 118.

Georges Dumézil (1970a), *Archaic Roman Religion*. Chicago: Univ. of Chicago Press.

Georges Dumézil (1970b), *The Destiny of the Warrior*. Chicago: Univ. of Chicago Press.

Bruce Lincoln (1986), *Myth, Cosmos, and Society: Indo-European Themes of Creation and Destruction*. Cambridge, Mass.: Harvard Univ. Press.

C. Scott Littleton (1982), *The New Comparative Mythology: An Anthropological Assessment of the Theories of Georges Dumézil*. 3rd edition. Berkeley and Los Angeles: Univ. of California Press.

C. Scott Littleton and Linda A. Malcor (1997), "Did the Alans reach Ireland? A reassessment of the 'Scythian' references in the *Lebor Gabála Érenn*." In John Greppin and Edgar C. Polomé, eds., *Studies in Honor of Jaan Puhvel. Part Two: Mythology and Religion*. Washington, D.C.: Institute for the Study of Man.

T. F. O'Rahilly (1946), *Early Irish History and Mythology*. Dublin: Institute for Advanced Studies.

Jaan Puhvel (1987), *Comparative Mythology*. Baltimore: Johns Hopkins Univ. Press.

Ceridwen Lloyd-Morgan (1988), "Triadic Structures in the Four Branches of the *Mabinogi*." *Shadow* 5/1.

T. L. Markey (1982), "The Cosmology of Lear and His Daughters." In Edgar C. Polomé, ed., *Homage to Georges Dumézil*. Washington, D.C.: Institute for the Study of Man.

Alwyn Rees and Brinley Rees (1961), *Celtic Heritage: Ancient Tradition in Ireland and Wales*. London: Thames and Hudson.

Alby Stone (1996), "The Three Destinies of Lleu Llaw Gyffes." *At the Edge*.

Jane Webster (1989), "The Celtic Iron Age Pantheon in Literature versus the Celtic Iron Age Pantheon in Archaeology." *Shadow* 6/1.

3rd Stone

Quarterly Review of Archaeology, Folklore and Myth

A modern miscellany of extraordinary wonders of the ancient world

Recent articles have looked at:
Stone Circles and Megaliths • Folk Memory
Archaeology of the Undead • British Hill Figures
Stonehenge Bluestones • English Giants
The Wicker Man • Folk Medicine

Four issue airmail subscription (one year)
US$50.00 (UK£35.00), £24.00 UK, £28.00 Europe, £36.00 Elsewhere

Visa/Mastercard/US & UK cheques and well-concealed cash accepted.
Please make all cheques payable to 3rd Stone. Subscriptions can also be made with Visa or Mastercard online at www.thirdstone.demon.co.uk.

3rd Stone, PO Box 961, Devizes, Wiltshire, SN10 2TS. UK
www.thirdstone.demon.co.uk email neil@thirdstone.demon.co.uk

Divine Traces in the Nibelungenlied, *or Whose Heart Beats in Hagen's Chest?*

Michael Moynihan

The old Germanic tale of the Nibelungs has lost none of its power over the centuries. Combining mythic and heroic overlays with a historical backdrop that ultimately traces back to the pre-medieval age of tribal struggles, there are a handful of different retellings that have been preserved.[1] These medieval variants of the tale continue to be read and studied both in their original versions and in translation, and the stories they tell have served as the inspiration for modern works of art, prose, and film. The most notable examples of this phenomenon are Richard Wagner's operatic *Gesamtkunstwerk* "The Ring Cycle" and Fritz Lang's silent film adaptation, both of which continue to fascinate audiences around the world.[2]

Some of the primary written sources of the story of the Nibelungs are to be found in Icelandic manuscripts that were rediscovered in the 18th century. In the Old Norse *Poetic Edda*, dating from the 12th or 13th century, appear a number of lays that relate the story of Sigurðr's life and tell of his infamous exploits slaying the dragon, Fafnir. The *Volsunga saga* is the prose retelling of the same story that was probably written down sometime in the thirteenth century.

These Icelandic tales are, however, just one branch of the northern literary tradition. If we shift our location to the continent, we find that the same stories were being told by the court poets of Germanic Europe. The particulars are sometimes different, and the Icelandic versions appear to preserve evidence of far more archaic customs, but the same legendary heroes appear in the continental epics, and in many ways the gist of their exploits is similar. All evidence thus points to the existence of a set of older (and now lost) heroic "*ur*-sagas" revolving around these figures. These "*ur*-sagas" migrated together with the poets who kept them alive orally, and the trappings of the stories mutated over time and according to the social contexts in which they were recited.

The most famous version of the legend that we are dealing with is *Das Nibelungenlied* (The Song of the Nibelungs), a Middle

High German epic written down by an unknown poet from the region of Bavaria. Here we find a remarkably different atmosphere from the aforementioned Icelandic sources, although the text itself dates from a roughly contemporaneous time. The *Nibelungenlied* links together two stories: the first part relates the saga of Siegfried (i.e., the continental version of Sigurðr) at the court of Worms, and his ultimate demise; the second part-unfolding as an inevitable consequence out of the first—tells of the downfall of the Burgundians after they travel to the court of Etzel, the king of the Huns.

In comparison to their Icelandic counterparts, the primary figures in the *Nibelungenlied* are much more developed literary characters, and the social structure they operate within is notably more "modern" than that of the *Eddas* or sagas. The *Nibelungenlied* is set firmly in a continental medieval realm of the 12th or 13th century, with all the details of noble chivalry, knightly contests of jousting and games, and courtly ladies watching from the castle windows as the gallant men compete below for their fancy. The protagonists in the story are civilized and Christian. Yet seething under the surface—and one needn't scratch deeply to discern this—are the archaic values and more brutal forces of the older Germanic world. Jan De Vries, the esteemed Dutch scholar of Germanic and Celtic religion, alluded to this situation of co-existing impulses when he aptly described the *Nibelungenlied* as being "like a good hunk of boar's meat smothered in a delicious sauce from the French kitchen."[3]

Siegfried of the *Nibelungenlied* is a markedly different figure from the Sigurðr in the *Volsunga saga*. Here we no longer find an initiate of the god Odin, nor is he versed in the magic of the runes; he is simply a champion fighter who is revered for his strength and prowess. His invincibility largely derives from the fact that when he slew the dragon he bathed in its blood, causing his skin to become like the dragon's own armor. He does carry some magical weapons which he gained when he captured the Nibelung treasure hoard, most prominent among them his *Tarnkappe*, or cloak of invisibility. But despite all of these assets, Siegfried himself is not a particularly compelling figure in the story. He comes across as naïve, devoid of any real intelligence, and he readily debases himself whenever the Burgundians hold a carrot in front of him—in this case, the prize of King Gunther's sister Kriemhild. In short, he is a something of an oaf. Worst of all, Siegfried seems utterly oblivious to his own fate.

Divine Traces in the Nibelungenlied

In contrast, the person who murders Siegfried is an *agent* of fate: a knowing harbinger of doom. Siegfried's murderer is Hagen. The warrior known in the Icelandic sources as Högni appears in the *Nibelungenlied* as Hagen von Tronje. Arguments about how to best interpret the nature of Hagen's character have been extremely partisan. He presents a serious conundrum for many commentators, as his actions in parts one and two of the epic seem difficult to reconcile with one another. For a reader or literary critic enamored of Siegfried, Hagen will be interpreted as a darkly sinister figure since he is the one who treacherously murders the cheerful hero. Yet in the second half of the epic Hagen himself takes on a compelling and undeniably heroic dimension, even as he leads his fellow Burgundians to their destruction. He is the unyielding opponent to the vengeful Kriemhild, and the two of them act as opposite poles in a dynamic but deadly equation. Like an accelerating, expanding whirlpool, their mortal struggle eventually drowns everyone in its wake.

In his role as both a hero and a foreboding agent of fate and death, Hagen is the most complex and compelling figure in the epic. His actions are fundamental to the progression of the story to a degree that is far more important than that of the famous Siegfried (after all, Hagen kills him off in the first half of the tale). Given his central but seemingly contradictory nature, one begins to wonder: what really lies behind the character of Hagen—what force or forces are at the root of his behavior? These questions have vexed scholars and readers for centuries, and they have likewise provided the stimulus for the present essay. As a prelude to analyzing Hagen's persona in search of an answer, it will be useful to first relate some of the key events of the *Nibelungenlied* specifically in terms of his role in the story. The following concise account of his deeds on the physical plane will simultaneously provide much of the material for a consideration of what may lie behind Hagen on a deeper, metaphysical level.

Hagen's Actions in the Part One of the *Nibelungenlied*

Hagen is a prominent warrior lord and the most trusted advisor in King Gunther's court. His name is often invoked with a certain degree of awe. When Siegfried of the Netherlands first arrives at Worms with his twelve men to seek the hand of Kriemhild in marriage, no one is initially able to recognize who the strangers are or what their visit portends. Gunther then asks Hagen to look out upon the new arrivals, for Hagen "knows our lands and foreign lands as well."[4] Hagen gazes at them from afar and says:

> "It would come as no surprise—
> Although I never saw him with my own eyes—
> If that were Siegfried walking so proudly along."[5]

Hagen then goes on to relate various stories of Siegfried's past, including his slaying of the dragon and his possession of the hoard of the Nibelungs, the cloak of invisibility, and the mighty sword called Balmung.

From this opening scene, Hagen shows himself to be possessed of an uncanny knowledge of the whos, whats, whys, and wherefores of the world—both inside and outside of the Burgundian court. When the Danes and Saxons soon make advances and declare war on the Burgundians, Hagen convinces his king that if they simply enlist the aid of Siegfried they will be able to ride against their foes and conquer them—and so it happens. And when Gunther decides he desires to woo the hand of Brunhilde in Iceland, Hagen advises him that to be successful he must again enlist Siegfried's aid—and so it happens.

The next major development in the epic comes after Siegfried has helped Gunther to subdue and thereby marry Brunhilde (and in return for providing this assistance, Siegfried receives Gunther's sister Kriemhild for his bride). As an ingredient in their deception of Brunhilde, Siegfried also pretends that he is a mere vassal of Gunther's. The only person fooled by this is Brunhilde. These acts of dishonesty are exposed a short time later when Kriemhild maliciously reveals to Brunhilde how the latter has been tricked, and tells her that it was in fact Siegfried in disguise who overpowered her in the bedroom on her wedding night, not her husband Gunther. Brunhilde demands vengeance for this humiliating affront on the part of Kriemhild, and it is Hagen who steps in with total determination to see that vengeance will be made manifest. The decisive turning point—on myriad levels—arrives when Hagen sets this new chain of events into motion.

A ruse is hatched involving a phony Burgundian war declaration which causes the Danes and Saxons to again attack, and Siegfried's aid is once more requested in battle. He agrees. Hagen then visits Kriemhild in private and asks if there is any place on

Siegfried's body where he is vulnerable to injury, since Hagen promises to watch over Siegfried and says that he will guard this spot in particular. Believing Hagen is a loyal ally, Kriemhild tells him of how when Siegfried bathed in the dragon's blood, a linden leaf fell between his shoulder blades. As a result, this spot untouched by the blood was not made impenetrable. Kriemhild even agrees to sew a small cross on Siegfried's battle shirt so that Hagen will know its exact location.

Shortly after Hagen has ascertained this information, the phony war is called off and all the warriors return home to Gunther's court. Hagen then announces he will lead a hunt in the woods and Siegfried accepts an invitation to come along. A champion on the hunt just as he is on the battlefield, Siegfried has the greatest success and bags the largest quantity of game—yet he has no intimation whatsoever of what awaits him on this fateful afternoon. Hagen claims to have ordered a supply of wine for the huntsmen to enjoy, but says it was mistakenly sent to the wrong location. As a result, when the heroes are thirsty, they race to a stream in the woods to take a drink. Hagen then hides Siegfried's sword and picks up a spear. Hagen brutally stabs Siegfried in the back, impaling him through his one point of vulnerability.

If the killing of her husband were not enough to enrage Kriemhild to blood-vengeance, Hagen adds insult to injury by having the corpse gruesomely dumped in front of her door. A long funeral ceremony for Siegfried then ensues, and despite Gunther's denials, Kriemhild knows that her husband has been murdered in an act of betrayal by her own kin. Before Siegfried's burial, the fact that Hagen is the murderer is supernaturally revealed when he approaches the corpse and the wounds on the body begin to bleed.

Kriemhild's revenge becomes an ominous inevitability that looms over the rest of the epic. During the time of the funeral she begins making personal gifts of money and treasure to many warriors throughout the Burgundian realm. And rather than return to the Netherlands with Siegfried's family, she makes the strange decision to remain at the Burgundian court, surrounded by those who have wronged her. It is through actions such as these that her vengeance, which will eventually consume everything, is incubated.

Kriemhild lives in a special house built for her at the court, and she maintains a red-hot hatred for Hagen. At this point the poet of the *Nibelungenlied* emphasizes repeatedly that it was

THE SACRIFICE OF SIEGFRIED AT THE HANDS OF HAGEN.
STILL FROM FRITZ LANG'S "DIE NIBELUNGEN"
(RELEASED 1924 BY DECLA-UFA).

Divine Traces in the Nibelungenlied

Hagen alone who propelled Siegfried to his ultimate fate. Yet the Burgundians have a vested interest in good relations with Kriemhild, for she has inherited the Nibelung treasure that was formerly Siegfried's. Eventually they convince her to have it brought to Worms. Kriemhild continues her gift-giving, which Hagen alone has the foresight to realize will amount to her buying the personal loyalties of many Burgundians—a serious potential threat.

The Burgundian leaders confer and decide that it would be best to wrest the treasure away from Kriemhild's control, but no one—save for Hagen—wants responsibility for the deed.

> "I swore to her an oath," cried Gunther the king,
> "That I would cause her no more suffering.
> She is my sister. That oath I'll not disclaim!"
> Hagen spoke once more: "Then let me take the blame."[6]

The next few lines of the poem continue:

> All their oaths were broken. Her vast wealth
> They took from her, a widow; Hagen, by stealth
> Got the key to it all . . .[7]

When two of Kriemhild's brothers learn what is transpiring they curse the misdeed, yet are peculiarly unable to bring themselves to halt the procession of events. Hagen takes the treasure to Lochheim and sinks it in the Rhein. And while the oaths of kinship to Kriemhild have been essentially broken by all those around her, Hagen has the Burgundian lords swear a new oath to him that they will keep the location of the Nibelung hoard secret until they die, and that no one shall ever inherit it. The one object of Siegfried's that Hagen does retain is the sword Balmung, which he now carries as his own.

Hagen's Actions in the Part Two of the *Nibelungenlied*

After thirteen years pass, the second half of the epic begins. King Etzel of the Huns, whose wife has died, decides to send messengers to the Burgundians to ascertain whether he might wed the widowed Kriemhild. When Etzel's envoys reach the court of

Worms, only Hagen recognizes who the strangers are. All of Gunther's men are excited at the idea of the marriage (which would serve as a wealthy political alliance), and they urge the king to approve of it—all of them, that is, except Hagen, who alone seems to foresee the consequences of such a union. But Gunther and his lords do not heed Hagen's warnings, and Kriemhild accepts the marriage proposal with her owns goals in mind—and only after she demands Etzel's envoy to swear an oath that the Huns will avenge any wrong that might ever be done to her.

Kriemhild then travels east and weds King Etzel. Thirteen years again pass. All the while, her lust for vengeance simmers, and she finally convinces her husband to invite the Burgundians to come to visit for a feast at the Hunnish court. She does this knowing that Hagen will have to accompany them if they accept, for he is the only one who knows the route they must travel.

As another retinue of Etzel's envoys arrives at Worms, Hagen alone recognizes them and knows who has sent them. When Etzel's invitation is recited to Gunther, all of his lords urge him to accept it—except Hagen, who whispers the eerie warning to the King: *"iu habt iu selben widerseit"* ("You call down war on yourself!").[8] Hagen knows what awaits them, and furthermore he knows what his own fate will be as the slayer of Kriemhild's husband. The lords tell Hagen he may remain at home, but he insists he will accompany them if they go, and that they must arm themselves well for the trip.

On the eve before the Burgundian lords depart for the land of the Huns, Gunther's mother Uta has a dire, portentous dream and warns them against making the trip. Hagen insists that they ignore the omen from the queen and forge ahead with the journey, and that he will lead the way. His own past warnings having been overruled, he is now grimly determined to allow the cycle of fate to play out, and even to prod it along in its revolutions.

When they reach the Danube, the river is raging with such high waters that there seems no way to cross it. Hagen dismounts, declaring he will find a ferryman. He goes by foot down the shore a distance and discovers some water sprites bathing in a spring. Knowing that these magical creatures can divine the future, he steals their clothing as ransom to force them to tell him what tidings the journey to the Huns will bring. The first sprite lies and informs him that he and his men will receive the honors of great heroes; hearing this good news he returns their clothes. The other

Divine Traces in the Nibelungenlied

sprites then reveal to him the real future, issuing a warning: "While you still have time, turn back again and do it soon."[9] They inform him that not a single man will survive the trip, except for King Gunther's chaplain. Hagen is dauntless, and angrily demands that the sprites tell him how to cross the waters. They reveal to him where a lone ferryman can be found. As he storms off, they tell him to be sure to pay the ferryman and to treat him kindly, for his brother rules over the lands on the opposite shore that they will have to travel through.

Hagen masks himself and attempts to trick the ferryman, who does not wish to carry any strangers into his brother's territory. A fight ensues, and Hagen decapitates the ferryman in a rage of fury and hurls his head into the depths of the river. Hagen commandeers the ferry, and in a feat of superhuman strength he rows the entire army across—nine thousand men in all!—with many trips of the small boat. He then proceeds to test the prophecy of the water sprites. He grabs the king's chaplain away from the company of the Burgundian warriors and throws him into the river. The other warriors try to stop him, but Hagen is determined to drown the chaplain—to kill him and thus disprove the prophecy. Despite the fact that he cannot swim, the chaplain somehow manages to get free and makes it back to the far shore from which they had come. Hagen knows then that his premonitions—and the water sprites' prophecy—have been confirmed, and thinks to himself, "All these men must die."[10]

Hagen reveals to the rest of the men what has transpired with the water sprites, what he did to the ferryman, and also tells them why he tried to drown the chaplain. He warns them that they will never return home alive, but orders every man to arm himself well and gird for battle. After a few further incidents (which include the killing of the ferryman's brother), they finally reach Etzel's court.

Animosities immediately begin to flare up, and Kriemhild enlists a small army of Huns to slay Hagen. She stealthily leads them by night to his quarters, but Hagen is sitting outside with his stalwart companion Volker. Although Kriemhild has an army of 460 men behind her, Hagen insolently refuses to even stand up to acknowledge her, and simply lets the sword laying across his lap— Siegfried's sword Balmung—shine in the moonlight. She asks who sent for Hagen to come to the Hunnish court, and he replies that "No one sent for me."[11] He came as a loyal lord accompanying his king. When she demands to know why he killed Siegfried, his only retort is to proudly boast of the deed. The warriors behind Kriemhild now have blatant cause to attack him, yet out of fear none dare to make a move. Nevertheless, it is unquestionable that warfare is imminent.

At a dinner feast in the Hunnish court, King Etzel tries to maintain good relations but violent quarrels break out among Burgundians and Huns outside the hall. A warrior named Dankwart slays one of Kriemhild's men and sets off a bloodbath. Upon hearing that Dankwart has decapitated a Hun, Hagen's response conveys a remorseless sentiment of might makes right:

> "Little harm in that.
> People say that if a man be dead,
> And if it be at the hands of some great hero
> So much the less excuse for lovely women's sorrow."[12]

In an act that further turns the tide toward oblivion, Hagen slays the young son of King Etzel and Kriemhild right before their eyes; the boy's severed head lands in Kriemhild's lap. At this point Hagen literally goes berserk. In a frenzy he begins cutting down Etzel's men in front of the king. A veritable slaughter breaks out in the hall. Theoderic of Bern—a legendary hero of epic proportions himself—is also present and upon seeing the carnage he shouts: "Hagen here serves out the bitterest wine of all."[13] This notion of Hagen's "wine" will be dramatically elaborated upon in a more literal sense a few scenes later.

At one point a brief truce is called in which Gunther concedes that he has no personal qualm with Etzel and therefore the Hunnish king may leave the building, along with his wife and any of his men who have not been openly involved in the provocation. The remaining Huns inside are killed; this leaves only the Burgundians holed up in the hall. They proceed to cruelly toss many of the Huns' corpses out the windows. Kriemhild now offers a huge reward to anyone who will kill Hagen. A Dane name Iring accepts the offer and attacks Hagen and the other Burgundians. Initially wounded by him, Hagen proclaims that his foe is marked for death. Iring escapes, but Hagen challenges him to return—at which point he seizes Iring's own spear and drives it through his head, fulfilling the proclamation.

Unable to get her antagonist, Kriemhild then has the hall set on fire, and in a remarkable scene Hagen exhorts his men to drink blood from the helmets of their dead enemies in order to survive the inferno. Ironically, certain commentators on the poem have tried to explain this scene as being an allusion to Christian symbolism,[14] but it seems far more likely that it simply depicts a reversion to the most ancient and barbaric of war customs. The blood vivifies the men as the hall is catching flame all around them. Hagen says:

> "Great lords and good, if you are plagued by thirst,
> drink this blood—
> In heat like this, finer than wine by far;
> At least you'll not do better now, the way things are!"
>
> One of the warriors went where a man lay dead,
> And kneeling by the wound, untied from his head,
> The helmet case, and drank the flowing blood.
> Strange though it was to him, it seemed exceedingly good.
>
> "God bless you Hagen," said the tired knight.
> "For teaching me to drink with such delight.
> Rarely have I been served a drink so fine.
> Should I live a while, I'll thank you for this wine."[15]

There can be no doubt that by this point a much more brutal code of Germanic warfare has risen to the surface of the *Nibelungenlied*. The façade of medieval Christian civilization has now been entirely stripped away. In the accelerated scenes that follow, everyone is devoured in violence. After the final battle, the only warriors who have not yet been slain are Theodoric and Hildebrand, another mighty hero of Germanic legend, and Gunther and Hagen, the two surviving Nibelungs. The few others that remain alive are those who stayed on the sidelines of the battle such as Etzel and Kriemhild.

Theodoric and Hildebrand confront Gunther and Hagen, and try to convince them to surrender. They promise to escort them home safely and to treat them with respect if they will just offer atonement for their actions. Hagen will have none of it, and vows to fight to the death rather than relinquish his personal authority or make amends to anyone. Hagen and Theodoric then engage in combat, and Hagen is wounded. Theodoric says he would gain no honor by killing such a great hero, so he takes Hagen as a hostage and delivers him to Kriemhild. Theodoric then captures Gunther in the same fashion and likewise hands him over to her; they are imprisoned separately. Kriemhild approaches Hagen and offers to let them return home to Burgundy if he will only reveal the location of the Nibelung treasure. Hagen defiantly refuses, and Kriemhild has Gunther's head cut off and brought before him.

The poet describes the scene:

> When, sick at heart, he saw his master's head,
> Hagen the warrior, turning to Kriemhild, said,
> "And so your will is done, and you have brought
> An end to things, and all has turned out as I thought."[16]

Enraged at Hagen's unwillingness to confess where the sunken treasure lies, she draws Siegfried's sword, Balmung, from its sheath and brings it down upon Hagen's neck, slicing off his head.

King Etzel is witness to this, and cries aloud:

> "God help us! Here lies slain
> At a woman's hands, alas, the finest thane
> Who ever carried shield or went to war.
> My heart is sad, for all the enmity I bore."[17]

The hero Hildebrand also sees what has happened, and shouting out that he is avenging Hagen's death, he slays Kriemhild with his sword and cruelly hacks her apart. The poet concludes his epic with the lines:

> I cannot say what afterwards occurred,
> Except that ladies, knights, and squires were heard
> Lamenting for the death of kin and friend.
> This is the Fall of the Nibelungs, and of this tale the end.[18]

Spiritual Undercurrents in the *Nibelungenlied*

As we have noted earlier, the *Nibelungenlied* is set firmly in the Christian era; the Burgundians attend mass, pay their respects to god, and so on. The only overt heathens in the poem are the Huns, and in the poet's description of the Hunnish feasts there are some lively elements which probably harken back to older customs. We have also seen how certain later battle scenes depict a far more bloody, archaic type of warfare than would normally be encountered in a continental courtly epic. Some commentators have argued that the entire story is a negative allegory about the evils of war and greed—but is there really a strong Christian message to be discerned here? Certainly the Christian god plays no direct role in the events described, despite whatever moral one may wish to perceive in the tale. Ursula Mahlendorf and Frank Tobin have remarked that, unlike other contemporary medieval tales where the "courtly hero is saved from ruin because he suddenly discovers an absolute system of values inherent in the order of the universe in the light of which he can redirect his strivings," in the *Nibelungenlied* there is "no transcendental superstructure by which the characters can orient themselves and resolve their struggles."[19]

The one central figure in the story who can be seen acting in ways that bear a metaphysical or even spiritual dimension is Hagen. When I originally read the work in its entirety, a recurring feeling arose that there is something more to Hagen than meets the eye—his role seems to transcend the limitations of a human protagonist. His unique essence sets him quite apart from his fellow Burgundians, and it repeatedly takes on spiritual connotations. Holger Homann, for example, has noted how Hagen operates on two levels, in accordance with both earth-bound and higher duties. This becomes overtly apparent after Hagen has attempted to drown the chaplain: "the loss of the chaplain deprives the Burgundians of their spiritual leader, a role which Hagen will assume later."[20] In Homann's view, Hagen "has become the agent of a superhuman, otherworldly force."[21] The fact that he is so often referred to by commentators as "demonic" is also an confirmation of this, despite that it may be a negative or inverted spiritual hue they are ascribing to him.

In the remainder of this essay we will look more intensely at a number of Hagen's actions and their deeper implications. When these are considered alongside the details of his attributes and physical appearance, a larger-than-life presence becomes evident: a presence no less than that of the Germanic high god Odin himself. This is not an entirely new revelation, as an investigation of secondary sources will turn up occasional inferences in this direction, although rarely does anyone make an overt connection. One notable exception is the American scholar Edward Haymes, who considers Hagen to be an archetypal Germanic "dark figure" or "dark hero" sharing similar attributes with a number of other figures in medieval Germanic literature.[22] Haymes goes a step further: "As we look at the Hagen figure, it will be useful to draw on other Germanic instances of the dark hero. The bright hero who almost invariably dies young in Germanic legend is the god Baldur. The dark hero can be identified with Odin/Wodan, the god of battle and death. The dark hero shares his wisdom, his closeness to the other world and in some cases his appearance."[23]

Starting with the physical and moving to the metaphysical, we will begin by looking at Hagen's appearance, and from there assess his behavior and deeds, before finally exploring the deeper, non-material correspondences between Hagen of the *Nibelungenlied* and Odin.

Hagen's Appearance

Hagen's physical presence is foreboding and imposing. He is repeatedly described with the word *grimme* ("grim, fierce"), which seems to sum up his entire mental and physical bearing. Grim Hagen is grey-haired and battle-scarred. If the *Nibelungenlied* is a courtly tale, Hagen is its proverbial Black Knight, and in one passage the poet describes him as being dressed in clothes of *rabenswarzer varwe* (raven-black color).[24] An intriguing fact is that he is also the only character in the epic for whom a genuine physical description is given:

> A man of heroic build, truth to say:
> Broad in the chest, his hair all streaked with gray;
> His legs were long; a look that terrified
> Flashed from his face; he walked along with a splendid stride.[25]

In the wider realm of Germanic literature, such a physical description is not only unique to Hagen. Pursuing a strand that would be taken up by Edward Haymes and other scholars many years later, the German psychologist Martin Ninck had written already in the 1930s about certain figures of uncannily similar aura who appear in the Scandinavian sagas. One of the most prominent is the Danish hero Starkaðr, whom Ninck says embodies the "archetype of the grim elder and the loyal weapon-

Divine Traces in the Nibelungenlied

master."[26] He is described by Saxo as having a "wild stare, wolfish snout, grey hair, hanging shoulders, rough skin, and a neck covered in scars."[27] Like Hagen, he is also decapitated when he dies. Ninck continues: "Even in death his head grimly bites into a clump of dirt, 'and thus his wildness culminated in the fury of his dying mouth' (Saxo)"[28] Ninck refers to this as "a dark, realistically drawn image which bears much likeness to the German Hagen, and stands in sharp contrast to Siegfried, a figure of light."[29]

Some additional details of Hagen's physical appearance can be discovered if other medieval sources are consulted which deal with legends related to the *Nibelungenlied*. The tenth century work *Waltharii Poesis* (The Poem of Walther) is a Germano-Latin epic which tells the saga of Walter of Aquitaine. We need not got into the minutiae of the story, but one incident is revealing. In the culmination of a series of events, Gunther and Hagen launch an attack against Walther. In the midst of this battle, Gunther's leg is sliced off, and Hagen manages to cut off Walter's hand, but Hagen also suffers a permanent wound—his right eye is gouged out. In the *Thidreks saga* (The Saga of Thidrek of Bern[30]), the Old Norse prose compilation of many of these same tales, Hagen (or in this case, Högni) is described in more detail:

> Högni . . . had black hair that hung down with some curl in it. He was long-faced, and had a large nose and hanging brows. He had a dark beard and he was dark in coloration everywhere. His face was grim and he had only one eye. He was rather fierce and bold. He was tall and stout in all his limbs, and when he put on his armor, he was noble in appearance, but still frightening. He was the strongest of all men and the best knight and no less of a dueller and warrior. He was a wise man and able to see the future. He was quiet, cold, grim and brave. He had a good heart and was courageous, quick in everything he wished to do, obstinate of disposition, straightforward, hardminded and merciless. . . . His shield, as well as all his other equipment, was inlaid with silver and the eagle was painted with red paint. If he carried it in the sunlight, his silver-inlaid shield glittered so brightly that one could not look at it for a long time. This was a wise trick, as one would expect from him. It has now been incorporated in the laws of the Germans that no one shall carry a shield or

HAGEN THE GRIM.
STILL FROM FRITZ LANG'S "DIE NIBELUNGEN"
(RELEASED 1924 BY DECLA-UFA FILMS).

buckler with silver inlays into battle. His eagle did not wear a crown, because he was not a king.[31]

If a composite picture of Hagen is drawn from these various descriptions, the striking similarity becomes evident between his appearance and that of the awe-inspiring, grey-haired and grey-bearded Odin, who has sacrificed one of his eyes in order to drink from Mimir's Well of wisdom.

A final interesting consideration is that of Hagen's pedigree. While this is not described in the *Nibelungenlied*, the *Thidreks saga* tells us that he is of the supernatural realm: "An event took place one time with [Queen Oda] when the king was not at home in his castle. When she was least aware, a man came to the queen and remained a while beside her and she got a son from this. His name was Högni. Even though he seemed to have been a man, he was an elf."[32] This could be seen as another similarity with Starkaðr, whose bloodline includes a giant.[33] The "dark figure" of *Egils saga*, Egill Skalla-Grímsson, too, has certain supernatural elements in his ancestry.[34] In all these cases a resonance can be seen with Odin himself, who is of mixed parentage, his mother being the giantess Bestla. Can there be mere coincidence in the fact that both Starkaðr and Egill proclaim Odin as their patron god?

Hagen's Deeds and Attributes

One of Hagen's most obvious attributes is his vast knowledge—not only of his own realm, but also of the people and landscapes beyond it. Whenever the Burgundians encounter strangers, Hagen is the one who instantly identifies them. In the *Nibelungenlied* there is nothing supernatural about this capability, it is simply a prominent trait in his character. In certain cases past "historical" events provide an explanation for his knowledge,[35] but this is not always so.

Through his deeds, Hagen often curiously controls the action of the story itself. Siegfried is reputed to be the greatest and bravest of warriors, but it is Hagen who cunningly directs Siegfried's behavior in some of the key scenes early in the tale. Hagen will suggest, "Why, we should have Siegfried do that for us," and Siegfried does so—whether it is leading the campaign of the Burgundians against the Danes and Saxons, or helping Gunther to win Brunhilde in Iceland.

Hagen's other deeds largely revolve around battle and, as importantly, murder. His preferred methods of killing seem to be via spearing or decapitation. His most infamous murder of the first type is the slaying of Siegfried. This powerful deed has been described by some prominent scholars as a "ritualistic murder" with the qualities of a sacrifice.[36] In this regard, I would propose that certain Odinic sacrificial practices are worthy of consideration.[37] There is a variety of evidence for a pre-Christian Germanic practice of sacrificing human men to Odin by stabbing them with a spear (often coupled with hanging). One prominent reference to this occurs in the following episode concerning Starkaðr in the *Víkars saga* (incorporated into the *Gautreks saga*). When King Víkarr has trouble at sea, a divination is performed which reveals that Odin wishes for a man to be hung in sacrifice. The victim is to be determined by drawing lots, and King Víkarr is the one who draws the fateful lot. That night Odin visits Starkaðr disguised as "Horse hair Grani." He orders Starkaðr to send King Víkarr to him, and for this purpose provides a spear that appears like a reed stalk. The next day Starkaðr proposes that they arrange a mock sacrifice so as to avoid actually killing the king. Starkaðr prepares the sacrificial site using a stump; a low, slender branch that stretches up nearby; and calf entrails for the noose. He informs the king that his gallows is ready, and that it does not look dangerous. The king concurs, but also says that if somehow he is nonetheless harmed, then that is his fate. The king climbs on the stump and Starkaðr puts the noose around his neck. Starkaðr then pokes the king with the reed stalk, saying, "Now I give you to Odin." At that moment he also lets the branch loose. The reed stalk turns into a spear and goes straight into the king, the stump falls from underneath him, the calf entrails turn into a strong withy, and the branch whips upward, hanging the king to death.[38]

In his dissertation on the sacral origins of Germanic death penalties, Folke Ström elaborates upon the connection between hanging and Odin, noting the importance of the spear-thrust as a key element of an Odinic blood sacrifice:

> Such a supposition agrees well with the fact that the spear is the specific attribute of Odin in Scandinavian mythology; Odin is *geirs dróttinn* ["lord of the spear"], *Gungnis váfaðr* ["shaker of Gungnir"; Gungnir being the name of Odin's spear]; Odin started the first battle in the world by flinging his spear; according to the Ynglinga saga he marked himself with his spear when dying; in Helgaviða Hundingsbana II Dagr sacrifices to Odin and receives the spear of the god, with which he kills his enemy. In a symbolic form we find the Odin sacrifice in the story of Eiríkr the Victorious in Þáttr Styrbjarnar Svíakappa. The king receives from Odin a spear (reed) which he is to fling over the army of the enemy with the words: "Odin shall have

you all.". . . And finally, mention may be made of Odin's hanging of himself in the world-tree in Hávamál 138, which illustrates the specific features of the Odin cult, namely, hanging in a tree and wounding with a spear.[39]

E. O. G. Turville-Petre likewise remarks how Óðinn "was most readily placated with royal or princely victims . . . the spear was Óðinn's favourite weapon. . . . It was, thus, natural that a victim sacrificed, or 'given' to Óðinn should be transfixed with a spear."[40]

In light of this we can see how Hagen's killing of Siegfried (who is also a king) may have a deeper mythic/religious resonance, although here there is no element of hanging involved. The deed takes place in a forest, surrounded by trees, and curiously in one of the extant *Nibelungenlied* manuscripts the place where it occurs is stated as the Odenwald (located near present-day Heidelberg, the name literally means "Odin forest").[41] Hagen's attitude about the slaying he commits is also worth noting. Despite the manifold consequences that are likely to result from the event, he feels no remorse and in a profound sense is indifferent to, or detached from, his own action.[42] He insists it was a necessary occurrence, and maintains this position resolutely from that point onward.[43]

Hagen's removal of Siegfried has other consequences that should be considered in a broader mythic context. In many ways, the Nibelung treasure can be seen as a tangible symbol of Siegfried's strength, and just as Hagen sacrificed Siegfried, he now takes possession of the treasure and sacrifices it to another realm—a realm where it continues to exist as a legendary or mythical object. By doing so, he inherits the powers that belonged to the champion, and he also becomes intertwined with Kriemhild on a more subtle and fateful level than Siegfried may have ever been. Hagen's killing of Siegfried also abruptly ends the deception that had been perpetuated regarding Siegfried's status in Burgundian society. Through Hagen's act of violence, the true social order or hierarchy is reestablished. For the rest of his earthly days, Hagen now carries Siegfried's sword Balmung as his own; it is a fierce weapon invested with an even greater symbolic power. Henceforth in the story the Burgundians are also mysteriously referred to by the poet as "Nibelungs"—through Hagen's deeds they too begin to take on a mythical aura that transcends mundane history. This is an important point we will revisit at the end of this essay.

Archaic spiritual and sacrificial undertones arise once more in the poet's language and description of when Hagen decapitates Etzel's son Ortlieb, a scene with a "decidedly atavistic quality."[44] The young prince is carried to the table in an almost ceremonial fashion. When Hagen suddenly slays him, he accompanies this with the unusual exclamation:

> *Nu trinken wir die minne   und gelten's kuneges wîn.*
> *Der junge vogt der Hiunen,   der muoz der aller erste sîn.*

("Now drink a toast for the dead and pledge the wine! The scion of the Huns shall be the first in line.")[45]

Discussing the implications of the language used here by Hagen, Holger Homann explains:

> De Boor comments on these lines that they are reminiscent of "ursprünglich germanische(m) Brauch" [original Germanic customs] and ascribes to them "feierlich-sakrale(n) Klang" [a ceremonial-sacral quality]; Weber echoes when he speaks of "Worte uralten germanisch-sakralen Brauchtums" [words relating to ancient Germanic-sacral customs]. Both are alluding to the ritualistic "Minnetrunk," the ceremonial conclusion of a sacred meal in honor of and a sacrifice to the gods and the dead. If we see this together with Hagen's reply to Etzel's expression of fatherly pride, namely that to him the boy looks *veiclîch getân* 'destined for death' . . . then Ortlieb's death takes on aspects of a ceremonial sacrifice: the young innocent prince, chosen by fate, must be sacrificed so that the battle may begin. . . . And Hagen is the one who speaks the ritual words and delivers the death blow, who assumes the role of the priest and makes the horror possible.[46]

Hagen's Nature, Speech, and "Demonic" Character

The contrast between the characters of Siegfried and Hagen adds another dimension to the latter's triumph over and removal of the former. Whereas Siegfried is a rather two-dimensional embodiment of pure warrior strength but little intelligence, Hagen is the most canny and keenly perceptive figure in the entire epic. Discussing the respective deaths of these two characters, Theodore Andersson makes the following interpretation:

> They must die . . . but they transcend their fate with a display of personal qualities. . . . Siegfried's display is limited to an exhibition of matchless strength; he has the surplus vitality but also the unconsciousness of youth. Hagen is older, more experienced, more vulnerable, but completely aware of the world around him. His heroism is the triumph of consciousness.[47]

Along with Andersson, many others have recognized Hagen's consciousness and awareness. In their important essay "Hagen: A Reappraisal," Mahlendorf and Tobin explore the nature of Hagen's intelligence in great detail. In contrast to other commentators who have presented one-dimensional assessments of Hagen, they note he is "perhaps the most interesting figure in the whole poem. . . . His complexity has been repeatedly oversimplified."[48] After analyzing and comparing the various descriptive epithets used by the poet to describe both Siegfried and Hagen, they elaborate on the latter's intelligence, contrasting him with the typical courtly hero:

> Nowhere in medieval literature do we find a practical intelligence that can match his. The courtly hero, led by his author into adventures to fulfill his quest, stumbles into situations, fights his way out of them with the help of the author and of God, and finally acquires that hindsight called wisdom. Unlike the courtly hero, . . . Hagen never acts blindly. . . . He is ageless, and his ability to reason neither grows nor fails him completely. . . . To achieve a definite goal he assumes roles inconsistent with his character so that the unity in character can only be grasped if one perceives what motivates him to assume the role. . . . Hagen may sometimes get out of his depth and be at a loss what to do, as in the encounters with supernatural beings as Brünhild or the *merwîp* [water sprite]. Yet after some deliberation, he is able to use such beings to serve his ends.[49]

Mahlendorf and Tobin also draw attention to Hagen's eloquence of speech, and how his "words are unrivaled in the poem in rhetorical force, subtlety, and proverbial aptness. [They] at once penetrate to the heart of the matter."[50] Hagen's position as a key advisor to King Gunther is not solely based upon his knowledge, but also on his powerful way with words. His incisive proclamations are consistently accurate, and if ignored the outcome is always to the Burgundians' detriment. But Hagen's powers of speech are not limited to any one style of utterance: "With great versatility Hagen adapts his speech to the demands of the occasion. He can be persuasive as when bringing Kriemhild to divulge Siegfried's secret. He can be gentle and reassuring as when comforting Giselher when taking over the night watch, or firm and aggressive as when commanding an army. Double meanings give his speech an ominous tone."[51]

Most commentators have been less kind in their appraisal of Hagen, however, preferring to see in him a ruthless and "demonic" figure. Holger Homann analyzes Hagen in terms of his repeated lies, deceptions, and tricks.[52] Jacob Stout, the author of a dissertation on Hagen that often offers a very negative interpretation, even goes so far as to state at one point: "Hagen has made God his enemy. The epic poets have personified in him the devilish, the antichrist."[53] A caustic, polemical assessment is also given by Harold Dickerson, who claims the real meaning of Hagen is as "a destroyer of values, a creator of voids" and also "living proof that a perversity dwells in all things."[54] He sees Hagen ultimately as representing a destructive force which is determined to tear apart society, and seems appalled that any overall positive assessment could be made of "this drinker of human blood, who leads an entire people to destruction."[55]

Despite these contradictory appraisals, all of the foregoing traits borne by Hagen are also characteristic of the god Odin. The latter represents expanded consciousness and the quest for knowledge on a grand scale. He is also a multifaceted deity, possessed of innumerable nicknames which attest to his shape-shifting character and ability to assume almost limitless roles. It is not surprising, therefore, that Odin was referred to with myriad names that reflect aspects of his multiform nature. Furthermore he is the patron of poets and inspired speech, and other Odinic literary figures such as Starkaðr and Egill are blessed with similar rhetorical abilities. On various occasions the god also uses deception for

Divine Traces in the Nibelungenlied

his own ends, emphasized by another of his names: *Bölverkr*, "Evil doer." Turville-Petre notes that Odin is a "god of war and dissension, delighting not least in fratricidal strife,"[56] and Georges Dumézil observes how the "character of Odin is complex and not very reassuring. His face hidden under his hood, in his somber blue cloak, he goes about the world, simultaneously master and spy. It happens that he betrays his believers and his protégés, and he sometimes seems to take pleasure in sowing seeds of fatal discord. . . . he is the god par excellence who receives or even requires the sacrifice of innocent men."[57] Given this darkly ambiguous nature, it is no wonder that in later Christian times Odin was transmogrified into an evil demon, and such assessments of Hagen might be taken in the same spirit.

Hagen and Fate

We have seen how Hagen is a formidable warrior and possessed of many physical attributes which serve to induce respect—not to mention fear and awe—in those around him. But Hagen's most vital function emerges on a level beyond the physical plane, and this concerns the realm of fate. Here, too, we find a powerful link to the god Odin, lord of battle and death, who both knows of, as well as succumbs to a catastrophic downfall along with his divine companions.

In addition to possessing his worldly knowledge of people, places, and travel routes, Hagen is also the only character who knows, or who can intimate, what the future (i.e., fate) holds for him and his comrades. In numerous scenes he proclaims such presentiments aloud. It is therefore no accident that Hagen is King Gunther's most trusted lord and advisor—despite the fact the king often refuses to heed his warnings. Hagen's foreknowledge frequently revolves around death. This is alluded to by the poet when, after Kriemhild has invited the Burgundians to visit her at Etzel's court, the envoys return to inform her of the response. She specifically asks them what Hagen's reaction was to the invitation. They tell her: "When they spoke of coming here and gave their word / It seemed the name of Death that grim Hagen heard."[58]

He is invariably the one who takes action to direct a turning point of potential events. There are many lesser examples of this, but the most dramatic instance is when Hagen rows nine thousand men across the Danube after having slain the ferryman.[59] This crossing of the river signals a point of no return, a fact that is emphasized when Hagen attempts unsuccessfully to drown the chaplain. This is the most bold example of where Hagen deliberately and tangibly "provokes fate."

After Hagen has gotten his fellow men across the river, the future seems grimly determined. Holger Homann notes that the relationships among the company have also changed:

> Hagen loses his position as guide and leader, a position for which he is eminently qualified and which was accorded to him as a matter of course. . . . This is quite an extraordinary event, so important apparently that the poet reports it twice. . . . Hagen accepts this development without demur. We may assume that he approves of it, that he willingly surrenders his responsibility as the company's guide to his successor Volker. He is freed of an obligation, without losing any of his influence. He no longer leads the way to a local destination, but rather to a destiny of death and destruction.[60]

All of Hagen's dealings with Kriemhild can also be viewed in light of his propulsion/provocation of fate, especially the scene when he refuses to rise and address her, but sits with Siegfried's sword across his lap, letting the glint of the moonlit blade shine back into her eyes. Their unique interplay culminates in the final events in the epic, as the dynamic between Kriemhild and Hagen forces the fulfillment of a scenario of what "Kriemhild would call revenge, Hagen the fulfillment of destiny."[61]

The position of Odin as a battle god is well-known, and likewise his connection to death and relationship to the world of the dead. This latter function is exemplified in Odin's recruitment of the slain warriors who have fallen in battle. But Odin must also be understood as a god of fate. The following quotation from Jan De Vries, taken from his important survey *Altgermanische Religionsgeschichte* (History of Ancient Germanic Religion, 2nd ed. 1956/1957), provides insight into the interrelationship of human attitudes toward fate and the understanding of this aspect of Odin:

> The human being can enter into a very different relationship to the force of fate ruling in the darkness. Life as a

whole is not thought of as a lot thrown down by the gods; it is determined from beginning to end by an inner law that lies in the essence of the person. . . . There exist, however, catastrophes that unsettle the human being in his deepmost soul; these will tend to be ascribed to outwardly active and suddenly intervening forces. What these forces are is not clearly determinable; the answer is dependent upon the respective soul-structure of the person. In the age when the figure of Odin had attained a paramount position in heroic life, he was the fate-determining god. We recall the calm words of Sigmund (*Volsunga saga* 12): "Odin does not wish for us to wield the sword since it is now broken into pieces; as long as it has pleased him I have fought battles." Yet when we take a deeper look, we see that Odin too is subject to fate; when he calls the heroes to him from battle, it so happens that this occurs in order to prepare for the coming doom, and he must admit that he does not know when the gray wolf will attack the seat of the gods. The Voluspa clearly shows us gods who go to meet an inescapable fate, *ragnarök*. . . . Under the blows of fate the person attains an insight that, far above life, lofty forces determine his earthly lot.[62]

As its title clearly indicates, psychologist Martin Ninck likewise acknowledges this relationship throughout his *Wodan und Germanischer Schicksalsglaube* (Wodan and the Germanic Conception of Fate, 1935). The work of both Ninck and De Vries in this area was also informed by that of another scholar, Hans Naumann, who in 1934 published his short treatise *Germanischer Schicksalsglaube* (The Germanic Conception of Fate).[63] Naumann even remarks in the foreword that he might have more appropriately titled his book simply *Odin* or *Wodan*. Considering that this work has never been translated, it is worth quoting some passages at length. In an effort to elaborate upon what he terms the "typical Germanic bearing," Naumann states:

Fate itself is determined and is not to be altered; indetermined and thus regulatable are only its onset and its course in their particulars, and above all the bearing of the soul maintained during its course. Often enough for the hero of the aristocratic warrior stratum, fate is simply identical with honor as a nobleman, honor of the clan, honor of the warrior—in short, with the laws of the cycle of life to which he belongs and which he cannot give up without giving up himself; which he may not deny; which he must defend or reestablish.

Thus the hero knows already of his fate to a great extent, and this knowledge influences his heroic bearing. If he does not know it, then he brings about the knowledge itself. He wants to know of it. Only by this does he obtain peace in the disquiet, shed his fear in the face of the threat, and become a hero. After all, exactly this is the function and meaningful role of the great and highest leader-god. As we have seen, Odin precisely and unceasingly explores the fate of the world—which, astonishingly, contains his own fate within it. He desires to know it. Precisely in him one clearly gauges how the Germanics elevated this bearing to a metaphysical category and a world-principle, since it corresponded to one of the fundamental needs of their soul.[64]

Naumann, basing his assessments upon a profound knowledge of Germanic philology, later draws a parallel to the events in the second half of the *Nibelungenlied*:

> The Nibelungen guests thus know the downfall they go to meet at the court of the Huns. As Odin explores the fate of the world and of the gods, so does Hagen explore the fate of his lords and friends. Uta's dreams, the sayings of the water sprites and their testing in the episode with the chaplain—these numerous warnings of a varied sort are the circumstances through which fate shows itself.[65]

Using the first person to denote the eternal validity of these underlying fate conceptions, Naumann then remarks:

> My fate must become my summoning. I have to wrestle with it; through this it blesses me. I must court the contest with it like young Ekka courts his single combat with King Thidrek of Bern in the dark night in the forest by Osning,[66] or just like a lover courts the favor of his beloved. Worry and menace turn into love and loyalty. Odin courts. Loyal to his fate up to its final fulfillment, up

to the *unio mystica* with it—that is the highest spiritual air which can really be felt upon the earth. And thus Iring in the *Nibelungenlied* goes to his raging death. This is the only moment where the human becomes superhuman and becomes a god: in heroic language he is called "hero," in religious vernacular he is called "saint."[67]

Hagen the Fated Hero

As we have noted when discussing his character and deeds earlier in this essay, Hagen could be seen as a treacherous, evil, or negative figure in the first half of the *Nibelungenlied*, and the poet often says as much. Through his actions in the latter half of the epic, however, Hagen ensures his own renown in a highly positive sense. This is plainly evident at the conclusion of the poem when King Etzel—whose men Hagen has just butchered in a series of battles, and whose own son he has just decapitated before the king's eyes—vocally laments Hagen's death and calls him "the finest thane who ever carried shield or went to war."[68] Taking this and other similar statements in the latter half of the poem as a starting point, Edward Haymes has compellingly argued that he is best interpreted as an archetypal hero rather than a villain.[69] This position is controversial, since Hagen plays such a pivotal role in a chain of events that leads to seemingly senseless mass destruction. But just as Odin must heroically fight to the death during the twilight of the gods—despite the fact that he is already aware of what its catastrophic outcome will be—so too does Hagen wage his battle to the end, although he has long known it will mean violent death for himself and his fellow men.[70] The closing scenes of the *Nibelungenlied* are a veritable *ragnarök*—a final conflagration of forces which, in the interplay of cause-and-effect, have seethed antagonistically for years. And calling to mind Hagen's presence in all this, what Georges Dumézil once said regarding Odin is equally apt: "When the unknown one-eyed figure appears in battles . . . then the moment of destiny is at hand, and those involved are left in no doubt of this fact."[71]

By acting as the agent who consistently provokes both war and fate, Hagen helps to provide the opportunity in which his companions will meet their moment of destiny. Indeed, he not only spurs forward the unfolding of his own fate and that of those immediately around him, but also the greater fate of his entire people, the Nibelungs. In the foregoing discussion, the implication has often been that fate is synonymous with death, and that it is one's attitude or bearing toward this inevitable death that elevates the human to a higher level. But there is more to the equation than this, for it is also through the heroic deeds enacted prior to death that one's name lives on across future generations. This is the true immortality available to a human being. In the famous words from the *Edda*, uttered by Odin himself:

> Cattle die, and kinsmen die,
> And so one dies one's self;
> One thing I know that never dies,
> The fame of a dead man's deeds.[72]

As a conclusion to our exploration of such matters, it is fruitful to ponder the downfall of the Nibelungs from a more timeless or metaphysical standpoint. We can then ask the question: did these figures really *die* as a consequence of all that transpired—or did they themselves become immortal and enter the realm of the mythic? After all, their names and deeds as told in the *Nibelungenlied* are still very much alive, centuries later, invoked on the lips of scholars, artists, and even their own remote descendants. In this sense the *Nibelungenlied* heroes have ensured their eternal glory. And had a darkly ambiguous and ultimately divine force not played a key role in the epic—a force which found its perfect embodiment in the figure of Hagen—their legacy might well have been long forgotten.

Notes:

1. A useful survey of the extant sources is Edward R. Haymes and Susann T. Samples, *Heroic Legends of the North*, (New York: Garland, 1996).
2. Numerous other modern artistic works inspired by the legends can be found detailed in *The Nibelungen Tradition: An Encyclopedia* (New York and London: Routledge, 2002).
3. Jan De Vries, *Heroic Song and Heroic Legend*, (London & New York: Oxford, 1963), p. 63.
4. Frank G. Ryder, trans., *The Song of the Nibelungs* (Detroit: Wayne State Univ. Press, 1962), st. 82.
5. Ibid., st. 86.
6. Ibid., st. 1130.
7. Ibid., st. 1131.
8. Ibid., st. 1458. For the original MHG of all these quotations, the reader may consult Karl Bartsch's standard text of *Das Nibelungenlied*, edited by Helmut de Boor (Wiesbaden: Heinrich Albert Verlag, 1996).
9. Ibid., st. 1540.
10. Ibid., st. 1580.
11. Ibid., st. 1788.
12. Ibid., st. 1954.
13. Ibid., st. 1981.
14. See D. G. Mowatt & Hugh Sacker, *The Nibelunglied: An Interpretive Commentary* (Toronto: Univ. of Toronto Press, 1967), p. 134.
15. Ryder, st. 2114–2116.
16. Ibid., st. 2370.
17. Ibid., st. 2374.
18. Ibid., st. 2379.
19. Ursula R. Mahlendorf and Frank J. Tobin, "Hagen: A Reappraisal," *Monatshefte*, vol. 63, no. 2 (1971), p. 139.
20. Holger Homann, "The Hagen Figure in the *Nibelungenlied*: Know Him by His Lies," *Modern Language Notes*, vol. 97 (1982), p. 766, n. 15.
21. Ibid., p. 767.
22. For a collection of essays on this general theme, see Edward R. Haymes and Stephanie Cain Van D'Elden, eds., *The Dark Figure in Medieval German and Germanic Literature* (Göppingen: Kümmerle, 1986).

23. Edward R. Haymes, *The Nibelungenlied: History and Interpretation* (Urbana and Chicago: Univ. of Illinois Press, 1986), p. 80. As Haymes and other scholars such as Otto Höfler and Martin Ninck before him have noted, the contrasting "bright hero" on the human-heroic plane would, of course, be Siegfried.

24. Line 3 of stanza 402.

25. Ibid., st. 1734.

26. Martin Ninck, *Wodan und Germanischer Schicksalsglaube* (Jena: Diederichs, 1935), p. 20.

27. Ibid., p. 21. Similarly, in the *Gautreks saga*, Starkaðr describes himself as having "ugly jaws, the long snout-shaped mouth, the wolf-grey hair and the tree-like arms, the bruised, rough-skinned neck." Cf. *Gautrek's Saga and Other Medieval Tales*, trans. Hermann Pálsson and Paul Edwards, London: Univ. of London Press, 1968, p. 41.

28. Ninck, p. 21.

29. Ibid.

30. This is the same "Theodoric" who appears in the *Nibelungenlied*.

31. Edward R. Haymes, trans., *The Saga of Thidrek of Bern* (New York & London: Garland, 1988), p. 116. Although merely a minor circumstantial point, it is worth recalling that the eagle is also an Odinic symbol. One of the god's many secondary names is *Arnhöfði*, "Eagle-headed." The "raven black" clothing Hagen wears in the *Nibelungenlied* is likewise circumstantially resonant with Odin as *Hrafnáss*, "raven god," who has two ravens as totem animals that survey the world for him. There are a number of other names that relate Odin symbolically with the raven, emphasizing this deep connection.

32. Ibid., pp. 110–111.

33. Ninck provides a detailed summary of Starkaðr and his ancestor the water giant (also named Starkaðr) on pp. 19–24 of his *Wodan und Germanischer Schicksalsglaube*.

34. For a detailed discussion of Egill's bloodline and his dark attributes, see Jesse Byock, "Egill Skalla-Grímsson: The Dark Figure as Survivor in an Icelandic Saga" in Haymes and Van D'Elden, eds., *The Dark Figure in Medieval German and Germanic Literature*.

35. For example, Hagen is said to have been raised in fosterage at the court of King Etzel.

36. Mowatt & Sacker, *The Nibelungenlied*, p. 93.

37. These are discussed in H. M. Chadwick, *The Cult of Othin* (London: Clay & Sons, 1899), pp. 13-16, and in more detail in Folke Ström's exemplary study *On the Sacral Origin of the Germanic Death Penalties* (Lund: Håkan Ohlssons Boktrykeri, 1942), pp. 137–145. Cf. also related explorations in James L. Sauvé, "The Divine Victim: Aspects of Human Sacrifice in Viking Scandinavia and Vedic India," in *Myth and Law Among the Indo-Europeans: Studies in Indo-European Comparative Mythology*, ed. Jaan Puhvel (Los Angeles: Univ. of California Press, 1970), pp. 173–191.
38. The same story is also told in Saxo Grammaticus's *Gesta Danorum*, with minor variations.
39. Ibid., pp. 142–143
40. E. O. G. Turville-Petre, *Myth and Religion of the North: The Religion of Ancient Scandinavia* (New York: Holt, Rinehart and Winston, 1964), p. 47.
41. This is the location given in Manuscript C (see entry for "Odenwald" in *The Nibelungen Tradition: An Encyclopedia*, New York and London: Routledge, 2002). Manuscript B, which serves as the primary text for the Bartsch edition, gives the location as "Waskenwald."
42. Hugo Bekker finds this attitude indicative of Hagen's "demonic nature." See Bekker, *The Nibelungenlied: A Literary Analysis* (Toronto: Univ. of Toronto Press, 1971), p. 130. But referring to Hagen as "demonic" is a common refrain, and one with deep roots. The author of *Div Chlage*, a related contemporary MHG text that is appended to most *Nibelungenlied* manuscripts, even has Hildebrand call Hagen "the devil [*valant*] . . . who was the cause of it all." See *The Lament of the Nibelungen (Div Chlage)*, trans. Winder McConnell, (Columbia, South Carolina: Camden House, 1994), p. 61.
43. One might even be tempted here to pursue a interpretation—admittedly esoteric—through the lens of Dumézilian tripartite theory: a "first function" figure of higher perception attempting to permanently resolve (albeit with deception, but this is in line with his Odinic nature) the problem of a reckless "second function" figure, a warrior who has exhibited a dangerous lack of restraint and thus threatens both the mundane hierarchy as well as the more subtle cosmic balance that underpins it. This proposal may well be an oversimplification, although Jaan Puhvel touches on similar considerations in the internal context of the archaic

warrior stratum in his article "The Warrior at Stake" in *Homage to Georges Dumézil*, ed. Edgar Palomé (Washington, D.C.: Journal of Indo-European Studies, 1982). For an intriguing discussion of types of human sacrifice considered in Dumézilian terms, cf. Donald J. Ward, "The Threefold Death: An Indo-European Trifunctional Sacrifice?" in *Myth and Law Among the Indo-Europeans*, pp. 123–142.

44. Ibid., p. 769.
45. Ryder, st. 1960.
46. Homann, "The Hagen Figure in the *Nibelungenlied*," pp. 768–769.
47. Theodore M. Andersson, *A Preface to the Nibelungenlied* (Stanford: Stanford Univ. Press, 1987), p. 165.
48. Mahlendorf and Tobin, "Hagen: A Reappraisal," p. 125.
49. Ibid., p. 129.
50. Ibid., p. 130.
51. Ibid.
52. Homann, "The Hagen Figure in the *Nibelungenlied*," pp. 759–769.
53. J. Stout, *Und ouch Hagene* (Groningen: J. B. Woulters, 1963), p. 325. He makes this particular comment in reference to Hagen's attempt to drown the chaplain.
54. Harold J. Dickerson, Jr., "Hagen: A Negative View," *Semasia* 2 (1975), pp. 55, 57.
55. Ibid., p. 45.
56. Turville-Petre, *Myth and Religion of the North*, p. 65.
57. Georges Dumézil, *Gods of the Ancient Northmen* (Los Angeles: Univ. of California Press, 1973), p. 30. It should be noted that Odin is also known to wear black, such as when he appears before Sigmund in the *Volsunga saga*.
58. Ryder, st. 1500.
59. Yet another of the many circumstantial resonances can be seen here, as nine is a number sacred to Odin.
60. Homann, "The Hagen Figure in the *Nibelungenlied*," p. 766.
61. Ibid., p. 767.
62. Jan De Vries, *Altgermanische Religionsgeschichte*, vol. I, (Berlin: Walter de Gruyter, 1956), pp. 268–269.
63. Hans Naumann, *Germanischer Schicksalsglaube*, (Jena: Diederichs, 1934). A translation of one chapter from this work recently served as the basis for Stephen Edred Flowers's article "Toward the Birth of an Odian Philosophy: Hans Naumann and Nietzsche's *Ewige Wiederkunft*," *Rûna* 9 (2001), pp. 29–32.

64. Naumann, *Germanischer Schicksalsglaube*, pp. 81–82.
65. Ibid., p. 85.
66. Naumann refers here to an early episode in the *Thidreks saga*.
67. Naumann, *Germanischer Schicksalsglaube*, p. 87.
68. Ryder, st. 2374.
69. See Edward R. Haymes, *The Nibelungenlied*, pp. 73–90, and "Hagen the Hero," *Southern Folklore Quarterly* 43 (1979), pp. 149–155.
70. An interesting circumstantial parallel can also been seen here between Hagen/Högni and Odin. In the *Thidreks saga*, on his last night alive after being mortally wounded by King Thidrek in the final conflagration of the Niflungs (Nibelungs), Högni fathers a son to avenge him. Odin likewise has a son, Viðar, who will avenge him after he dies during *ragnarök*.
71. Georges Dumézil, *Mitra-Varuna* (New York: Zone, 1988), p. 140.
72. "Havamal," stanza 78. The translation is from Henry Adams Bellows, *The Poetic Edda* (New York: American-Scandinavian Foundation, 1923), p. 44.

Thanks to Edward Haymes for kindly supplying me with his articles on Hagen, to Kent Jewell for assistance in obtaining other secondary material, and special gratitude to Ingrid Wultsch for helpful suggestions regarding the translation of some of the German passages quoted in this article.

I would like to dedicate the present essay to Dr. Louis J. Elteto, a teacher who has generously imparted much wisdom and in whose stimulating Middle High German course I first had the pleasure of making Hagen's close acquaintance.

Indo-European Religion after Dumézil

EDGAR C. POLOMÉ
University of Texas, Austin

CONTENTS

Romulus and the Fourth Function
N. J. Allen
The First Function: A Critical Analysis
Wouter Belier
Today, after Dumézil
Enrico Campanile
Penser Les Mythologiques (Dumézil, Eliade, Lévi-Strauss)
Daniel Dubuisson
Broadening the Perspective on Dumézil's Three Functions
Emily Lyle
Indo-European and non-Indo-European Elements
in Germanic Myth and Religion
Edgar C. Polomé
After Dumézil, What?
Jaan Puhvel
Tripartition in Early Ireland: Cosmic or Social Structure?
William Sayers
Archaeology, Language and Comparative Mythology
Jens Peter Schjødt

Journal of Indo-European Studies
Monograph Number Sixteen
ISBN: 0-941694-51-8, 196 Pages
$36.00 plus postage: US $3.50; Foreign $5.00
(Mastercard/Visa Accepted)

1133 13th St., N.W., #C-2
Washington, D.C. 20005
Tel: 202-371-2700 Fax: 202-371-1523 Email: iejournal@aol.com

The Goddess Zisa

Nigel Pennick

Zisa is a Central European goddess whose city exists to this day in Bavaria, where her memory is kept. Her existence is recorded in two medieval manuscripts, the *Codex Monac* of circa 1135, and the 12th–13th century *Codex Emmeran*, and also in Goldast's *Rerum sue. Script. Aliquot veteres*, published at Ulm in 1727. These texts, "taken from Gallic history", come from an account of Velleius the Gaul who left us a record of a Swabian victory over invading Roman forces during the first century BCE. Velleius's account speaks of a city called Zizarim, situated on the border between the Suebi (Swabians) and the Bajuwarii (Bavarians), which is the present-day Augsburg. The name of the city came from the goddess Zisa (otherwise Cisa), "whom they worshipped with extreme reverence". Tacitus, in his *Germania*, tells how the Suebi worshipped the goddess Isis, clearly his *interpretatio Romana* version of Zisa. A later Old High German gloss refers to *Ziuwari suapa*, "People of Ziu, Swabians".

The city of Zizarim was a strongly defended place, surrounded by a rampart and ditch. The Roman commander, the Praetor Titus Annius, had poor intelligence of the military situation, for he made the mistake of setting siege to the city just before the most holy day of Zisa, which fell on September 28th. Just at the time when the Roman legion of Mars had encamped, a vast throng of Swabian warriors had also come to Zizarim to take part in the annual festival of games and celebrations in honour of the goddess. On her holy day, suddenly they sallied forth against the besieging Romans. Empowered by their goddess, the Swabians overwhelmed the enemy forces, virtually wiping them out in a famous victory. In later years, under the Emperor Augustus, the city was stormed again, and this time, it was overrun by the Roman forces. After the conquest, it was reconstructed as a Roman city, and re-named Augusta Vindelicorum (or Augusta Rhaetica) after the emperor. Its present name, Augsburg, recalls its Roman re-foundation. But Zisa was not forgotten.

Zisa's temple at Zizarim, on the hill called Zisenberck, appears to have been on the local high point where the present church of

St Peter am Perlach stands. In the German tradition of named urban watchtowers (such as Nordlingen's 'Daniel'), the church tower of St Peter's, the Perlachturm, as the central tower of the city, was dedicated to St Michael ('Turamichele'). His day, September 29th, (clearly in continuity of Zisa's holy day) is celebrated annually to this day at St Michel's altar in the western Perlachturm chapel.

According to the ancient writers, Zisa's temple on the Zisenberck was "surrounded by wood in the barbarian manner". This place is mentioned by the bard Küchlin sometime between 1373 and 1391 in a poem he wrote for the Burgomeister of Augsburg, Peter Egin the Younger. The goddess is also acknowledged by Sigmund Meisterlin (who died in 1484), in the *Augsburger Chronik* (written in 1456, and published in 1522), where she is shown standing atop a pillar. In 1615, a gilded windvane in the shape of Zisa, designed and made by Elias Holl, was set up on top of the Perlachturm. She is depicted holding the pinecone that is her emblem. As the Stadtpyr, the cone is the emblem of the city of Augsburg. The Zisa vane, having undergone several restorations and re-gildings, still stands guard over the city.

Zisa is depicted as the tutelary goddess of Augsburg in the Golden Hall of the Rathaus (City Hall). Destroyed in the Second World War, the entire renaissance building has been faithfully restored, complete with images of the goddess as foundress and protectress of the city. She is depicted in a prominent painting above the hall's main door as wearing a red dress, which also appears in a devotional altarpiece in St Peter am Perlach. Painted around the year 1700 by Johann Melchior Schmidtner, here the female divinity is Our Lady, in her rarely encountered aspect as *Maria Knotenlöserin* (Mary Undoer-of-knots). Maria Knotenlöserin is shown unravelling the tangled thread, appearing as an extra Weird Sister who undoes our *örlog*. Our Lady in red appears to be an aspect of Zisa, whose presence in Augsburg in the year 1700 was well understood. The church itself is actually described as "Wallfahrtskirche zur Gottesmutter Maria Knotenlöserin" (The Pilgrimage Church of Mary Undoer-of-knots, Mother of God).

Other known shrines of Zisa existed in present-day south Germany at places called Zeise, Zeislsperg, Zaissenperig, and in present-day Switzerland at Cisuris (now Zitgers, Rhaetia), where she was known under the name of Cisara. Jakob Grimm quotes Ladislaus Suntheim's *Chronica* that records a Pagan duke of Swabia called Esenerius, who had a castle at Hillomondt, in Vertica, the modern Kempten (Cambodunum). Duke Esenerius venerated images of the gods Edelpoll and Hercules and the goddess Zisa in his chapel. To this day, not far from the church of St Peter am Perlach in Augsburg stands a fine renaissance fountain of Hercules. In Kempten, a Gallo-Roman temple of Hercules has been reconstructed in recent years.

Zisa's festal day, September 28th as recorded in several medieval texts that go back to reliable sources (see Grimm, 1878, III, 269, 275), was held 59 days after August 1 (Lammas). Zisa's holy day, September 28th, was easily assimilated with the Christian Michaelmas, September 29th. This is the high festival of the year, but also each Tuesday (Zîstag, Zistig, Zaistig) is the day of the goddess. Zisa was so strongly venerated in the region that, when the Christian church set up its rule as the Diocese of Augsburg, the name of the weekday was banned. Instead, Zîstag was called by the descriptor, '*Aftermontag*' (the day after Monday).

Additional evidence of the power of Zisa locally is that the day-name Zîstag appears only in this part of Germany. Generally, in other Germanic regions, this day, the day of Mars, is associated with the god variously known as Tîwaz, Tiw, Tiu or Týr (hence the Anglo-Saxon Tiwesdæg, the modern English Tuesday).

The goddess's day falls during the harvest period, and in my drawing, made for the perpetual goddess calendar published in Stuttgart in 2000, I have shown her with the cornucopia, the attribute of an abundant harvest. The pinecone, Zisa's emblem *par excellence*, contains the living seeds of the generation yet to come. It is a symbol of protection, regeneration and continuity. The cone, protector of the seeds within it, denotes Zisa's role as protectress of the city and its inhabitants. Zisa is a perfect example of the continuity that underpins the European Tradition, appearing when she is needed, in whatever form is appropriate to the age.

Bibliography:

Avesta and Pennick, Nigel: *Göttinnen in Mitteleuropa: Immerwæhrender Kalender.* Stuttgart, 2000.
Breuer, Tilmann: *Die Stadt Augsburg.* Munich, 1958.
Grimm, Jakob L.: *Deutsche Mythologie.* Leipzig, 1878.
Green D. H.: *Language and History in the Early Germanic World.* Cambridge, 2000.

The Dark Side of the Mountain

Annabel Lee

The peaks of the mountains, beautiful and sublime, have inspired many a rapturous outpouring of words attempting to convey the mysterious power of nature. Travelers through the dramatic landscapes of granite and glaciers are often struck by the immense proportions, the dazzling and sometimes deadly display of natural forces, and the stark contrast between the white snow-covered peaks, blue luminescent lakes, and fertile green valleys. Poets and writers throughout the ages have already put an avalanche of metaphors on paper attempting to capture the peaks in words and sentiment, but as Julius Evola comments, "the mountain itself appears . . . to be the best antidote . . . [for] in few of its manifestations does nature give us the sense of what, in its greatness, purity, power, and primordial nature, is far above the insignificant lives and artificial lyricism of ordinary people."[1]

The alpine environment is a unique and fragile ecosystem, even more hostile to living beings than the arctic region.[2] The growing season is shorter, the wind stronger, the sun harsher, and oxygen scarcer. Because the ground remains frozen for most of the year, alpine plants have adapted in a number of unique ways. For instance, in order to take advantage of the warmth found underground, they have developed long and powerful root systems which are larger than the leaves and stems themselves. Some plants grow almost exclusively underground. There is a high altitude moss that grows at the rate of a third of an inch in ten years and produces an astonishing *two leaves* per year. The taproot of this plant, however, is typically five feet long. Some alpine plants are able to produce their own heat and can even flower under the snow. Other adaptations include the fine, white, hirsute surface of the delicate edelweiss plant, which reflects the precious sun back into the leaf to keep it warm. The warmth of the sun at high altitude is too slight for a darker exterior to offer any advantage.

The mountains of northern Europe, from Great Britain to Scandinavia, are the remains of an archaic plateau that rose up long before the rest of the continent came into existence. They were once as high and jagged as the Alps, but were worn down over the millennia by waves of glacial ice.³ Certain mountains are thought to be the world axis. The peak is the heavenly home of the gods, such as the "heavenly castle" Himinbjörg where Heimdall guards Asgarð, and Óðinn's high seat Hliðskjálf. The sides of the mountain are the middle world where humans and animals live, and the inside of the mountains—in the caves, volcanoes, holes, and harrows—is where the legends, the monsters, and the myths dwell.

In numerous sacred traditions—ranging from those of the peoples of the Himalayas, to Sufism, to northern Europe—the orientations of "North" and "up" are synonymous. The North is where enlightenment and wisdom originate for the shamans of the Himalayas. For Hindus it is where the sacred mountain Kailash lies; Shiva meditated on her summit for thousands of years.⁴ The North is understood to be on the vertical axis, symbolized by the Pole Star at the heavenly pole or summit of a mountain, and indeed the star shines directly over the "solar and polar."⁵ At the other end is the nadir, "the well of darkness where the element of light is held captive."⁶ This esoteric relationship between "North" and "up" is reflected in the environmental similarities between arctic tundra and high altitude mountains. The "well of darkness" can also be understood as the invisible world of legend and myth hidden inside the mountains.

The royal titles of "Highness" or "Serene Highness" originate in the ancient symbolic connection between "mountain" and "pole" as well.⁷ Regions elevated above the earth, such as Montsalvat in the Grail saga, are conceived of as the realm of "salvation" or "health." The gods occupy the heights. The term *paradise* stems from the Sanskrit *paradesha* and has the precise and literal meaning of "height" and "high land." Julius Evola writes: "In this context I think it is legitimate to make a reference to Mount Olympus . . . [and] to all the other mountains in various traditions that are the dwelling place of the gods."⁸ The most famous human challenger of the gods, Prometheus, is bound eternally on the side of the mountain, with the unattainable summit in view. According to legend he suffered this fate upon the loftiest peak in Europe, Mount Elbrus, a lovely breast-shaped mountain.

In the Irish *Lebor Gabála* (The Book of Invasions) it is explained that the mysterious Tuatha dé Danann first came to Ireland obscured by clouds, landing on a mountain. An ending to the story was added in the 12th century in which the Gaels, after defeating the Tuatha dé Danann, made an agreement to share the earth: the surface went to the Gaelic people and the Tuatha dé Danann went underground into ancient barrows. Thus natural and supernatural beings coexist.[9] The divine geography of heathen Germany is more obscure. Literary references to the gods are few and particulars, such as where the gods lived, are fewer. But traces of a connection in the minds of the people between the mountains and the supernatural realms can be found, left over, in folklore.

There are many legends of men and titans scaling the summits of mountains in order to know or to challenge gods. The love of wisdom has driven flesh-and-blood man to ascend mountains in order to become acquainted with the divine—sometimes for eternity. However it would be a mistake to say that the symbolism of the mountain as sacred is a universal phenomenon. While the Greeks placed their twelve most beloved gods on the peaks of the mountains, the Romans regarded the Alps as misshapen lumps on the landscape and generally ignored them, appreciating them only in their role as a good barrier against the barbarian North. Mountains were considered by some Christians to be a punishment by God—ugly bumps marring the smooth surface of the perfect egg-shaped world he had originally created.[10]

In 1646 a traveling Englishman, John Evelyn, described the Alps as he crossed them as "strange, horrid, and fearful crags and tracts."[11] Thomas Burnett found them not only loathsomely ugly but morally repugnant as well: "'Tis prodigious to see and to consider of what extent these heaps of stones and rubbish are! . . . They have neither form nor beauty, nor shape nor order. . . . There is nothing in nature more shapeless and ill-figured than an old rock or a mountain."[12] Even Mount Blanc, the loftiest mountain in the Alps, the eternal standard of mountainous perfection, is tainted by its association with St. Bernard who banished the devil there, thus turning the inside of the mountain into hell.[13] Nevertheless in many instances European mountains have maintained a Christian religious importance and numerous pilgrims make their way to the peaks in honor of Saint Bridget, Saint Patrick, and others. Saint Patrick is said to have climbed many mountains, most importantly Croaghpatrick in County Mayo.[14]

Mountains are dense and impenetrable, mysterious and unknowable, even to those who live directly beneath them. They are merciless and vast to the human form, easily devouring it, easily thwarting access. It is not inconceivable that even the most explored mountain has nooks and crevasses that might conceal lost armies or obscure creatures. The great mountaineer Reinhold Messner spent years not only scaling to the remote summits of the highest and most challenging peaks in the world, often without assistance or oxygen, but also undertook a serious search for the most famous legend of the Himalayas, the Yeti. In his book on the subject he writes: "There is more behind our thirst for monsters than curiosity or escapism. There is the fear that the earth is losing the last regions where myths can flourish."[15] This fear is grounded in the reality that man is well on his way to contaminating every last inch of the globe.

The Germanic words for mountain reflect the legends about them: the words mean both "elevated" and "concealed." The Latin-derived English word "mountain" has only the blunt meaning of "projecting part." The German word for mountain is *Berg*. The re-constructed Indo-European form is **bhergh*, meaning "high, raised, lofty."[16] The oldest forms of the word in the Germanic languages relate to "high, with derivatives referring to hills and hill forts," for instance *Burg* (mountain compound or fortified place), *Burgher* (townspeople), Burgundy (region), and Burgundian (Germanic tribal name meaning "Highlanders"). **Bhergh* also means "to hide, protect," and the German verb *bergen* still has this meaning. *Bergen* is also the plural form of *Berg*. The English word "to bury" shares the same origins, as does the previously mentioned home of the Tuatha dé Danann, "barrow." The proper name Bridget also finds its roots in **bhergh*.

*Kel is another Indo-European root which carries the dual meaning of "elevated" and "concealed or concealed place" and "to save, protect." From this root come such words as "hell" (the place), *Hölle* (hell in German), *Höhle* (cave in German), Hel (the Norse goddess and her underworldly domain), hall (from Old English *heall*), Valhalla, hole and hollow (from Old English *holh*), helm and helmet.

These words, with their seemingly contrary meanings suggesting ascending and descending movement, could reflect the descent of the Germanic gods from the mountaintops or heavens into the underworld, a descent which is reflected in the transformation of the gods into heroes or monsters. Aspects of lost heathen gods can still be found concealed in the popular legends about heroes sleeping inside mountains or strange women who live in the mountains. This was a belief held by the Christians as well, and volcanoes were used as geological proof that the underworld was hell, the molten lava a testament to the veracity of the description in the Bible.

The mountains are where heathen gods and rare creatures wait in exile. "Excellently suited to our mythology is the idea of removal," states Jakob Grimm, and he explains the difference between that which has *metamorphosed* and that which has been *banned*—the former has its significance changed, while the latter remains the same but is hidden from usual view. "What is *banned* becomes imperceptible, and can only become corporeal again under certain conditions."[17] This emphasizes the importance of wilderness, the place where the possibility of understanding such banned things lies, the place opposed to civilization.

A number of kings sleep in mountains in Germany and Austria. The most famous is Frederick I, Barbarossa (1123–90), who sleeps in a cave at the Kyffhäuser mountain. He is expected to reawaken and emerge with his army to defend the Germans in their greatest moment of need. The legendary Siegfried rests in the castle Geroldseck on top of a mountain. The legends surrounding Charlemagne (742–814) extend far beyond the boundaries of his kingdom, and one has him resting inside Mt. Etna in Sicily.[18]

But most stories still told in Germany about people captivated by the mountains are related to Frau Holle (Holde, Helle). Like the powerful and deep root of the high altitude moss with its two leaves, a modest plant by any standards, the simple legends of Frau Holle appear as didactic stories, but they simultaneously conceal, sustain, and are in return nourished by an immensely deep taproot. Frau Holle is considered to be the most popular and lively figure of the Grimm collections,[19] and the stories related to her are where Jakob Grimm's notion of *banishment* becomes applicable. He connects the many legends about "white women" or "white-robed maidens" in the mountains who often visit shepherds, with the banishment of Frau Holle to the mountains. Shepherds have grazed their herds on the same fields for generations. The taproot is deep and she is still visible to them, one of the "divine and half-divine beings of heathendom, who are still visible to the gaze of the mortal at certain times."[20] A bold attempt was made by Karl Simrock to reconstruct a Germanic goddess named *Hilde* as a holistic combination of the ON *Hel* who represents darkness, and Holle who stands for light.[21] Holle embraces the world, she is concealed beneath the earth, and she covers the world in snow.

The moral ambiguity in the folktales about Holle retains elements of a primordial state of divine holism in which "good" and "evil" were not so forcefully delineated. The disparate meanings of her name, from "mother" to "witch," also reflect this ambiguity. In particular this seems true in the pantheon of the northern gods who are eternally neutral, realizing that there must be a proper balance between order and disorder. This essentially active and dynamic world thrives on the tension between the perfection of the peaks and the pulsing currents of the depths. The inner journey of northern man is one of action, not rest and meditation.

An underlying current in these themes of moral ambiguity is the negation of duality—the divisive, limiting worldview so adored in modern times. This holistic world "beyond good and evil" should not be mentioned without recalling a few words from Nietzsche's famous mountain climber Zarathustra. He scaled the peaks in search of truth, skipping gracefully from "peak to peak," and was pushed back down to his cave and into the valley by the omnipresent force of gravity from which mortals cannot escape—no matter how high they climb—and challenged by the "voice that spoke without a voice." The paradox of conscious existence has rarely been so eloquently expressed as in this delirious poem: "O heaven above me, pure and deep! You abyss of light! Seeing you, I tremble with godlike desires. To throw myself into your height, that is *my* depth. To hide in your purity, that is *my* innocence."[22]

The holistic reconstruction of a cultural heritage requires the consideration of "both sides": the peaks and the valleys, the feminine and masculine, folklore and scientific lore, the heavens and the underworld, gods and mortals, the inside and outside of the mountains, the outer sun and the inner light. It is not just in otherworldly divine stories and heroic legends that we find this dynamism. On the human and material level, a similar perspective comes after death. The options of where to put a corpse seem as narrow as these two: to be lifted into the air as fire and ash (or carried aloft in the bodies of birds who have eaten the corpse), or else lowered into a hole in the dark earth. Thus, as the cycle turns and matter is transmuted, even our mortal remains will be accorded their ultimate view from the peaks—or from deep in the underworld.

Notes:

1. Julius Evola, *Meditations on the Peaks* (Rochester, Vermont: Inner Traditions, 1998), p. 39.
2. All environmental descriptions from Margaret Fuller, *Mountains* (New York: Wiley Nature Editions, 1989), p. 9ff.
3. Edwin Bernbaum, *Sacred Mountains of the World* (Los Angeles: University of California Press, 1997), p. 114.
4. Christian Rätsch, Claudia Müller-Ebeling et al., *Shamanism and Tantra in the Himalayas* (Rochester, Vermont: Inner Traditions, 2002), p. 78.
5. Julius Evola, *Meditations on the Peaks*, p. 114.
6. Henry Corbin, *The Man of Light in Iranian Sufism* (New Lebanon, New York: Omega, 1994), p. 62.
7. Evola, *Meditations on the Peaks*, p. 113. The subsequent comparisons also derive from Evola's commentary.
8. Ibid.
9. Dr. Daithi O hOgain, *Myth, Legend & Romance* (New York: Prentice Hall, 1991), p. 407.
10. Bernbaum, p. 121.
11. Ibid.
12. Ibid.
13. Ibid., p. 124.
14. O hOgain, *Myth, Legend & Romance*, p. 359.
15. Reinhold Messner, *My Quest for the Yeti*, (New York: St. Martin's, 2000), p. 164.
16. All definitions from *The American Heritage Dictionary of Indo-European Roots* (Boston: Houghton Mifflin, 2000) and *Das Herkunftswörterbuch* (Mannheim: Dudenverlag, 1989).
17. Jacob Grimm, *Deutsche Mythologie*, (Graz, Austria: Akademische Druck, 1968), vol. 2, p. 794.
18. Ibid., vol. 2, p. 796.
19. Elizabeth Wylie-Ernst, *Frau Holle and the Re-creation Myth* (Ph.D. dissertation, University of Pittsburgh, 1995), p. 2.
20. Ibid., p. 83.
21. Ibid., p. 14.
22. Friedrich Nietzsche, *Thus Spoke Zarathustra* in *The Portable Nietzsche*, trans. Walter Kauffmann (New York: Penguin: 1954), p. 258.

Dominion Press Is Proud to
Announce the Publication of

Confessions of a Radical Traditionalist
by John Michell

Confessions of a Radical Traditionalist is a wide-ranging collection of colourful essays by English author and philosopher John Michell. For those readers only familiar with his better-known writings on Earth Mysteries, unusual phenomena, and eccentric figures, much of the material here will be a pleasant surprise.

Since its inception, Michell has regularly contributed to the monthly magazine *The Oldie*, one of Britain's best-kept publishing secrets. Michell's column, "An Orthodox Voice," is a perpetual font of erudite insights, charming commentaries, wittily scathing pronouncements, and divine revelations. Writing in clear, exquisite language, he deftly applies traditional wisdom to various aspects of the modern conundrum. In author Patrick Harpur's words, "If Socrates had ever written a column, this would be it."

Divided into nine sections, *Confessions of a Radical Traditionalist* presents Michell's thoughts on a wealth of heretical topics, from ancient echoes of a Golden Age to the madness of modernity and the unfolding apocalypse. Undergirding these ruminations is the rarely heard perspective of an enlightened, idealistic Platonist. Even when slaying sacred cows or lancing contemporary buffoons, he never forgets that the elusive "paradise of the philosophers" is within reach for those with the strength of vision to see it. In our inverted modern world, these disarming orthodox writings have the delicious flavor of forbidden fruit.

The 108 essays in this volume have been carefully selected and introduced by Joscelyn Godwin, a long-time admirer of John Michell's work and himself an acknowledged authority in matters esoteric and metaphysical.

The book itself is beautifully typeset and produced, making use of traditional design and sacred measurements. The cover features a stunning tempera portrait of John Michell painted in 1972 by Maxwell Armfield (1881–1972), as well as artwork by Michell himself.

John Michell was born in London in 1933 and educated at Eton and Trinity College, Cambridge. His early books *The Flying Saucer Vision* (1967) and *The View Over Atlantis* (1969) exposed new generations to the lost wisdom and sacred sciences of the ancient world. His voluminous subsequent writings have chronicled forgotten eccentrics and illuminated the mysterious worlds of crop circles, ley lines, simulacra in nature, Stonehenge, and sacred geometry. Some of his recent works include *At the Center of the World* (1994), *The Temple at Jerusalem: A Revelation* (2000), and *The Measure of Albion* (with Robin Heath, 2004). An exhibit of his geometrical and other watercolour paintings was held in London in 2003 at the Christopher Gibbs Gallery. He lives in Notting Hill, London.

Clothbound, with full-color dustjacket, 5¾" x 9¼",
352 + xxi pages, Dominion, 2005, ISBN 0-9712044-4-6

"Refreshingly original, yet genuinely grounded in tradition. John Michell is wise, amusing and mischievous. He has expanded the frontiers of British sanity, and enriches the lives of those who know him and his works."
—*Rupert Sheldrake*

"A delightful read. Maybe there's some hope for the world after all!"
—*Thomas H. Naylor*, The Vermont Review of Books

As a special offer for readers of *TYR*, *Confessions of a Radical Traditionalist* is available for $25 postpaid in the U.S.A. and $60 airmail postpaid to the rest of the world. Please send check or money order payable to:

Dominion
P.O. Box 129
Waterbury Center, VT
05677

Inquiries and Paypal payments may be directed to our email address:
dominionpress@comcast.net

On the Spiritual Arts and Crafts: Practising the Ancient Skills and Wisdom of Europe

Nigel Pennick

> The objective of all the arts is beauty.
> And beauty is nothing other than the intense, intoxicating joy
> that is produced for us by sounds, words, shapes and colours.
> —August Endell (1871–1925)

Introductory Note

This essay is not an historical appraisal of a movement known as "Arts and Crafts," which lost its momentum in the early 20th century partly as the result of the twin catastrophes of the Great War (1914–1918) and the Great Depression after 1929. The "Arts and Crafts" movement of the late 19th and early 20th century, however, did have a spiritual as well as a social dimension whose message remains relevant in the present day. The Spiritual Arts and Crafts I write about here are a continuing process that comes unbroken from the roots of our culture. Because they are timeless, they are immediate, necessitating a direct involvement with the here-and-now. Whilst recognizing that admiration and respect is due to the great masters, named and unnamed, of bygone times, and taking what they have left us as inspiration, we, like them, have to work within our given *örlog*, which is the present condition. If we understand and apply true principles to our work, then we, like our forebears, can be in harmony with the world and its underlying essence. The European Arts and Crafts have a solid spiritual basis. It is up to us to know what we have to do, and to do it.

Ancient Skills and Wisdom: True Principles

The rubric "ancient skills and wisdom" was coined in Cambridge in 1969 by John Nicholson. It describes a culture that recognizes, celebrates and uses the knowledge, traditions, abilities and the spiritual understanding of how to do things. To practise these ancient skills and wisdom requires an understanding of one's personal place in the continuity of culture over thousands of years. It necessitates being present in one's own tradition, based upon place and the accumulated understanding of countless ancestral generations. Ancient skills and wisdom are timeless because the basic true principles of existence do not change. Things that are made that follow these essential principles are in themselves also timeless.

An understanding of these true principles is a fundamental tenet of the European Tradition. It can be found in the writings of Plotinus (3rd century CE), most especially his *Enneads*, where he explains that the arts are not an imitation of Nature, but human-mediated expressions of the spiritual source of which Nature is only the outward manifestation. "If anyone thinks meanly of the arts, on the ground that they only mimic Nature," Plotinus writes, "there is a threefold answer. Firstly, we must note that all Nature is itself an imitation of some other thing. Secondly, we are not to imagine that the arts merely imitate the seen thing: they go back to the principles of form out of which Nature is generated. Thirdly, in many of their creations, they go beyond imitation: because they possess beauty, they provide whatever is lacking in the perceived object."

This understanding of true principles has informed the arts and crafts of Europe through their most creative periods. It has been present both in the formal, courtly arts of aristocratic and commercial patronage, as well as the everyday handicrafts of the working class. Throughout time, most have worked at their profession, producing arts and crafts that satisfied the needs and aspirations of their place and time. Few have left writings that express the inner principles that can be seen in their surviving works. From the 19th century onwards, however, there are some notable insights provided by the great masters. French master sculptor Auguste Rodin observed that "An art that has life does not restore the works of the past: it continues them." The Catalan master architect Antoni Gaudí (1852–1926) noted in the 20th century, "Originality consists of a return to the origin."

Craftsmanship taught according to the traditional European guild system, where ancient skills and wisdom is handed on directly from master to apprentice, is not separated from the spiritual dimension of life. In ancient times, craftwork was made mindfully of the Gods who symbolize the inner principles and uses of the work in hand, and the Divine Harmony that is their expression. Later, under Christianity, it was made in honour of the single Creator and His divine harmony. And later still, in a more pluralistic age, Theosophical and abstract spiritual principles have been similarly expressed. What has remained important throughout time is the system of values, not what dogmas are outwardly professed. Whichever deity or guiding ethos is kept in mind, the inner principles remain the same.

The Question of Form

The inner essence of anything we make mindfully is necessarily expressed in form. As with all things, this is not fixed, for all forms change over time. But if the essence remains the same, then the form will express it even when a comparison of two forms will seemingly show them to be disparate. This is the principle of evolution from one form to another over time that was recognized in different ways by J. W. von Goethe and Charles Darwin. The basis of forms, Plotinus tells us, is the source: "this source cannot be the beautiful objects themselves: were it to be so, then it would also be a mere part. It can be no shape, no power, nor the sum of shapes and powers that have had the genesis that puts them here; it must stand above all the powers, all the patterns. The origin of all this must be formless; formless not as lacking shape but as the very source of shape . . . this formless form is beautiful."

Order emerges out of Chaos as a function of Chaos itself; not as the imposition of order from outside. Another significant principle was noted by the English nature philosopher and poet Samuel Taylor Coleridge (1772–1834). It was he who described the fundamental difference between "organic form" and "mechanic form." Organic form is drawn out by human skill from the inner nature of materials. Mechanic form, on the other hand, is imposed from outside, regardless of the inner nature of the material. Organic form is the way of Nature; mechanic form that of the spiritless. The guiding ethos of the Spiritual Arts and Crafts naturally brings organic form into being. The English 'Arts and Crafts' architect M. H. Baillie Scott (1865–1945) noted that the art of building is undermined by what he called the "mechanical ideal" of regularity and smoothness that devalues the part played in construction by the craftsmen. The work of a craftsperson is literally personal. Conscious attempts to erase the mark of the craftsperson's hand is literally depersonalizing the artifact.

There are ways of doing things that can have a spiritual basis, and other ways that do not. Practising the spiritual arts and crafts is not just a matter of understanding how organic form can be brought into being. It is also a matter of being true to our true selves as well as being true to the materials we use. Plotinus again: "We possess beauty when we are true to our own being: ugliness is going over to another order." When we are compelled to do that which is against our true selves, whether by being forced to do work for which we are not fitted temperamentally or spiritually, or by having to produce harmful, brutal or meaningless products, we have been forced into the mechanical form of another order.

The great Manx master Archibald Knox (1864–1933), whose inspired spiritual works express a transcendent spirit, talked of how the distinctively individual Self Nature is the combination of Outside Nature and our own Nature. Just as Hans Poelzig later observed that form emerges from the Mystic Abyss, Knox originated individuality in the recesses of the unknown. It is from this archetypal realm—the outer, cosmic, realm, and its microcosmic reflection in the inner, human, realm, that all individual forms originate. In traditional terms, they were referring to the principle of reflexiveness embodied in the maxim of Hermes Trismegistus, "as above, so below."

When the Arts and Crafts are conducted according to European Traditional Spirituality, then the raw materials are gathered mindfully, and with rites and ceremonies that reflect the needs both of humans and the divine. Their preparation and manufacture, too, are conducted in an atmosphere of spiritual awareness. This imbues them with certain qualities and virtues that have real meaning to those who ply their craft in creating works that are reflections of the Divine Harmony. As embodiments of the Divine Harmony, they are ensouled artifacts. Writing of such artifacts, animated by harmony, the 16th century Italian spiritual teacher Guilio Camillo Delminio quotes ancient words ascribed to Hermes Trismegistus, "in Egypt there were statue makers who were so skilled that when they had given a statue perfect proportions, it was found to be animated with an angelic spirit: for such perfection could not be without a soul."

Ensoulment of artifacts is only possible if craftspeople are mindful of the spiritual dimension of their work. Doing everything in a spiritual state of mind is the key to the Spiritual Arts and Crafts. The great Russian master illustrator Ivan Bilibin "Ivan of the Iron Hand" (1876–1942), taught his students to meditate before beginning work, in the tradition of the Orthodox icon painters. By so doing, he imbued his work with spirit. When the doer and the act are in perfect spiritual harmony, then the artifact produced will embody this as long as it exists.

In former times, this was always done with sacred architecture, such as in building churches. But to apply this only to what we may hold to be holy or divine unavoidably degrades the rest of existence into the profane or unsacred. If we make only the overtly spiritual according to true principles, then the rest of the world is left to rot. And when the "profane" world rots, then it is not long before the rot spreads everywhere, and nothing is sacred. Then, even the outwardly holy has been made without reverence and spiritual consciousness. Such a loss of awareness is already largely accomplished in a culture whose mindfulness has been distracted by simplistic materialism. The ensouled world comes about not by chance but only by the appropriate application of true principles. "Although it is held that the house should be convenient and aptly fitted to its material functions" wrote M. H. Baillie Scott, "it is but a mean thing if it does not express something of the aspirations of the spirit of its builders, and indeed possess, as it were, a soul of its own." It is the successful enabling of this soul to come into being that is the crowning achievement in the Spiritual Arts and Crafts.

Creation and co-production necessitates involvement at many levels, dealing robustly with the bewildering complexity and destructiveness of the human world, neither falling into naïvity nor dogmatism. Forgetting that humans are involved in the creative process of bringing the idea into physical reality, as Baillie Scott warns us against, is compounded by the practise of not crediting those who have made essential contribution to the work.

Spiritual Practicality

In understanding the spiritual dimension of the Arts and Crafts, we need to learn to see the world from the individual's experiential viewpoint. Our approach to the world requires a sense of wonder that acts without feelings of powerlessness, arrogance, dismissal, or sentimental projection. It requires the appreciation and cultivation of the inner visionary mind, always avoiding literalism and remaining grounded in reality. In 1905, the German master August Endell wrote, "There are so many things that are immediately accessible to us, yet so few of us see and appreciate them; a wonderful, magnificent world directly before our eyes, so exquisite, so full of colour, and so rich that there is absolutely no need for us to invent imaginary worlds. Today; the present; reality: these are the most fantastic and incredible of all; the wonders made up in literature are utterly paltry in comparison. It is only our stupidity that prevents us from using this treasure. We have no need of another world above the clouds or in the past; the greatest marvels are found here in our world, in our own time: true, they are invisible to the eye that is dull, but clear and tangible to the eye that sees."

The Stark Alternatives

In some cases, there are alternative ways of performing the same task or achieving the same construction. Yet although they may appear different from one another, nevertheless if they work equally well then they are both manifestations of true principles. Different ways of doing the same thing may exist as a result of the *örlog* of the situation, and thus embody a cultural meaning. Thus, for example, the street sweepers in London, Stuttgart and Rome all use different kinds of broom to accomplish the same task. The type of broom used to sweep a street is only an instance of the myriad variant ways of doing things that, cumulatively, define the character of each place. When, through unthinkingness, a wish for "modernity" or "improvement," something ancient and individual is altered needlessly, that which supersedes it is frequently a product of the globalized industrial environment. Even if it works "just as well," what comes in its place is something that has no relationship, historical or spiritual, with the place where it is being used. Individuality, the historical sense of meaning and belonging to a place, to a culture, is wiped out at once. True principles also include appropriateness.

Traditional things, honed to perfection for a particular purpose at a particular place by generations of users, embody the soul of that place. They have local names in the local language that convey precise meaning. These names denote the local application of true principles that are without name, for they operate without name or description in the world outside the realm of humans. As with the local languages from which they come, they embody more than just a means of description. When they are destroyed, "winter falls upon the legendary remembrance of a people." Even the knowledge of the possibility that such a thing can exist fades away. A cultural catastrophe has taken place, unrecognized in the hastening twilight of awareness.

The Spiritual Arts and Crafts are nothing if not unified. Each part, each necessary activity, emanates from the spiritual source. It is this that decides and defines the direction and "style" of all the work. To do otherwise is to dissipate one's energies. To practise the Spirtual Arts and Crafts does not require mystical revelation, but application. It comes from direct experience of the natural world, tempered by the knowledge of "how to" and the ability so to do as the result of practice and experience. The inner mystery of the nameless art is that of life itself.

Sources and Further Reading:

Bowe, Nicola Gordon: *The Life and Work of Harry Clarke*. Dublin, 1989.
Bryce, Derek: *Symbolism of the Celtic Cross*. Felinfach, 1989.
Carpenter, Edward: *The Art of Creation: Essays on the Self and its Powers*. London, 1904.
James, William: *The Varieties of Religious Experience*. London, 1902.
Kandinsky, Wassily: *Über das geistige in der Kunst*. Munich, 1911.
Lauweriks, J. L. M.: *De ladder von het zijn*. Amsterdam, 1904.
Lethaby. William R.: *Architecture, Mysticism and Myth*. London, 1891.
Macleod, Fiona: *The Winged Destiny: Studies in the Spiritual History of the Gael*. London, 1910.
Martin, Stephen A.: *Archibald Knox*. London, 2001.
McAllister, Isabel: *Alfred Gilbert*. London, 1929.
Olbrich, Joseph Maria: *Ideen von Olbrich*. Wien, 1900.

Schoenmaekers, M. H. J.: *Het Nieuwe Wereldbeeld*. Bussum, 1915.
Scott, M. H. Baillie: *Houses and Gardens*. London, 1906.
Thomas, Patrick: *A Candle in the Darkness: Celtic Spirituality from Wales*. Llandysul, 1993.

Julius Evola: A Philosopher for the Age of the Titans[1]

Joscelyn Godwin

It is a pity that no researcher, while there was still time, ever spoke to the friends and relations who knew Julius Evola (1898–1974) in his youth. Like other occult philosophers (Blavatsky and Gurdjieff come to mind), Evola covered his tracks, putting his apprentice years out of reach of the curious, then constructing an idealized biography.[2] After his crippling injury in World War II he became an obscure and private figure, of little interest to the world in general, so that no one was prompted to go to Sicily, for instance, to try to find some cousins or to establish the status of the title "Baron" to which he sometimes answered. His few disciples, for their part, would never have had the bad manners to poke into the Master's past, or to search out his aging school-fellows for insights into a level of his personality which he affected to despise.

I must confess to a frustrated scholar's curiosity about how such a man developed: a man whose first impact on the world was at the age of 21, with an exhibition of 54 paintings in the most modernistic style,[3] and who promptly laid down his brush, to reappear as commentator and translator of the *Tao Te Ching*;[4] a man who by his mid-twenties had completed a series of essays on Magical Idealism, a scholarly study of Tantra, and an 800-page treatise on the Absolute Individual.[5] But Evola, like his early hero Nietzsche, seems never to have been a child, but to have come into the world fully-formed, ready for his life's mission at a time when most young men are still finding themselves.[6]

When Evola sent a summary of his treatise to the most eminent Italian philosopher of the time, Benedetto Croce, he stated that:

> For some years I have tried to organize my philosophical views into a system, mainly contained in an unpublished work entitled *Theory of the Absolute Individual*. . . . I will release this volume, which has cost me several years of work, without any remuneration. . . . For a number of reasons that I cannot go into here, the publication of the

principal work represents something quite important to me, since, in the discipline I have followed, it is the opportunity to address freely and without reserve those for whom the general effect of my doctrine, expounded theoretically, is not merely an abstract scheme.[7]

This treatise, divided by its first publisher into the two volumes *Teoria dell'Individuo Assoluto* (Theory of the Absolute Individual) and *Fenomenologia dell'Individuo Assoluto* (Phenomenology of the Absolute Individual), is based on premises adumbrated by Novalis, Fichte, and Schelling, but generally quite foreign to Western philosophy. They are more familiar to readers of the Taoist, Tantric, alchemical, and magical texts with which Evola was simultaneously concerned. The Absolute Individual is the Self, seen as identical to the source of all being. Like the philosophy of Plotinus and other Neoplatonists, and even more like the philosophic writings of India and China, Evola's doctrine includes the dimensions of religious experience and mysticism. His twin volumes contain a history of subjective idealism, and a practical philosophy of life, based on the assumption that the Absolute Individual is the ultimate object of human aspiration and attainment. Evola, at least, must have been familiar with the experiences about which he was writing; apart from the authoritative tone of the second volume,[8] there is the additional evidence of an entire life lived most rigorously in the spirit of this philosophy. It is an open question whether his youthful experiences of the Absolute were temporary *samadhis* (to use the language of Yoga) that confirmed him in the truth of his intellectual convictions, or whether they effected a permanent change in his being, leaving him, no matter what his outer activities and circumstances, in the condition of absolute consciousness known as *sahaja samadhi*. But there is no point in discussing this question without the consent of an audience for whom such states are valid possibilities.

Evola's concept of the Absolute Individual is inseparable from the other theme which he treated in this early period: that of Magical Idealism. "Magic" is the blanket-term for the methods taught in East and West that aim at the realization of the Absolute Individual. The choice of term is not a happy one, because of its associations with occultism, not to say stage-magic. But how else is one to fling a net so wide that it includes alchemy, Taoist breathing-practice, the higher forms of Yoga, and little-known mind-altering procedures that use sex or drugs?

There are two reasons why Evola's Magical Idealism is a landmark in the history of modern occultism (another inevitable blanket-term). First, he raises questions that have scarcely ever been addressed to practitioners or answered by theoreticians of the occult sciences, concerning the ultimate motivation and validity of the latter. The answers that one could expect from most occultists are either of a very lowly order, aiming at personal power, knowledge, wealth, etc., or else, in more serious figures such as Eliphas Lévi and A. E. Waite, they give way to dogma, making magic a handmaid to Judeo-Christian religious notions. The second reason is that Evola was not content to stay within the Western streams of magic, philosophy, or mysticism, but needed for the completion of his experiential system the input of the East.[9] He did for magic what the Theosophists had done for the theoretical study of esotericism: opened it to the whole world.

By the time he was writing to Croce, Evola had already met Arturo Reghini (1878–1946)[10] and become a close associate of this esoteric activist, founder of journals and societies, and member of fringe-masonic groups.[11] Reghini performed two important services for the younger man. By his own example as a kind of Pythagorean nationalist, he convinced Evola—hitherto a student more of German Idealism and of the East—of the value of his native Italian heritage; and he introduced him to the writings of René Guénon.

At the beginning of 1927 Evola founded an esoteric group, the "Gruppo di Ur," and edited its eponymous journal,[12] with the support of Reghini and including a number of the latter's previous collaborators. Simultaneously with their writing, the group conducted magical and occult experiments, not of a superstitious kind but more in the practical mode of Rudolf Steiner's "spiritual science"; for the group included some of Italy's chief Anthroposophists.[13] I do not know of a more solidly-based, sensible and comprehensible treatise on magic from any period to compare with the three volumes of *Ur* and *Krur*.[14] The responsibility for this goes mainly to Evola's guiding hand and to the contributions by himself and Reghini.

One consequence of the friendship with Reghini was the theme of Evola's next book, *Imperialismo pagano* (Pagan Imperialism), which was so polemical against the Catholic Church that it later became an embarrassment to him, and was never reissued during his lifetime. It is subtitled "Fascism Facing the Euro-Christian Peril,"[15] and argues, as Reghini had been doing since the end of World War I, for the restoration of the Roman pagan tradition as the proper spiritual foundation of the new Italian republic.[16] The insistence, henceforth in Evola's work, on "Tradition" is the legacy of Guénon, whose early writings[17] had propounded the idea of a single primordial tradition from which the various religions were offshoots, and which contained in symbolic form the basic metaphysical truths about the universe and man's self-realization. The Absolute Individual that Evola had found in Taoism and Tantra, Guénon had expounded as the Supreme Identity of the Vedanta. It seemed clear to both of them that the same ultimate truths and teachings were to be found as the deepest layer of every authentic tradition.

Unlike Guénon, Evola was dubious about the status of the Judeo-Christian tradition, which was so displeasing to him on a political and aesthetic level. But he did not fail to discern other strands that had kept the authentic tradition alive in the West, foremost among which was alchemy. His contributions to *Ur* and *Krur* included many essays on this subject that he later gathered and expanded into a book on the Hermetic Tradition.[18] In the history of alchemy in the twentieth century, Evola's work represents a third stream, distinct from the practical, laboratory alchemy of Canseliet, Frater Albertus, and their schools, and equally distinct from the psychologized alchemy of Jung and his followers. Evola's Hermetic Tradition is instead a cosmology, combined with a method for self-realization, in which sulphur and mercury, conjunction, transmutation, etc., are the names of otherwise undefinable states of mind and soul. Although it is not made explicit in the text, Evola's alchemical method, like much else in occult practice, centers on the deliberate separation of consciousness from the body and on operations performed in the "astral world" or the world of the Imagination (taking this term in the sense used by William Blake or Henry Corbin), which require more than the usual degree of concentration and courage.

The more one mentions things of this kind, the greater is the tendency to associate Evola with other modern occultists, in the broad sense of the term. But his next book drew the line firmly between himself and them, being a denunciation of the "Mask and True Face of Contemporary Spiritualism."[19] It was based on articles he had already published critical of Spiritualism, Psychoanalysis, Theosophy, Anthroposophy, the French occultists, etc., and it served the same purpose as Guénon's earlier works against Theosophy and Spiritualism:[20] defining the field, the sources, and the individuals that were unacceptable to "traditionalists." Like *Pagan Imperialism*, *Mask and Face of Contemporary Spritualism* evidenced a dualist trend that had always been latent in Evola's character, but which in his earlier works had not yet become the source of his creative energy. Now it was not enough to speak of the various royal paths by which the "superior man" (in Taoist terminology) achieves the Absolute Individual: the machinations of inferior men and women had to be laid bare, and war had to be declared against them.

Just as Evola's early explorations in art, philosophy, psychedelics, and magic had found their expression in the dissertation-like *Theory* and *Phenomenology of the Absolute Individual*, so now he gave vent to his paganism, his sense of tradition, his political consciousness, and his contempt for most of the human race in his most important and representative work: *Rivolta contro il mondo moderno* (Revolt Against the Modern World).[21] This revolt was urged in the name of a primordial tradition whose metaphysical and cosmological principles occupy the first half of the book, while the other half is concerned with the process that led to the modern aberration. The fundamental assumption, without which *Revolt* makes no sense whatever, is the cyclical principle of history that is most fully developed in the Hindu system of four Yugas or world-ages (Satya, Treta, Dvapara, and Kali Yuga), and also known to the Greeks as the Ages of Gold, Silver, Bronze, and Iron. Evola accepts this, just as Guénon did, with the corollary that modernity is a phenomenon of the last part of the Kali Yuga or Age of Iron—after whose cataclysmic ending a new Golden Age will dawn, as certainly as the sun rises every morning.

Whether there ever was a Golden Age with a perfectly ordered primordial tradition, situated, as Guénon and Evola both maintained, in the region of the North Pole, is beyond proof or disproof. One might call it a romantic idea, for there have been plenty of romantic adherents to it, or to some version of it. Be that as it may, Evola's evocation of the orderly cosmos of Tradition and its fall is at least a work of art on a Wagnerian scale, that like a great opera does not have to be "true" in order to be an inspiration and an enrichment to its audience. The greatest value of

Revolt may be its quality as an epic work of the imagination, which like all epics offers an escape into a world better-ordered than our own, if no less tragic.

If the cyclical interpretation of prehistory and history is correct, then modernity is nothing but the inevitable consequence of the tail-end of the cycle. There is nothing moral or immoral about it, any more than about night, winter, or natural death. Yet Evola and the other Traditionalists write as if to condemn it, with scathing comments on its social organizations, its confusion of gender-roles, its materialism and vulgarity, its racial and spiritual degradation. Above all, there is Evola's pervasive theme, apparently derived from his early reading of the Swiss anthropologist Bachofen, of the superiority of the masculine over the feminine, especially in spiritual terms of the virile, primordial, Arctic, "Uranian" and "Olympian" way, contrasted with the Southern, orgiastic, sentimental, Dionysian way of the Mother-goddess. The former, one gathers, is the path to the Absolute Individual, while the latter leads only to extinction on the wheel of the Eternal Return.

Gianni Ferracuti[22] has pointed out that only in modern times could someone have thought and written as Evola did, refusing his native environment (whether one thinks of this as Italian Catholicism or as the rootless materialism of the Western world) and deliberately choosing an invented, or at least a foreign (because fundamentally Eastern) mode of thought. The critic of modernity is an essentially modern phenomenon.

This cultural pessimism, as it is generally known today, was a natural reaction to events in Europe which none could ignore, least of all one of Evola's warrior disposition. For all the lapidary certainties of his writing, Evola was looking for something to hold on to during the 1930s. He had been disappointed as Fascism compromised itself with the bourgeois and proletarian world, even though he never found it so degraded as the rival systems of American capitalism or Soviet communism. During this decade his glance wandered continually to Germany, hoping to find there a political realization closer to his ideals. Fluent in German, he made several semi-official visits to Germany and Austria between 1934 and 1941 to give lectures and to meet dignitaries of the *Schutzstaffel*. But these encounters also left a residue of mutual disillusionment: his hosts found him too unworldly and idealistic; he found National Socialism too narrowly Pangermanist; and the

Italian regime became so uneasy about his activities that in 1942 it withdrew his passport.[23]

Two themes dominated Evola's thought after the completion of *Revolt Against the Modern World*. One of them had been present incidentally in that book: the theme of race, and in particular the connection of the primordial tradition with a pure Hyperborean race that had interbred, after the destruction of its Arctic homeland, with the inferior races of the South. As Mussolini's German allies began to exert pressure on a Fascist system that had been, at the outset, quite innocent of racism, Evola became a self-appointed authority on this topic. Some of his contributions were purely scholarly;[24] some addressed the "Jewish problem";[25] others proposed his own theory,[26] which was that there are three types of race. One of these is the sense in which "race" is generally used, to indicate physical and genetic types: this Evola calls the "race of the body." The others are the race of the soul, which is expressed in art and culture, and the race of the spirit, expressed in religion, philosophy and initiation. Only a man's spiritual race was of ultimate importance to Evola, for it was there, whatever his genetic heritage, that he differentiated himself from the rest of humanity.[27] Evola's fundamental disagreement with the racism of the National Socialists was that, like cattle-breeders, they considered only people's biological or bodily race: in his view, the least significant of the three. It is no wonder that the SS found him unworldly.

The other theme that occupied Evola in the pre-war years was also connected to his Germanophilia: he developed an admiration for the high Middle Ages that resulted in a book on the Mystery of the Grail.[28] For whatever reason,[29] his historical allegiances had now changed, and it was no longer ancient Rome, from Romulus to Augustus, that seemed to him to incarnate the last worthy manifestation of the tradition, but the "Holy Roman Empire of the German People" inaugurated by Charlemagne's consecration in the year 800. In his book, Evola connects the Grail myths on the one hand with the prehistoric Hyperborean tradition, and on the other with the resurgence of the imperial and knightly spirit in the Middle Ages: no matter that Charlemagne was the pitiless suppressor of Nordic paganism, or that the Holy Roman Empire derived its authority from the church that Evola had so reviled in *Pagan Imperialism*. This medievalism, exacerbated by Evola's later indulgence towards Catholic supremacists,[30] continues to puzzle

PASSPORT PHOTO OF JULIUS EVOLA, CIRCA 1940.
COLLECTION OF GASPARE CANNIZZO. PUBLISHED IN "JULIUS
EVOLA: SCRITTI PER VIE DELLA TRADIZIONE 1971–1974"
(PALERMO: EDIZIONI DI VIE DELLA TRADIZIONE, 1996).

those (including the present writer) who would prefer him to have taken the side of the Renaissance Neoplatonists, of whom he seems to have had no appreciation.

During the first years of World War II, Evola turned to yet another tradition, that of Buddhism, and wrote one of his best books, by any standard: *The Doctrine of Awakening*,[31] which for many years was his only work available in English. The quality of the work is a function of its scholarship, based on solid English-language sources (Evola could hardly be expected to know Pali), its insights into the human condition that Buddhism addresses, and the calm spiritual height from which it speaks. The temporary habitation of Oriental modes of thought seems to have enabled Evola to forget the politics and the polemics which contemplation of the modern West so easily provoked from him. At the same time, the work is revisionistic in its preference for Hinayana Buddhism. The Western impression of Buddhism, abetted by nineteenth-century incomprehension and by Theosophical influence, has always been condescending to the primitive Hinayana (the word means "lesser vehicle") in comparison with the "greater vehicle" of Mahayana Buddhism, to which belong the schools of Japan and Tibet that have been such successful exports. To Evola, the contrary was true: the Mahayana was a late and decadent development, sullying the original purity of Buddha's philosophy with its sentimental and religious accretions (just the sort of thing Westerners *would* prefer!), while the uncompromising Hinayana was the original teaching, fit only for Aryas, i.e., the élite, in terms of their spiritual race.

The trauma of his war-injury in 1945 and the years-long hospitalization left Evola disabled. This is how he described his condition in a letter to a fellow philosopher: "The last war made me the gift of a lesion in the spinal cord, which has deprived me almost entirely of the use of my legs: a contingency, however, to which I do not attach much importance." After his return to Rome, he only once left his apartment at 197 Corso Vittorio Emanuele II.[32]

The postwar years were not favorable to Evola, who now bore the stigma of having fought for the losing side. Now that "fascism" had become a term of abuse, it was applied to him, who had never joined the Fascist or any other party, indeed who had risked much with his criticisms of the government.[33] It was difficult for him to re-establish the career as a journalist which had supported him before the War.[34] He first returned to print with a thorough recasting of his early book on Tantra.[35] Then he was rediscovered by some of those who were still faithful to the principles of the Right, and for them he wrote the booklet *Orientamenti* (Orientations).[36]

Evola paid dearly for this act of idealism. In April 1951 he was arrested at his residence and accused of being the "master," the "inspirer," with his "nebulous theories," of a group of young men, who were accused in their turn of having hatched organizations for clandestine struggle and attempted to reconstitute the dissolved Fascist party. (How redolent of the accusations against Socrates: misleading the young, and not believing in the gods of the city but in other, strange gods!) Evola, confined to his wheelchair, was held in the Regina Coeli prison until the trial, which lasted from early October until 20 November, 1951, when he was acquitted.[37]

In the early 1950s he was still hoping for some counter-revolutionary movement, somewhat in the spirit of the "Conservative Revolution" of post-World War I Germany, that would restore the Right to power. *Gli uomini e le rovine* (literally, "The Men and the Ruins"),[38] a book largely about public, social and political matters, addresses the potential leaders of such a movement. It is an analysis of the postwar world, somewhat like an updating of *Revolt Against the Modern World*, that ends with an outline of what would be needed for the healing of Europe: a Europe that would no longer be the playground and victim of the rivalry between the USA and the USSR. Evola hopes—but knowing that it is probably beyond hope—for a resurgence of the Imperial ideal, which would endow the separate nations with a spiritual unity, but not with a forced, political one. His description of how Europe should *not* become united is an uncanny anticipation of what would, in fact, transpire. For example, he writes: "Democracy on the one hand, and a European parliament on the other, which would merely reproduce on a large scale the cheerless and despicable comedy of the European democratic parliaments, would make the idea of One Europe ludicrous."[39] In the end, he puts his faith in the foundation of an Order, if among the ruins there are sufficient men left to stand up and constitute one.

To trace accurately the development of Evola's thought during the 1950s it would be necessary to analyze his journalism, for he published no more books for five years after *Men among the*

Ruins. That his thought did develop is clear.[40] The next time he addressed the élite, he no longer envisaged any possibility or desirability of changing the world itself: it was too far gone on the road to perdition and the conclusion of its cycle. The only place for revolution was now inside oneself. The title of the work in question, *Riding the Tiger*,[41] refers to a Taoist emblem of how the superior man behaves towards a chaotic world: following the principles of "actionless action" and of "doing that which is to be done," he uses it to fortify his own higher individuality. In contrast to the public themes of *Men among the Ruins*, *Riding the Tiger* treats more private domains such as existential philosophy, belief and non-belief, sex, music, drugs, and death, always in the spirit of Tradition and from the point of view of their use for the man in quest of his Absolute Individual.[42]

In between these two last statements of Evola's revolt against the modern world, he published a book on the "Metaphysics of Sex" that was extraordinary for its time, well before the sexual revolution of the 1960s. Sex has always been one of the secret weapons in the magician's cabinet; but Evola was the first, and to date the only writer to treat it from the point of view of "traditional" metaphysics, so as to explain why it has this function.[43]

Most of Evola's remaining titles are anthologies of his earlier articles and journalistic essays on various subjects—genres to which he contributed prolifically up to his death.[44] Only two more original books appeared: his autobiography *Il Cammino del Cinabro* (The Cinnabar Path); and his definitive judgment of the Fascism and National Socialism that had been, and will always be, the first thing with which his critics associate him.[45]

Evola is a very useful figure for students of esotericism to keep in mind, as a touchstone against which to judge less self-aware and articulate ones. In this survey, the occult or magical side of Evola may seem to have taken second place to the philosophical and political man, until it is realized that all of his work was conducted in a magical spirit—the spirit of "Magic as the Science of the Self." The kind of questions that outsiders discuss, such as whether magic is an irrational belief-system, or a reaction against modern science, would have been totally irrelevant to him. In his world, magic and the order of things classified as occult were nothing if not the object of direct, intuitional knowledge. By stripping them of all superstition, all Christian-Kabbalistic accretions, he reduced them to a form in which, at last, they could be sensibly discussed.

By writing this elementary introduction to Evola, I hope to draw the attention of historians and other interested parties to the Italian strain in modern esotericism. Besides Evola, Giuliano Kremmerz and Arturo Reghini also merit attention on the grounds of their stature as thinkers and movers, at least equal to those of the much-researched Golden Dawn or to the French school of Papus, Guaïta, and the like. The fact that so much of Evola's enormous output of books and articles is available in European languages bears witness to a stratum of readership to which there is no parallel in Britain or the USA, and whose influence as a ferment within the political, cultural, and academic worlds, especially in Italy, cannot be ignored. One can say, in conclusion, that Evola is currently the only esoteric and magical philosopher to have any impact whatever on the "real world."

Notes:

1. "The age of the gods is over, and we are entering the age of the titans." Ernst Jünger, in *The Details of Time: Conversations with Ernst Jünger*, trans. Joachim Neugroschel (New York: Marsilio, 1995), p. 69.
2. *Il Cammino del Cinabro* (Milan: Scheiwiller, 1963).
3. For the catalogue of Evola's Rome exhibition of 20–31 January 1920, see Elisabetta Valento, *Homo Faber. Julius Evola fra arte e alchimia* (Rome: Fondazione Julius Evola, 1994), p. 19n. This book includes color plates of Evola's surviving paintings, some of which are in public collections (Civici Musei d'Arte e Storia, Brescia; Kunsthaus, Zurich; Galleria Nazionale d'Arte Moderna, Rome).
4. Evola completed his version (the second one ever to appear in Italian) and introduction in September 1922. The book was published as *Il libro della Via e della Virtù di Lao-Tze* (Carabba: Lanciano, 1923), and reprinted, together with his later version, as J. Evola, *Tao Tê Ching di Lao-tze* (Rome: Edizioni Mediterranee, 1997), with an introductory essay by Silvio Vita.
5. *Saggi sull'Idealismo Magico* (Todi, Rome: Atanòr, 1925), reprinted Genoa: Alkahest, 1981; *L'Uomo come Potenza. I Tantra nello loro metafisica e nei loro metodi di autorealizzazione magica* (Todi, Rome:

Atanòr, 1926; see also note 35 below); *Teoria dell'Individuo Assoluto* (Turin: Fratelli Bocca, 1927); *Fenomenologia dell'Individuo Assoluto* (Turin: Fratelli Bocca, 1930); the latter three books reprinted by Edizioni Mediterranee, Rome.
6. Evola completed his university studies in engineering, but disdained to receive a diploma, then served in World War I as an artillery officer. He never held a salaried job.
7. Evola, letter to Croce, 13 April 1925, quoted in Piero di Vona's introduction to *Teoria dell'Individuo Assoluto* (Rome: Edizioni Mediterranee, 1998), pp. 7–8.
8. Evola revised the first volume, *Teoria dell'Individuo Assoluto*, during his convalescence, and the resulting "second edition" of 1973 is a completely rewritten book. He never rewrote *Fenomenologia*. See Appendix: "'Teoria' prima e seconda" by Roberto Melchionda in *Teoria dell'Individuo Assoluto*, 3rd ed. (Rome: Edizioni Mediterranee, 1988), pp. 195–204.
9. In both these respects, Evola's philosophical journey resembles that of Aleister Crowley, who, for all the difference in personal style, would probably not have disagreed with many of his principles.
10. Evola was introduced to Reghini by the Futurist painter Giacomo Balla. See Valento, p. 18n.
11. Massimo Introvigne, in *Il Capello del Mago* (Milan: SugarCo, 1990), p. 179, mentions the journals *Atanòr* [1924], *Ignis* [1925, 1929], and *Ur* [1927–28] (the latter run jointly with Evola); the orders of Memphis and Misraïm and the Rito Filosofico Italiano; Martinism, the O.T.O., and the Italian Theosophical Society.
12. *Ur* ran for two years, 1927–28. Then after Evola's break with Reghini, it was retitled *Krur* and ran for one more year (1929) under Evola' s sole control. Much of the contents of the two journals (but excluding the essays by Evola that were later incorporated into his books) has been reissued in three volumes as *Introduzione alla Magia quale Scienza dell'Io* (n.p.: Fratelli Melitta, 1987). The definitive work on the Gruppo di Ur is Renato Del Ponte, *Evola e il Magico Gruppo di Ur* (Borzano: SeaR Edizioni, 1994). The main text of the latter work has been included as the introduction to the English edition of vol. 1 of *Introduzione alla Magia* (see note 14).
13. Evola devoted a chapter to the criticism of Anthroposophy in his *Maschera e volto dello spiritualismo contemporaneo* (Turin: Fratelli Bocca, 1932).

14. The formidable bulk of this work has been largely translated into French in six separate publications by Edizioni Arché, Paris and Milan (Evola's contributions, trans. Yvonne Tortat and Gérard Boulanger, as *Ur 1927*, 1983; *Ur 1928*, 1984; *Krur 1929*, 1985; *Tous les écrits de Ur & Krur et "Introduction a la Magie" signés Arvo, Agarda, Iagla*, 1986; Reghini's contributions, trans. Philippe Baillet and Yvonne Tortat, as *Tous les écrits de . . . Ur 1927–1928*, 1986; those of Guido De Giorgio as *L'instant et l'éternité*, 1987). The German edition, translated by H. T. Hansen, has so far covered the first two volumes of *Introduzione alla magia*, as Julius Evola/Gruppe von Ur, *Magie als Wissenschaft vom Ich. Praktische Grundlegung der Initiation* (Interlaken: Ansata-Verlag, 1985), and Julius Evola, *Schritte zur Initiation. Magie als Wissenschaft vom Ich. Band II Theorie und Praxis des höheren Bewusstseins* (n.p.: Ansata-Verlag, 1997). The English version of vol. I, translated by Guido Stucco and edited by Michael Moynihan, is entitled *Introduction to Magic: Rituals and Practical Techniques for the Magus* (Rochester, Vermont: Inner Traditions, 2001).

15. *Imperialismo pagano. Il fascismo dinanzi al pericolo euro-cristiano* (Todi, Rome: Atanór, 1928).

16. Mussolini, more alive to political necessities than swayed by "traditional" spirituality, dealt the death-blow to these pagan dreams in 1929 with his Concordat with the Roman Church. The Duce remained a reader of Evola and his protector, up to a point, despite the philosopher's fearless criticisms of Fascism. The literature on Evola, Fascism, and National Socialism is large, but see especially H. T. Hansen's introduction to *Men among the Ruins* (see note 38 below).

17. Especially *Introduction générale á l'étude des doctrines hindoues* (1921), *Orient et Occident* (1924), *L'Homme et son devenir selon le Védânta* (1925).

18. *La tradizione ermetica, nei suoi simboli, nella sua dottrina e nella sua "arte regia"* (Bari: Laterza, 1931). English translation by E. E. Rehmus, *The Hermetic Tradition: Symbols and Teachings of the Royal Art* (Rochester, Vermont: Inner Traditions, 1995).

19. *Maschera e volto dello spiritualismo contemporaneo. Analisi critica delle principali correnti moderne verso il "soprannaturale"* (Turin: Fratelli Bocca, 1932).

20. *Le Théosophisme, histoire d'une pseudo-religion* (1921); *L'erreur spirite* (1923).

21. *Rivolta contro il mondo moderno* (Milan: Hoepli, 1934). English translation of the 3rd edition (1969) by Guido Stucco, *Revolt*

Against the Modern World (Rochester, Vermont: Inner Traditions, 1995).
22. Gianni Ferracuti, "Modernità di Evola" in *Futuro presente* 6 (1995), pp. 11–26.
23. The passport was restored after Mussolini's personal intervention. For documentation of the reactions on both sides, see Dana Lloyd Thomas, "Il filo-germanesimo di Julius Evola: le reazioni dello Stato fascista" in *Politica Romana* 4 (1997), pp. 263–293; *Julius Evola nei documenti segreti dell'Ahnenerbe*, ed. Bruno Zoratto (Rome: Fondazione Julius Evola, 1997); *Julius Evola nei documenti segreti del Terzo Reich*, ed. Nicola Cospito and Hans Werner Neulen (n.p.: Europa, 1986).
24. *Il mito del sangue* (Milan: Hoepli, 1937) is a treatise on previous racial theories.
25. *Tre aspetti del problema ebraico, nel mondo spirituale, nel mondo culturale, nel mondo economico sociale* (Rome: Edizioni Mediterranee, 1936).
26. *Sintesi di dottrina della razza* (Milan: Hoepli, 1941); *Indirizzi per una educazione razziale* (Naples: Conte, 1941).
27. For an orientation to Evola's racial theory, written in a conciliatory spirit, see the anonymous Foreword to the re-edition of his manual for educators, *Indirizzi per una educazione razziale* (Padua: Edizioni di Ar, 1994), pp. 9–11.
28. *Il mistero del Graal e la tradizione ghibellina dell'Impero*. (Bari: Laterza, 1937). English translation by Guido Stucco, *The Mystery of the Grail: Initiation and Magic in the Quest for the Spirit* (Rochester, Vermont: Inner Traditions, 1997).
29. See the series of articles by Piero Fenili, in which these reasons are analyzed: "Julius Evola e la cultura della destra cattolica e neopagana [I]" in *Politica Romana* 2 (1995), pp. 41–68; "Julius Evola e la cultura della destra cattolica e neopagana II" in *Politica Romana* 3 (1996), pp. 15–73; "I miti evoliani del sangue e della crociata e la destra metafisica e massonica" in *Politica Romana* 4 (1997), pp. 14–69.
30. Such as the reactionary Donoso Cortès; see Fenili in *Politica Romana* 2, p. 47 and passim.
31. *La dottrina del risveglio, saggio sull'ascesi buddhista* (Bari: Laterza, 1943). The English translation by H. E. Musson was published in 1951 by Luzac, the London Oriental publisher, uniformly with a number of Guénon's works; currently in print as *The Doctrine of Awakening: The Attainment of Self-Mastery According to the Earliest Buddhist Texts* (Rochester, Vermont: Inner Traditions, 1995).

32. The owner, an aristocratic admirer, allowed him a free lease for life.

33. In this, as in many other regards, Evola resembles the anti-Nazi novelist Ernst Jünger (1895–1997).

34. Like many Barons and most magicians, Evola was not wealthy. Besides his books, which were hardly a lucrative enterprise, he wrote an enormous number of contributions to newspapers and journals, and many translations of books by others. The most complete bibliography is *Bibliographie Julius Evola* (Vienna: Kshatriya, 1999); also useful is the annotated bibliography by Renato Del Ponte, "Julius Evola: una bibliografia 1920–1994" in *Futuro presente* 6 (1995), pp. 27–70.

35. *Lo Yoga della Potenza, saggio sui Tantra* (Milan: Fratelli Bocca, 1949). English translation by Guido Stucco, *The Yoga of Power: Tantra, Shakti, and the Secret Way* (Rochester, Vermont: Inner Traditions, 1992).

36. *Orientamenti, undici punti* (Rome: Imperium, 1950).

37. See J. Evola, "Autodifesa" (Self Defense Statement) published as an Appendix to *Men among the Ruins* (see next note).

38. *Gli uomini e le rovine* (Rome: Edizioni dell'Ascia, 1953). English translation by Guido Stucco, with an introductory essay by H. T. Hansen, edited by Michael Moynihan. *Men among the Ruins* (Rochester, Vermont: Inner Traditions, 2002).

39. *Gli uomini e le rovine*, 3rd ed. (Rome: Volpe, 1972), p. 244.

40. On this process, see Philippe Baillet's Introduction to Isabelle Robinet's translation of *Chevaucher le tigre* (Paris: Guy Trédaniel, 1982), pp. xii–xiii.

41. *Cavalcare la tigre* (Milan: Scheiwiller, 1961). Translation in progress.

42. The language here is deliberate, for Evola does not seem to have considered woman as a likely candidate for this quest.

43. Evola chose never to marry or have children. It is common knowledge that he had ample heterosexual experience in his younger days.

44. One of these collections, *Meditazioni delle vette* (La Spezia: Edizioni del Tridente, 1974), has appeared in English translation by Guido Stucco: *Meditations from the Peaks: Mountain Climbing as Metaphor for the Spiritual Quest* (Rochester, Vermont: Inner Traditions, 1998).

45. *Il fascismo, saggio di una analisi critica dal punto da vista della Destra* (Rome: Volpe, 1964). The second edition (1970) is enlarged with *Note sul Terzo Reich*.

Hermann Löns:
An Introduction to his Life and Work

Markus Wolff

The literary output of Hermann Löns is part of a profound reaction against the soullessness of encroaching industrialization, big city life, and cultural and economic materialism. This reaction started in the 1890s and continued into the 1920s and can loosely be named *"völkisch."* A deep love for his *"Heimat,"* or homeland, fueled Löns's wide-ranging activities as a scientist, journalist, novelist, and poet. He also shared with the proponents of the *völkisch* movement an interest in Germanic myth and prehistory. Löns's character was defined by a fierce individualism that led him to triumph against great odds, and often over his own inner demons. His writing style has been praised for its directness, color, and intensity of expression. The depth and greatness of his animal characterizations made him a sort of German equivalent of Jack London and Rudyard Kipling, and have found a wide readership. His nature stories continued to be popular after World War II, while his other work, with the notable exception of *Der Wehrwolf*, has been almost entirely forgotten. Until recently, *Der Wehrwolf* was the only Löns work to be translated into English (under the title of *Harm Wulf*).

Hermann Löns was born on August 29th, 1866, the oldest son of a teacher in Kulm, Western Prussia. His father came from a family of teachers, but his grandfather, Diederich Löns, married a wealthy farmer's daughter. Löns's biographer Castelle speculates that this influx of peasant blood might well have inspired Löns's lifelong interest in peasant culture. One of his great-grandfathers on his mother's side was Moritz Bachofen, a notable poet and scholar from the Romantic period who issued books such as *Gunloda* and *Arminia* and published a periodical called *Das Nordlicht*. Like his descendent, Bachofen came to prefer his native landscapes and gods to the classical world championed by most of his contemporaries.

When he was one, Löns's parents relocated to Deutsch-Krone, where his father continued to teach high school. The young boy Hermann was to grow up there until he turned eighteen, in the process becoming intimately acquainted with the local surroundings. In his short autobiography *Von Ost nach West*, he later professed that "even as a very small child, it was my greatest pleasure to watch the flies on the window, and at age five a dead mouse lured me more than a piece of cake." Local peasants and playmates soon laid the foundations for his immense passion for the natural sciences. On entering school in 1873, Löns became one of the best students. His intensified interest in the natural world led him to seek out the solitude of the surrounding woods, heaths and moors. On these excursions, he had many a strange adventure with poachers and gypsies, once even stumbling upon a police commission investigating the body of a game-keeper murdered by wood thieves. "Once he fell asleep under a large oak. When he was awakened by the voices of the forester and woodsmen, he made a surprising discovery. In the meantime, on the other side of the tree, an old drunk had ended his life by hanging himself."

Löns's specialty during his early to mid teens was the investigation of local bird life. To this end, he assembled a sizable collection of stuffed birds for the high school, and at sixteen wrote a report about local bird life which lists 130 species. It was during these years that Löns developed the skills for minute observation that later served him so well while writing his nature and hunting stories.

During his years in Deutsch-Krone, Löns had wanted to become a painter, but his efforts were thwarted by an inability to learn the techniques. Throughout his life, he maintained an avid interest in art and many of his closest friends were fine artists. Löns continued to draw postcards, adding little verses in the manner of the great artist and story teller Wilhelm Busch, and sent them to friends. Although some of these were published after his death, they were meant as a private amusement.

In 1884, Friedrich Wilhelm Löns was called to teach in Münster in his native Westphalia. This move was of decisive importance to the further development of the young Löns. The house of his grandparents gave him an opportunity to connect with his family history and a sense of belonging awoke within him. After two years, according to *Von Ost nach West*, he "consciously became that which [he] had unconsciously always been: a Lower Saxon."

After graduating from high school, Löns went off to study medicine at the famed Greifswald University in 1887. In

Greifswald, a small city by the Baltic coast, he quickly sought and found new obsessions: fencing, dancing, and the opposite sex. He joined a students' association called "Cimbria," and it was not long before his face was scarred defending his honor in multiple duels. Relishing his new found independence and freedom, he continued his own studies in nature which led him to publish several zoological articles in scientific journals. Löns was already affirming his close connection to the countryside and its peasant inhabitants, gathering material, and formulating the guiding principles of his literary work. However, Löns also neglected his proper studies, which led to a bitter dispute with his father, who brought him back to study the natural sciences at the academy in Münster. He specialized in beetles, discovering a new species, as well as malacological studies, some of which were published.

It was during these student years that Löns first discovered his love for writing poetry, mainly under the influence of the works of Detlev von Liliencron and Annette Droste-Hülshoff. But his youthful mind also absorbed most of the other groundbreaking writing and thought of the day, such as that of Nietzsche. This was reflected in the rebellious tone of some of his early modernist poems, one of which demands "a new melody" and asserts that the old poetry concerns itself with "rotten corpses" and needs to be overcome. He would remain an ardent opponent of Naturalism in literature, once calling Thomas Mann's famous family novel *Die Buddenbrooks* "one of the greatest bores of the new century."

Soon after, Löns gave up his studies and tried his hand at journalism, at first being very unhappy with the reality of the trade. After a few short-term positions, he regained his inner strength after witnessing the cholera outbreaks in Hamburg. He decided to become a reporter and moved to Hannover at the end of 1892. The central position of Hannover proved to be a godsend for the young author. The city lies close to a variety of landscapes that he would come to love, write about, and even fight for: the Harz region, the Suntel, and especially the Lüneburg Heath to the North. After a year of successful reporting for the *Hannoversche Anzeiger*, he married Elizabeth Erbeck, whom he had known in Münster. Löns soon won local fame through his "Sunday Chats," a sharp and incisive column dealing with local issues that he wrote under various pseudonyms, the last one being "Uhlenspiegel." Soon he also took over editorial duties at the new *Hannoversche Allgemeine Zeitung* and oversaw its art and literature departments. The same year, 1902, saw him take over the editorship of the local

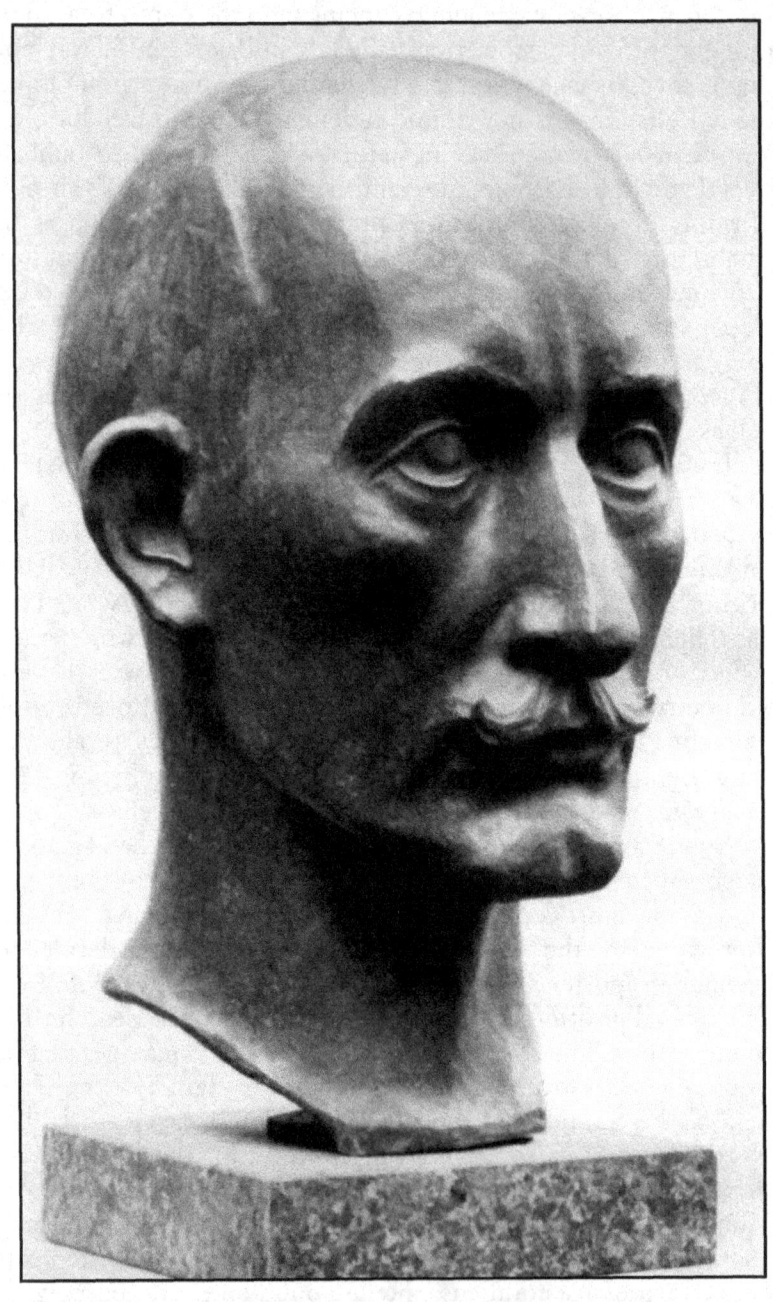

BUST OF HERMANN LÖNS — HANS HAFFENRICTER.

periodical *Niedersachsen* which dealt with local folklore and history. Fine art continued to be of great interest to Löns. Castelle goes so far as to say that "for Löns, colors signify emotions, creation, experience. His descriptive prose glows and bleeds with color. Löns sees the world through the eyes of a fine artist." In keeping with his anti-naturalist attitude, Löns's favorite artist was the Swiss symbolist Arnold Böcklin.

Hermann Löns's political side was very pragmatic during this period. He disliked most political parties, lamenting the lack of foresight and unity, and the petty squabbles and intrigues of Parliament. He was always fascinated by what he saw as the healthy, inborn strength that he experienced in his dealings with common people—as opposed to the pathological hypermodernity of the middle classes. This simple, straightforward world was what he later sought to portray in his novels.

Löns and his first wife divorced in 1901, ending an increasingly unhappy and childless marriage. Löns tried to find his bearings again in nature and vowed not to marry again. But only a few months later he fell in love with Lisa Hausmann. The pair married in the spring of 1902. A year earlier, he had published a volume of poetry, *Mein goldenes Buch* (My Golden Book). It contains vivid descriptions of hunting and country life. As he wrote later in his autobiography: "I . . . lived for weeks on end in a hunting lodge, lived for months among the peasants, and then, when I was back in the bustle of the city, that which the heath wind had told me took on a tangible shape and form." He had been hunting off and on since the early 1890s, taking out his notebook when confronted with an interesting scene or animal and recording every minute detail. The process, aura, and surroundings of the hunt seemed to interest him more than killing.

During the next few years, he worked on the short stories that would make up *Mein braunes Buch* (My Brown Book), which was published in 1907. The work was subtitled "Heath Impressions" and includes stories that take place in the Lüneburg Heath, an area that was only then being "discovered" by the rest of Germany as a unique and magical landscape, and becoming known for its red-brown soil, tall juniper trees, moors, and sandy dunes. One of these stories, "Die rote Beeke" is especially notable and was later published separately in an illustrated edition. The title translates as "The Red Brook," the stream that runs red with the blood of slaughtered Saxon chieftains. The story deals with a historic event from the time when the Christian Frankish king Charlemagne subdued the heathen Saxons by force. The story sings the praises of resistance against outside forces, a theme that Löns would continue and expand upon in *Der Wehrwolf*. Like the rest of the stories in *My Brown Book*, "The Red Brook" was distinguished by short, terse sentences and a loaded, colorful style that was by now becoming a Löns hallmark and coming to the attention of the serious literary establishment. In the coming years, he would gather enduring fame as the "poet of the heath."

The early history of Saxony and Germanic history in general was to be a continuing influence and interest for Hermann Löns. During this time, he adopted the old German names for the months, which to him were more intimately symbolic of the actual cycles of the year than the Latin names. In July 1912, Löns wrote to his friend Traugott Pilf, that he was "currently reading a lot of Tacitus, Caesar, Prokop, in order to become more closely acquainted with German prehistory. The Greenland and Färoe Sagas are splendid, the discovery of America and so on, and Egill the skald, poet, murderer, miser, and fine fellow." An inscription, also from 1912, in Pilf's copy of *Der letzte Hansbur* reads: "We should always remember that the Christian cross once looked like a swastika." And, starting at least as early as 1902, Löns adopted a personal insignia that had been in use among the peasants of Lower Saxony for generations: the *wolfsangel*. The variation Löns used has the shape of a reversed N with a vertical slash through the middle. Other forms found on old lower Saxon farmhouses often have a swastika-like shape.

In his poetic imagination, Löns visualized an interesting origin of these symbols. He speculated that peasants sat at their hearths watching and contemplating the different shapes that sparks took flying into the air, "drawing strange red runes through the darkness. Crosses were formed by their hasty flight, golden crosses, whose ends were bent into hooks." Elsewhere, he muses about the general significance of the fiery element: "Fire means community, just like running water and waves of grain. Those three know so much, and can tell us so much, but the open fire indeed knows the most, even though it speaks the quietest language. Ancient stories it knows, stories that men have long forgotten, stories from the age when Wode and Frigga were still venerated, when the wolf still pounced on the elk calf in the moor."

Swastika and *wolfsangel* figured prominently in two of Löns's best-known novels: *Der letzte Hansbur* and *Der Wehrwolf*. The cover of many editions of the former shows a bind rune formed out of the S-rune and a vertical *wolfsangel*, while various versions of the swastika were placed in a seemingly arbitrary manner as vignettes at the ends of some chapters. Löns himself never explained their use, but in later editions a note was added which mentions that the author might have been influenced by folkloric interpretations like "morning and evening sun" and "male and female." In *Der Wehrwolf*, the *wolfsangel* in its reverse N shape without the middle slash is used by the peasants as a symbol to leave behind marking their activities: "three axe marks, one this way, one that way, and one diagonally."

Hermann Löns's deep connection to his homeland, its people, and its natural beauty also had other consequences. The writer quickly became a conservationist and early supporter of the movements to establish National Parks and set aside unspoiled wilderness areas in Germany. He wrote numerous articles for periodicals expounding his views on the holistic concept of *"Heimatschutz."* In addition to the conservation of natural habitats, *Heimatschutz* concerns itself with the preservation of folk culture and worthwhile cultural features and monuments. To Löns, the preservation of beauty was always a driving motivation in these matters, as can be seen in his writing. Among other things, this led him to become involved in the project of the Harzer Heimatpark, and to write the text of an introductory brochure about the park. Together with Curt Flöricke, Löns was also instrumental in the creation of the protected area at the Wilseder mountain, the Heideschutzpark. The environmental changes in the Lüneburg Heath certainly brought out his most passionate concern, even leading him to compose some of the first outright ecologist poetry: "Die Letzten" (The Last Ones) and "Der Bohrturm" (The Oil Well), both of which are included in the 1909 collection *Mein blaues Buch* (My Blue Book), which also contains many ballads with references to prehistory, Germanic antiquity, and folk customs with roots in pre-Christian pagan times. "Die rote Rune" (The Red Rune), "Die Varusschlacht" (Varus's Battle), and "Das Osterfeuer" (The Easterfire, translated in this issue of *TYR*), are examples of this.

Of Hermann Löns's poetic collections, *Der kleine Rosengarten* (The Little Rose Garden) would prove to be the most popular. The tone in this book is generally lighter and more accessible than *Mein blaues Buch*. Many of these poems were later made into folk songs. Like most of his works, it is set apart by an extremely visual and immediate style of poetry that conquered the hearts and minds of his readership. Much later, in 1932, a movie was even made (*Grün ist die Heide* [Green is the Heath], named after a Löns poem that Karl Blume arranged into a popular song and which was featured in the film), loosely inspired by the settings and moods of Löns's popular fiction and poetry. It strove to recreate the life of the inhabitants of the Heath.

After several hectic years in Hannover, Löns increasingly yearned to live in the country and, in 1907, he took on a position of chief editor in the quaint, small town of Bückeburg. He was to stay there for four years, which would prove to be some of the most productive as well as unhappy years of his life. He had by and large completed his literary explorations of the natural world and now returned to the human sphere. This resulted in the peasant novels *Der letzte Hansbur* and *Der Wehrwolf* as well as the psychological novel *Das zweite Gesicht* (Second Sight).

Der Wehrwolf tells of the same tribe that fought Charlemagne under Widukind, only this time the tale is set 800 years later during the Thirty Years War, when Saxon farmers banded together to fight off Swedish marauders and other questionable elements that were trying to take advantage of the chaos of the war. In this tense novel, the peasants are torn out of their harmonious shell and faced with the daunting task of having to commit grave violence in order to prevent more bloodshed. This inner conflict is nowhere more apparent than in the novel's title, a word coined by Löns himself. Its meaning is explained by Lehnemann: "A 'werewolf' or 'manwolf' is a man that from time to time transforms into a raging beast. The 'Wehr-wolves', on the other hand, are human and remain human, since they are peasants defending themselves in a time of war, in order to survive." The "wehr" in "Wehrwolf" derives from the verb *wehren* which means "to defend." But "Wehrwolf" also refers to the savagery that the peasants employ in their war against the marauders, savagery that is perhaps justified during wartime but which could also threaten to undermine the ethical basis of their life. Obviously, Löns exploited the multiple meanings inherent in his word creation to the fullest.

Der Wehrwolf was Hermann Löns's greatest success as a novelist. The great German writer Ernst Jünger, who later in World War I led the very same company that Löns joined, described its language as "coarse and akin to a woodcut" and noted a spirit of the "old sagas." While reading it, Jünger was living in Kirchhorst, near the area where the action in the novel takes place. The novel was widely read during both wars and even inspired some groups of the German youth movement to adopt the *wolfsangel* as insignia.

While working on *Der Wehrwolf* in late 1909, Löns suffered a nervous breakdown, caused by stress from overwork and too many deadlines. On November 20th, 1909, he was nevertheless able to sign the *wolfsangel* at the end of the completed manuscript. For the design of the book cover, Löns recommended the kettle hook, the "most sacred object in the house, the symbol of ownership; oaths were made on it, possession was taken with it. . . . [The] protection [of the gods] was requested with it."

The last years of Löns's life were marked by the painful separation from his wife and their sickly son, and by constant disillusionment and restless travels in Austria and Switzerland. Nevertheless, even during this difficult period he was able to produce some notable works, such as the nature sketches in *Mein buntes Buch* (My Colorful Book) and the village chronicle *Die Häuser von Ohlendorf* (The Houses of Ohlendorf), leaving the latter manuscript behind in his drawer when he donned his army uniform.

Perhaps one of the most tragic aspects of Löns's early death was that some of his wide ranging plans for future works would never come to fruition. In his late letters, he was hinting at several novel ideas, one of them being an epic retelling the struggle of the Christian Franks with the heathen Saxons, pitting Charlemagne "the Saxon Slayer" against Widukind. During 1912, Löns was engaged in studies of the historical period he wished to depict. The other project was to be a novel called *The Antichrist*, a study of a new man whose "heart is warm and gentle, his mind cold and hard, and who does not stop at anything to help his blood brothers, his people . . . one who laughs when the enemy's bullet tears through him and who shakes the latter's hand and says: Thank you for saving me from dying a straw death and for facilitating my bodily exit!" As if trying to fulfill this ideal himself, the enthusiastic writer went to great lengths to join the regular army in 1914, and finally succeeded. Because of his reputation as a writer, he could have easily been a war correspondent, but Löns was driven to see actual combat. Perhaps also seeking to escape his inner torments and hardships, Löns seems to have almost welcomed death. After all, for him *Der Wehrwolf* had already been his "war song."

On August 24th, he was accepted by the 73rd Infantry regiment as fit for duty.

Even though Löns had joined the war filled with certainty about its necessity and its liberating, even cleansing possibilities, his war diary often tells a different story. Together with a whole generation, he found himself overwhelmed by the mechanization of war in which individual heroism seemed next to impossible. "I find that the din of battle reminds me of the noise of factories. It doesn't excite me, it only fills me with disgust." Two days before his death, Löns made the following entry: "From my bunk I watch the shooting stars. I think of the corpses, of the spy that was shot. Up in the night sky the same danger and distress. Life is death, coming into existence only leads to ruin."

Hermann Löns's date with death came on September 26th, 1914, on the Western Front, only one month after he had enlisted. A comrade in his battalion tells the story of Löns's last moments:

> I had never seen Hermann Löns so happy as on that morning. At five o'clock we went off, both of us in front, until we came to the stubble field, without any cover. Then suddenly we were under heavy fire from the French. It was like a hailstorm. "Lie down!" I shouted, and there we lay, he right behind me. The fire grew ever more heinous; at the edge of the field, there was an excavated passage, we had to take cover there otherwise they would have shot us to pieces. I called, "Keep crawling!" but in the midst of the hellish noise I heard a faint sound behind me, I turned around—the bullet had hit only too well, below the left shoulder and then into the heart. . . . Yes, and then we took cover in the passage until dark and couldn't move. At half past seven I crawled out and over the field. I had to see him . . . He still lay there like I had last seen him in the morning fog. The face was propped by his hands, deeply peaceful. He looked so calm and handsome. It couldn't have taken more than two seconds after the bullet had hit. I kneeled down by him and arranged his body and folded his hands. It was almost dark. Only here and there were the enemy lines lit up. His large clear eyes quietly gazed into the night. . . . Well, and then I got the shot through the mouth, right there next to him, and those fingers there are gone too. I would do it

again in a second . . . If we could only have kept him. We will not get a comrade like that again . . .

On the morning of January 5th 1933, as farmer Sohier was busy plowing his field near the French city of Reims, the soil suddenly turned up a German soldier's boots and some bones. The local cemetery warden handed the I.D. tag on to the proper authorities. The number on the tag, 309, I.R. 73, 4 Kp., identified the remains as those of Hermann Löns. His mortal remains had been presumed missing since he was hastily buried during that early fighting in 1914. By now, *Der Wehrwolf* had been bought over 400,000 times, and some adherents of the incipient German regime were eager to paint Löns as a precursor to a new era. At least one protected natural area near Würzburg was named after him. But although he was widely praised as a *völkisch* forerunner of the "blood & soil" ethos, Löns's peasant novels are rooted in an organic sense of community and fierce independence that is far removed from the centralized planning and stilted pageantry of the National Socialist state.

After several attempts at a state burial, his bones were finally given a simple military funeral near Fallingbostel in his beloved Lüneburg Heath, the area whose natural features and people he immortalized in his works. The poet, novelist, and conservationist himself would have preferred a quieter exit, as can be seen in this poem from 1912:

Evening Song

And if things should end, then leave me alone,
All by myself on the deserted heath,
Not to hear or see any more,
But to wither away like dead animal bone.

The grey heath moss my deathbed shall be,
The crow sings my funeral litany,
The death bell is tolled by the storm,
I shall be buried by beetle and worm.

And on my grave no stone shall stand,
No grave mound heaped from the sand,
No wreath shall lie in the place I died,
And no tear shall fall at the final rite.

I want to hear and see nothing more,
Only to waste away, like the grass and leaves.
I do not want a stone or mound,
Only to pass away without trace or sound!

Bibliography:

Beckmann, Karl-Heinz. *Die Bucherstausgaben von Hermann Löns*. *Loensia*, vol. 1, Ascheberg-Hebern: Wissenschaftliches Forschungsarchiv Hermann Löns, 1993.
Beckmann, Karl-Heinz, ed. *Die Letzten*. *Loensia*, vol. 2, Ascheberg-Hebern: Wissenschaftliches Forschungsarchiv Hermann Löns, 1994.
Beckmann, Karl-Heinz. *Hermann Löns—Sein Werk*. *Loensia*, vol. 3, Ascheberg-Hebern: Wissenschaftliches Forschungsarchiv Hermann Löns, 1996.
Brandes, Wolfgang. "Hermann Löns und Ernst Jünger: Zwei Schriftsteller erleben den Ersten Weltkrieg" in *Höret* 10, Walsrode: Verband der Hermann-Löns Kreise, 1996.
Castelle, Friedrich. Preface to Hermann Löns, *Grün ist die Heide*. Hannover: Adolf Sponholz, 1932.
Castelle, Friedrich. "Ein Lebensbild," *Löns-Gedenkbuch*. Hannover: Gersbach, 1917.
Deimann, Wilhelm. *Der Künstler und Kämpfer: Eine Lönsbiographie und Briefausgabe*. Hannover: Sponholtz, 1935.
Deimann, Wilhelm. *Hermann Löns: Ein soldatisches Vermächtnis*. Berlin: Ahnenerbe-Stiftung, 1941.
Lehnemann, Widar. Introduction in *Il Wehrwolf, Romanzo*. Seregno: Herrenhaus Edizioni di Andrea Sandri, 1999.
Löns, Hermann. *Von Ost nach West*. Berlin: Schriftenvertriebsanstalt, 1921.
Löns, Hermann. *Die Rote Beeke*. Hannover: Sponholtz, 1912.
Löns, Hermann. *Der letzte Hansbur*. Hannover: Sponholtz, 1928.
Löns, Hermann. *Mein blaues Buch*. Hannover: Sponholtz, 1909/1912.
Löns, Hermann. *Sämtliche Werke in acht Bänden*. Leipzig: Hesse & Becker, 1930.
Löns, Hermann. *Leben ist Sterben, Werden Verderben. Das verschollene Kriegstagebuch*. Frankfurt a. Main/Berlin, 1988.

Löns, Hermann. *Land und Leute. Über Natur- und Heimatschutz.* Dresden: Zeitenwende, 2001.
Thorstein, Ulf. *Hermann Löns und seine völkische Sendung.* Minden: Köhler, 1937.
Tönjes, Max A. "Hermann Löns" *Löns-Gedenkbuch.* Hannover: Gersbach, 1917.

English editions of Hermann Löns's works:

Harm Wulf: A Peasant Chronicle. Translation by Marion Saunders. New York: Minton, Balch & Co., 1931. (English edition of *Der Wehrwolf.*)
The Red Brook. Translation and introduction by Markus Wolff. Sandusky: Europa, 2001. (English edition of *Die Rote Beeke.*)

The Easter Fire

Hermann Löns

Across the heath I walked, the heath so wide and vast,
And solitude whispered sullen words in my ear.

It whispered of times dead and gone, when the aurochs still roamed,
When the eagle circled high in the sky above the marsh,
When the wolf, the fierce one, left death runes in the sand,
When the elk, the strong one, was still felled by the hunter's hand.

Before foreign ways turned good into evil,
And noble Wodan and Frigga were yet highly honored;
When manly courage, and not just worldly wealth, held sway,
When the hero maintained his right with drawn sword;
Not with cowardly words and cheap oaths;
This the deathlike solitude secretly taught me.

Our Gods were once called love and power,
Power to procreate, love to make pleasure bloom.

Our law was terse, our law was this:
Redeem love with love, and hate with hate.
A loyal hand to every man who proved a friend.
A bloody hand to the wight who approached as an enemy.

Different times passed across the heath,
Wodan's sacred woods fell prey to the treacherous axe;
Frigga, the loving lady, was turned into a witch,
Every holy stead dishonored as a loathsome site;

Wodan's noble raven was called now the gallow's bird,
Frigga's roguish little owl insulted as a savage corpse's hen;
And thirteen, that sacred number of secrets,
Was at once a number of misfortune and fear.

Among the oaks stood a single thatched-roof house,
From the mossy gable, horses stretched their necks;

Beneath it, a heart-shaped opening was cut for the owls, in
    keeping with a friendly age-old custom.
On the grey door, the sacred circle was displayed, carved and
    colored as in the days of old.
And the good sun rune right beside,
Just like the forefather's earnest, unyielding ways would have it.

On either side of the black wall of the hearth
Wodan's battle horse boldly reared up;
As if it wished to whinny to me with all its strength:
Even now I carry Wodan still, my friend, and you still
    trust Frigga.

I walked on further across the twilit land,
Behind which the sun sank down, round and red.
On the other side across the brownish marsh,
A glowing red flame rose toward a starless sky.

The white smoke billowed up before the pitch black forest,
Until it slowly disappeared in the evening clouds.
And I stood and stayed, gazing at the fire's glow,
And listened to the girls' cheering and the young boys'
    shrill shouts,
And I laughed and thought:
Despite it all, the joyful ways of our ancestors
Have been kept alive by my people.

Still they honor their God in the beautiful way of their forefathers,
    with glowing embers and white whirling smoke.
Still it remains as it was in ancient times.
Blue of eyes and mind, light of heart and hair.
They have kept their bodies and spirits yet strong,
Still healthy are their limbs, their blood and marrow.

Across the heath I walked, the heath so wide and vast,
And solitude whispered joyful words in my ear.

(Translation: Markus Wolff)

Infernal Proteus

Edelweiss	Allerseelen
Borage	Alio Die
Oak	Apoptose
Belladonna	Wolfskin
Mandrake	Alraune
Cornflower	Hekate
Yew	Waldteufel
Pine	S. Roden
Dandelion	In Gowan Ring

ILLUS. BY LICSI SZATMARI

A MUSICAL HERBAL. HARDBOUND BOOK WITH 4 CDS.
40 MUSICAL IMPRESSIONS OF FLORA
TENTATIVE RELEASE DATE: SUMMER SOLSTICE 2002

WWW.THEAJNAOFFENSIVE.COM
THE AJNA OFFENSIVE. POB 3003, ASHLAND, OR 97520 AJNA9@HOTMAIL.COM

The Saxon Songwriter:
An Interview with Fire & Ice's Ian Read

Joshua Buckley

Despite its rather marginal status, there now exists an entire subculture of "Euro-heathen" music. Pagan, Euro-centric, and often espousing a Nietzschean contempt for the masses, it is a genre that thrives in the post-Internet world. Once the province of a few geographically scattered initiates, unusual ideas are now available at the click of a button. Small music labels that would have been incapable of achieving global distribution fifteen years ago, can now sell their wares from Minneapolis to Moscow. New records or magazines appear and word spreads through the electronic grapevine in minutes. There is a significant chance that the journal you now hold in your hands was discovered over the Internet.

Once the lone province of the World Serpent label, Euro-heathen music is now being produced by a slew of independent entrepreneurs, many of them specializing in lavish packaging and special commemorative releases. Over the past ten years, CD compilations have appeared in honor of Julius Evola, the Roman legionary cult of Mithras, the Fraternitas Saturni, the *völkisch* artists Hermann Hendrich, Joseph Thorak, and the filmmaker Leni Riefenstahl. Predictably, much of the music one finds on these releases is heavily derivative of the original World Serpent stable—"apocalyptic folk" luminaries Current 93, Sol Invictus, and Death In June. Although one could quibble over whether or not these groups were the sole creators of the genre (Robert N. Taylor's outfit Changes was playing music that could be described as "Euro-heathen" way back in the 1960s), they have undoubtedly been the most influential.

Yet while many of these second generation Euro-heathen artists' interest in Germanic mythology, runes, and aesthetics is merely an imitation of their heroes, Ian Read's enduring fascination with the myth, magic, and mysteries of Northern Europe runs deep. A former collaborator with both Death In June and Current 93 (he appeared with Freya Aswynn on 1986's *Swastikas For Noddy* LP), Read soon ventured out to form Sol Invictus with Death in June alumnus Tony Wakeford. Combining traditional songs with newer material based on pagan themes, Sol's first few albums were grim explorations of European folklore, Spenglerian cultural pessimism, and Wakeford's own romantic misadventures. Read participated on the first three Sol releases: *Against the Modern World*, *Lex Talionis*, and *Trees in Winter*. In many ways, the latter set the stage for his solo work as Fire + Ice. The song "Michael," by far that album's brightest (darkest?) moment, is the ideal vehicle for Read's hauntingly evocative vocals. Shrouded in medieval ambiance, it conjures up an atmosphere that seems to hover outside time.

But as Sol Invictus experimented with new musical directions and increasingly personal lyrics, Fire + Ice has delved further and further into the Northern European tradition. In 1996 the group released *Rûna*, which constituted Read's "master work of lore" for the Rune-Gild. Featuring songs like "Of Midgard," "Holy Mead," and "Egil," it might be the most seamless musical expression of Odinist principles ever produced. *Birdking* (2000) soon followed, and is without a doubt Fire + Ice's most musically accomplished recording to date. Exhibiting a variety of styles, but rooted in Read's folk-traditional sensibilities, *Birdking* is at once a celebration of England's heroic tradition, and a lament for a world in which that tradition has been almost completely submerged:

> *Where have they gone, those proudest of dreamers?*
> *Their woods are all silenced and the bright halls stand free.*
> *Children sturdy and flaxen,*
> *Gewissæ bold and free,*
> *As the land they were Saxon.*
> *Tall grass is waving over their barrows;*
> *Their pastures unmown, and the meadows ghostly.*
> *Shadows are whispering, songs from the twilight;*
> *Their swords all shattered, and the spears just trees.*

In between musical endeavors, Read publishes the Germanic heathen magazine *Rûna*. With articles on topics ranging from herb-lore to the European warrior tradition, *Rûna* features some of the most polished, intellectually engaging writing currently being produced in the Ásatrú-Odinist milieu (and, we might add, it has played no mean part in inspiring our own efforts with *TYR*). Read was also kind enough to find time to respond to the following interview, which was conducted via the Internet in mid-2001.

How did you get involved with the occult? Was Crowley much of a catalyst?

As a child I saw *Mary Poppins* and thought to myself, "I would love to be a wizard one day." In 1974 I joined Sir Richard Bolles's Regiment of Foote in what was then called the King's Army but is now the English Civil War Society. They stipulated that all members had to learn the Elder Futhark so that we could communicate with each other secretly. We also worshiped Óðinn, although they were pretty basic and inaccurate rituals—but done in the right spirit. Being who I am, I looked deeper into rune-lore and a whole new world opened up in front of me (and, to some extent, behind me).

Crowley played no part in this initially. Only later did I look into his work, finding his magick of only vague interest, but his life and contribution to our age of great importance.

What about the Illuminates of Thanateros and Chaos Magic? Can you give us a little background as to how that became so important?

At that time I was unable to find any Odinists who had any interest in things more esoteric, beyond a vague desire to dabble with the runes (by which I mean the rune shapes and basic meanings). To some extent this is still true. So I needed another way of learning the basic techniques of sorcery. A magazine called *The Lamp of Thoth*, which had seen one issue, was revived and contained an advertisement for the IOT. I wrote to Pete Carroll announcing my intention of completing the syllabus for neophytes called *Liber MMM*, and then moved to Germany to live. A year later I visited England and saw Pete to hand over my diary. He told me that over a hundred people had written to him, but I was the only one to do the work. Later, when I started running groups, I realized that this was unusual because only one in a thousand typically do any work. Therefore, I became a member of the IOT because they were a working magical order that allowed their members to pursue any path they wished, which suited me because I wanted to work with others in the Germanic way.

Pete later reconstituted the IOT into the Pact of the IOT and asked me to run a group. As I already had some people, I asked them to move into the Pact and they agreed. After Pete retired, I took the reins until retiring a few years ago.

IAN READ IN SINTRA, PORTUGAL.
(PHOTO: ANNABEL LEE)

Was the Germanic Tradition always something you felt an affinity for, or was that more an outgrowth of these other explorations?

As you will see from the former question, the horse always came before the cart.

Before becoming involved in the Rune-Gild, were you part of the Odinic Rite or any other organized heathen group? I was under the impression that you'd collaborated with Freya Aswynn at some point.

My profession certificate into the Odinic Rite bears the number 17, so I was a fairly early member. Freya Aswynn ran a group in London that became a Hall in the Rune-Gild. For various reasons the core of this group all left with me to go our own way, and Freya stopped her association with the Gild. Around 1980, I wrote to Edred to order some material and sign up for his Institute of Runic Studies Ásatrú. After the split with Freya, he asked me to run the Gild in the UK and I agreed.

For those of our readers who might not be familiar with it, can you give us an overview as to the Gild's goals and history?

We can be fairly certain that there was an actual Gild in ancient times for several reasons, particularly the uniformity of change from the Elder to the Younger Futhark all across Northern Europe. We continue their work, which is to help people initiate themselves into the mystery system of our Folk. In order to do this, we run groups, research, and publish specialized works, as well as trying to find better methods for training people. This may ultimately be the only hope left for our Folk to become what they should be. It certainly will be of paramount importance.

Have you done any lecture tours lately? Is that something you plan to pursue in the future?

There have been no lecture tours for some time, although I do present something each year at the Rune-Gild International Moot, which has hitherto been held in the USA. Whether there will be further tours is in the lap of the gods.

What about your work with Fire + Ice? Do you think your music has been influential in promoting the Germanic Tradition to people who might not otherwise be exposed to this sort of thing? Has the music made people more receptive to your other projects?

Music is theoretically a great way to spread ideas, but in reality most people are completely undiscerning. Their preference for one band over another is just a matter of peer pressure or marketing. It would be nice to think that some are turned towards their natural way by my music, but I have no idea either way. To record albums or perform live in the expectation of this would certainly be a soul-destroying venture. Many don't seem to realize that the Ian Read who is Fire + Ice is the same one who works on *Rûna*. The old gnomic verse about taking a horse to water is as true now as it ever was.

Tell us about your background as a musician. Were you involved with other groups before Death in June and Current 93?

I used to sing for my own amusement and pleasure. Mainly in smoky halls at feasts or by bonfires at rituals. My singing at a gathering in London prompted Douglas P. to ask me to work with him in Death In June. Later Tony Wakeford, whom I knew through the religion and Viking re-enactment, asked me to form a band with him and that became Sol Invictus.

Have you always been interested in folk/traditional music? Were you around in the early seventies, when Steeleye Span and the Watersons were at their peak?

Even if I didn't like folk music, I would support and nurture it because it forms part of our sacred way. My favorite folk band is called Strawhead, but typically most people have never heard of them. I am not one to know facts in the way most people do. Consequently, although I listen to folk, I probably couldn't name more than a few performers just as, despite an abiding love of fighting skills, I don't know the names of more than a handful of boxers. My contempt for modern politics is such, for example, that I ignore the news and have read no newspapers for twenty years. It takes me on average two to three weeks before I find out the name of the new American President. And even then I would forget it if I could.

As an Ásatrúar, do you feel that this kind of music—and folk culture in general—has a deeper resonance for those of common European descent?

Of course. DNA will out, as it were.

Besides Germanic culture and heathenism, what other influences have contributed to your songwriting approach? Are there any specific authors or poets who have struck a chord over the years?

In the past I have spoken of my regard for Leslie Charteris's books about the Saint, and how he first introduced me to the idea of elitism. I read voraciously at all times. When traveling anywhere I carry a book because time is too precious to waste, and people should respect themselves enough to do this. Because of how many authors I have read and my focus on the point behind something rather than the specifics, I would be hard put to name any specific influences.

Do you feel particularly rooted in England, or are your allegiances more pan-Germanic? Has English history always been something you've looked to for inspiration?

My first allegiance is to a group of people all around the world (and not just in Europe), who I see as my real family. However, my love for England is well known. In reality, this is somewhat metaphysical as I well know that most Englishmen, like most people everywhere, aren't worth the cost of the ink on their birth certificates. It would be possible to have a pan-Germanic allegiance in theory, but in reality nothing is likely to ever bring these peoples together. Although it could happen if we weren't ruled by people who couldn't organize a piss up in a brewery.

As to your other question, is anyone not inspired by English history? We ruled the largest empire ever at one time for years and a history of the world that failed to mention England would be a booklet. One of our legacies is that more miles of road in the world demand one drive on the left than on the right, to the amazement of most who discover this.

How do you feel about the environmental movement? As a heathen, it's almost inevitable that you should feel a stronger connection to the natural world than your average Christian or urban secular humanist.

The environment would be helped by a drastic reduction in the human population.

On the *Birdking* album, you worked with a number of other musicians. Are there other collaborative projects planned for the future?

I have written no lyrics for more than a year now, so it is unsure if there will be any further music projects, let alone collaborative ones. We shall have to see.

Any other interesting (or prurient) details you'd like to mention? I've been told that you're a fanatical pipe smoker.

Anyone can smoke a cigarette. Pipe smoking is a more elite pursuit.

"Son of man, can these bones come to life?"
Review Essay: The Prisoner
A&E Video, VHS (12 tape set) and DVD (10 disc set)

Collin Cleary

1. Introduction

A&E's new release of *The Prisoner* bills this cult series as "television's first masterpiece." In truth, it is probably television's *only* masterpiece. *The Prisoner* is a triumph of acting, of photography, of design, of writing, of thought, and, less so, of music. More generally, of course, it is a triumph of audacity and imagination. Like a great work of art, it is timeless. Very little about *The Prisoner* is dated—even though it went into production more than thirty-five years ago. For the most part, the series looks as fresh as it did when first aired. And its message seems more relevant than ever.

Of course, what that message is is the central problem with *The Prisoner*. Fans love to emphasize the "open-endedness" of the series: everyone has their own *Prisoner*. But when we interpret a text (even a cinematic text) our goal should not be to arrive at a purely subjective, idiosyncratic understanding. Interpretations of *The Prisoner* are often wildly speculative and subjective—and often completely ignore the public statements that Patrick McGoohan (the series' creator) has made about it. Surely what we want is an interpretation which causes the text to open itself and reveal the meaning its creator put into it, if any. Serious-minded people don't treat texts as Rorschach blots. One begins the task of interpretation by carefully studying every detail of a text. One also studies the background of its author, and what its author has said about it.

Some interpretations work better than others. Some can explain the text as a whole, others only in part. The former is obviously preferable to the latter. For example, in the final episode of the series we at last discover the identity of the mysterious "Number One": he is the Prisoner himself. Can one interpret this in an atheistic, or "secular humanist" vein? Does the final episode teach us that Number One is God, but that God is really us? One could indeed interpret things that way—but only if one ignored the fact that McGoohan was (and is) a devout Catholic.

What I have attempted to do in this essay is to present an overall interpretation of *The Prisoner*, situating it within the tradition of 20th-century "anti-modernism." As an artist, McGoohan must be understood as belonging to the school of Pound, Yeats, Eliot, Joyce, Huxley, Lawrence, Kafka, and (to some extent) Orwell. It does not matter if McGoohan never read these authors; they would have recognized him as one of their own. It is my belief that such an interpretation is the most fruitful way to understand *The Prisoner*. But first, a little background information for the uninitiated . . .

At the time *The Prisoner* went into production, Patrick McGoohan was the highest-paid actor in British television. He was the star of *Danger Man* (shown in the USA as *Secret Agent*), in which he played a spy by the name of John Drake. But Drake was no James Bond knock-off. *Danger Man* premiered on September 11, 1960, almost two years before the release of the first Bond film, *Dr. No*. Incidentally, McGoohan was the first actor offered the part of Bond, but he turned it down. He felt that Bond's womanizing and killing were immoral. McGoohan made sure that Drake was never depicted in any amorous encounters with women, and that he never killed his enemies. But *Danger Man* was plenty violent. Fisticuffs were a major feature of the series (and also of *The Prisoner*). McGoohan was physically imposing in the role of Drake. He was tall, tough, determined, and deadly serious. McGoohan's odd, sing-songy voice (a product of being born in New York, and later raised in Ireland and Sheffield) was also crisp and powerful. He radiated enormous intensity and intelligence.

In 1966, McGoohan's contract for *Danger Man* ran out, and he decided to quit (even though the first two episodes of the new season—the only ones in color—were already in the can; they were later edited together as a seldom-seen feature called *Koroshi*). Lew Grade, the head of ITC, the firm that produced *Danger Man*, wanted very much to keep McGoohan on. When the star put to him the idea for *The Prisoner*, Grade immediately agreed to it. He had no idea what he was getting into.

The germ of *The Prisoner* was provided by George Markstein, script editor for *Danger Man*. Markstein had worked in British intelligence, and knew of the existence of a secret "rest home" called Inverlair Lodge, where old spies could live out their days without accidentally revealing their secrets when Alzheimer's set in. Somehow, Markstein, thought, this could be developed into an exciting series. This was basically the extent of Markstein's contribution to the series' format. *The Prisoner* was Patrick McGoohan's creation.

Here is the premise: a secret agent—whose name is never revealed in the entire series—angrily resigns his job and prepares to leave the UK on holiday. Unbeknownst to him, however, he is followed home by a man in a hearse, who knocks him unconscious using some kind of gas. When the secret agent awakens, he is in his own bedroom, but when he looks out the window, he finds that he is in a strange, cosmopolitan little town. He discovers that he is being held prisoner in this place, which is known only as "the Village." No one is referred to by name, only by number. The inhabitants wear colorful costumes, and spend a good deal of time parading and having fun, yet they are all curiously soulless. Underneath the Village is a complex of control rooms, from which a vast bureaucracy watches the Villagers' every move using sophisticated, electronic surveillance equipment.

The highest ranking authority in the Village is called "Number Two," and the office is constantly changing hands. Number One remains in the background. The location of the Village is never revealed—nor is it ever revealed "which side" runs the place. The Villagers are cared for from cradle to grave. Some seem to work, whereas others do nothing. The masters of the Village have at their disposal the most advanced technology imaginable. They can invade one's dreams, brainwash one into believing anything, switch minds from one body to another, and bring a dead man back to life. Escape is impossible. The perimeter of the Village is guarded by a mysterious creature that looks like a balloon and is called only "Rover." It lives at the bottom of the sea and can suffocate escapees, or merely stun them. Is it alive? Is it a machine? "That would be telling," says Number Two in the first episode (see the Appendix to this essay).

The men behind the Village want to know why our hero—who they call "Number Six"—resigned his job. He refuses to tell them, or to conform. They try to break his will in various ways. They drug him. They hypnotize him. They trick him into thinking he has escaped, only to reveal that he has never left. They raise him to the exalted position of Number Two, then literally beat him and deposit him back in his bed. They turn his old friends against him. They make him doubt his own identity. They perform a mock lobotomy on him. They trick him into believing he is a gunfighter in the Old West. They regress him back to his childhood, then "bring him up" all over again. They even allow him to actually escape, and then lure him back. Finally, with no more tricks left up their sleeves, the Villagers admit defeat and beg the Prisoner to lead them.

Oh, and aside from McGoohan, the only other regular is a dwarf.

This was—and is—quite simply, the most unusual thing ever made for television. Only David Lynch's *Twin Peaks* rivals it for sheer strangeness and originality. McGoohan arranged with Lew Grade to produce *The Prisoner* under the auspices of his company, Everyman Films, which he had set up in 1960. This gave him total control over every aspect of the production. ITC budgeted the series at £75,000 an episode, a huge amount in those days. Extensive location shooting was done at Portmeirion in Wales: an artificial village constructed over several decades by architect Clough Williams-Ellis. McGoohan planned out in detail the world of the Village. He contributed to the design of sets, props, costumes. The Village even had its own typestyle, which was also used for the opening and closing titles of the series.

The production included many *Danger Man* alumni. Particularly striking were the sets designed by art director Jack Shampan. They included a large, circular chamber which could be redressed to serve as several settings: No. 2's office, the sinister "Monitor Station," and others. These sets are ultra-modern and ultra-simple. They look as impressive today as they did in 1966. The music was one aspect of the production that McGoohan was less happy with. The original theme, contributed by Wilfrid Josephs, was deemed too avant-garde (though it still appears in the background in several episodes). Ron Grainer, the composer of *Dr. Who*, contributed the theme that was finally used. Albert Elms contributed background music which works brilliantly in the series, but sounds thin and repetitive when heard apart from the visuals (a series of CD's was released a decade ago or so).

The Prisoner is visually opulent and looks even more expensive than it was. The photography is crisp and provocative. Scenes call to mind Bergman, Fellini, and Hitchcock. The color is vivid. The editing is like that of a Bond film: fast-paced, each shot lingering only briefly, presenting only essentials. Indeed, every aspect of this series is polished and top-drawer. *The Prisoner* exhibits that same consummate, seemingly effortless professionalism that one finds in other British series like *The Avengers* and *The Saint*. Some of the best direction in the series came from McGoohan himself (he helmed five episodes, wrote three, and probably re-wrote all the rest).

The story goes that as production on the series went on, McGoohan began asserting more and more control over every aspect. He was a perfectionist, who delegated little. George Markstein quit, and subsequently attacked McGoohan in interviews for his "megalomania." But one can hardly argue with the results, for *The Prisoner* is a brilliant creation. Nevertheless, after a year in production, only thirteen episodes were completed and the stories were getting stranger and stranger. ITC decided to pull out, and told McGoohan to wrap things up with a final four episodes. When the last episode was broadcast, viewer reaction in Britain was so hostile that it is said McGoohan and his family felt they had to leave the country.

Originally McGoohan had only wanted to do seven episodes. Indeed, roughly ten of the episodes are fairly routine adventures, lacking much intellectual substance. The seven "primary episodes" are probably these:

"Arrival"

"Free for All"

"Many Happy Returns"

"Dance of the Dead"

"Checkmate"

"Once Upon A Time"

"Fall Out"

Like many television series, the episodes were not broadcast in the order in which they were filmed.

2. Interpreting *The Prisoner*

So, to quote No. 6 in "Arrival," what's it all about? *The Prisoner*, like many texts, has different levels. The exoteric *Prisoner* is an adventure series with lots of action, gee-whiz technology, and a dashing, intransigent hero. Even at this level, the series makes the viewer ask certain questions. Chief among these are:

1) What is the hero's name?

2) Who runs the Village?

3) Where is the Village?

4) Why did our hero resign?

5) Who is No. 1?

The first three questions are insignificant and will lead one astray. Anyone who thinks that these are important questions probably also thinks that the central question of *The Trial* is what the K in Joseph K. stands for.

The Prisoner is not John Drake. He is Patrick McGoohan, if Patrick McGoohan had been a secret agent. The Prisoner's birthday is March 19—the same as McGoohan's (this is mentioned *twice* in the series). In the final episode, he credits each of his stars—Leo McKern, Alexis Kanner, and Angelo Muscat—at the bottom of the screen, but bills himself as "Prisoner." Furthermore, the Prisoner shares other biographical details in common with McGoohan: he boxed in school and had a talent for mathematics ("Once Upon A Time").

But there is much else to the character that is not McGoohan. In fact, at times it seems No. 6 is *everything*. He can build a boat and navigate it, he can fly a helicopter, he can fence and shoot, he can speak several languages, he can water ski, he is a gymnast, he can ride a horse, he knows the sciences, he knows literature, etc. In truth, he is Everyman. He is all of us. (In Biblical terms, six is the number of man, for man was made on the sixth day.) What is he trying to say about all of us? I will address that in section four, below.

Of the above questions, only those concerning the Prisoner's resignation and the identity of No. 1 have any real significance.

It is made clear that the Prisoner resigned his job for matters of principle. ("The Chimes of Big Ben" has the Prisoner revealing that his resignation was "a matter of conscience"; in "Once Upon a Time" he says that he resigned for "peace of mind.") Part of McGoohan's message must surely be to convey that principle.

PATRICK MCGOOHAN AS THE PRISONER, STANDING BEFORE THE PENNY-FARTHING BICYCLE, THE SYMBOL OF "PROGRESS." (INCORPORATED TELEVISION COMPANY, LTD.)

In "Living in Harmony" the story of *The Prisoner* is played out in an Old West setting. The Prisoner resigns his job as sheriff, then is kidnapped and taken to another town where he is forced to become the new sheriff. He refuses to wear guns, however. Naturally, this calls to mind John Drake. So, did our hero resign his job because he could no longer stomach killing? This cannot be the case, for in the same episode he does put on his guns briefly in order to kill the homicidal "Kid." This shows that he is willing to kill, if he thinks it justified (he also kills with abandon in "Fall Out"). No, our hero did not resign because he thought it never right to kill; he resigned because he could no longer, in good conscience, kill for, and in the name of, his society. His act of resignation is a rejection of his society, and its regime (in "Once Upon A Time," when Leo McKern says "You resigned," McGoohan replies "I rejected").

One of the mysteries of *The Prisoner* is why the Villagers cannot see that this is all there is to it. But this is what one should expect: modern people find nonconformists to be thoroughly inexplicable creatures. How could anyone reject this wonderful world in which, to quote Ned Beatty in *Network*, "all necessities [are] provided; all anxieties, tranquilized; all boredom, amused." There *must*, they think, be another reason why he resigned!

Nevertheless, the Prisoner clearly has some vestigial loyalty to Her Majesty. In "Arrival" he insists that his loyalties don't change. In "A, B and C" he condemns B for working on the "wrong side." Almost every episode opens with No. 6 demanding of his captors "Whose side are you on?!" This is one of the two ways in which No. 6 is portrayed as being *misguided*. He is portrayed as a hero, and as an extremely virtuous individual, but he has failings nonetheless. In "The Chimes of Big Ben," No. 2 tries to set him straight on the issue of "whose side" they are on:

> *No. 2:* It doesn't matter which side runs the Village. Both sides are becoming identical. What in fact has been created [here] is an international community. When the sides facing each other suddenly realize that they are looking into a mirror, they will see that this is the pattern for the future.
>
> *No. 6:* The whole earth, as the Village is?
>
> *No. 2:* That is my hope.

"A, B and C" informs us that the Prisoner believes in "absolute truth." But he needs to realize that neither side (democro-capitalist or communist) embodies his ideals, and that neither side is salvageable. He tries to escape the Village to get back to "my world" (as he puts it in "Dance of the Dead"), thinking that it's "different" ("The Chimes of Big Ben"). But, in essence, they are the same. The Village is the essence of modernity laid bare. But No. 6 does not see it.

What he needs to see is that, as Heidegger claimed, the two sides are *metaphysically identical*. Both capitalism and communism are based on the supremacy of materialism, and on the rejection of man's higher nature. In "Arrival," No. 2 says, "We have everything here." But there is one thing conspicuously absent from the Village: a church. The Villagers are devoid of any spiritual dimension. They are happy, healthy, well-fed meat machines, with an army of psychologists at the ready to drug away their every doubt and blue mood.

The Village is a microcosm of modern society. (In fact, No. 6 calls it that in "Many Happy Returns.") First of all, it has no cultural or ethnic identity. ("Are you English?" the Prisoner asks No. 2 in "Dance of the Dead"; she does not answer.) Physically, the place is a mix of international architectural styles. ("It's very international," says a girl in the first episode.)

The authorities know everything about you—but no one cares, because it makes everyone feel "safe." Don't worry about car accidents, you aren't allowed to drive yourself anywhere (too dangerous). And don't forget to be in by curfew at 10:00 pm.

The Villagers pride themselves on their democracy, even though the whole process is rigged ("Free for All"). "Of the people, by the people, for the people," a sign proclaims. They think themselves free, even though their "freedoms" are things like the freedom to walk on the grass ("Arrival"). "You do what you want. . . . As long as it's what the majority wants," No. 2 tells us in "Dance of the Dead." Run for office by all means, but don't try and change anything if you win. ("You want to spoil things!" No. 6 is told in "Dance of the Dead.") Don't make the mistake, however, of thinking that the Villagers have no ideals. "Progress! Progress! Progress!" they scream in "Free for All." (McGoohan has said that the "penny-farthing bicycle," seen in the series as the Village's emblem, represents the ideal of progress.)

A cheery radio announcer makes sure that a light, informal tone is maintained at all times. To "simplify" things, everyone goes by number, rather than by name. Those who claim not to be numbers are laughed at ("Free for All")—and resented. The Villagers wear silly costumes—colorful capes, straw hats, striped sailor shirts. Dignity is, of course, a terribly old-fashioned idea, and, again, likely to stir resentment.

Everything is automated. The houses have radios and TVs that can't be shut off because, after all, why would anyone want to shut them off? Leaving for the Village store to buy processed food? Don't forget your credit card and identity card.

Got troubles? Go to the Citizen's Advice Bureau ("A Change of Mind"). Need work? Queue up at the Labour Exchange, where you will be given an aptitude test ("Arrival"). Suffering existential angst, or anti-social tendencies? "There are treatments for people like you!" ("Dance of the Dead"). Do you wonder "Who am I? Why am I here?" ("Schizoid Man"). Sign up for Group Therapy at the hospital. It "counteracts obsessional guilt complexes producing neurosis" ("Arrival"). And remember: "Questions are a burden to others; answers a prison for oneself" ("Arrival," and "Dance of the Dead"). In fact, "if you get [an] attack of egotism, don't wait. Go . . . to the hospital immediately" (No. 2 to the Rook in "Checkmate"). The Village treats men as soulless pieces of meat to be manipulated by science ("We mustn't damage the tissue," No. 2 cautions in "Free for All"). Pavlovian methods of conditioning are employed (methods first perfected—as No. 6 points out *twice* in "Checkmate"—on dogs).

When your mind is completely gone and you can no longer shop for yourself, you are retired to the Old People's Home, where you are encouraged to enjoy a second childhood.

3. *The Prisoner* as Anti-Modern Manifesto

In short, *The Prisoner* attacks modernity on the following grounds:

1) Modernity rests upon a materialistic metaphysics (all is matter), and champions materialism as a way of life (the focus on material comfort and satisfaction).

2) Modernity is spiritually empty (again, no church in the Village); it must deny or destroy what is higher in man.

3) Modernity destroys culture, tradition, and ethnic and national identity in the name of "progress" (called "globalization" today).

It is significant that we do not know where the Village is, for modern people are really "nowhere." As Nietzsche's "Madman" said, "Where are we headed? Are we not endlessly plunging—backwards, sideways, forwards, in all directions? Is there an up and a down anymore? Do we not wander as if through an endless nothingness? Do we not feel the breath of empty space? Hasn't it grown colder?" *(The Gay Science)*.

4) Modernity promises only trivial freedoms (e.g., the freedom to shop) while oppressing freedom of thought, freedom of religion, freedom of association.

5) Modernity involves the belief that nature (including human nature) is infinitely malleable; open to the endless manipulation and "improvement" of science. (In a 1977 interview with Canadian journalist Warner Troyer, McGoohan said, "I think we're progressing too fast. I think that we should pull back and consolidate the things that we've discovered.")

6) Modernity systematically suppresses ideals that rise above material concerns: ideals like honor, and dignity, and loyalty (the Village is filled with traitors).

7) Modernity preaches a contradictory ethos of collectivism and "looking out for No. 1."

8) Modernity banishes the sacred, and profanes all through an oppressive levity (masking cynicism).

9) Modernity places physical security and comfort above the freedom to be self-determining, to be let alone, and to take risks.

10) Modernity fills the emptiness in people's lives with *noise* (the TV and radio you can't turn off). Silence might start people thinking, which could make them unhappy.

In addition to the hostility to religion, the Village also seems to be hostile to marriage, sex, and procreation. It is not clear whether there are any married couples in the Village. Sex is probably forbidden. No children are seen until "The Girl Who Was Death," and those children are depicted as living in a kind of barracks. There is a touch of Plato's *Republic* in *The Prisoner*.

The Villagers are Nietzsche's "Last Men." In *Thus Spoke Zarathustra*, Nietzsche has his prophet proclaim:

Alas the time of the most despicable man is coming, he that is no longer able to despise himself. Behold, I show you the *last man.*

"What is love? What is creation? What is longing? What is a star?" thus asks the last man, and he blinks. . . .

"We have invented happiness," say the last men, and they blink. They have left the regions where it was hard to live, for one needs warmth. One still loves one's neighbor and rubs against him, for one needs warmth. . . .

One still works, for work is a form of entertainment. But one is careful lest the entertainment be too harrowing. One no longer becomes poor or rich: both require too much exertion. Who still wants to rule? Who obey? Both require too much exertion.

No shepherd and one herd! Everybody wants the same, everybody is the same: whoever feels different goes voluntarily into a madhouse.

"Formerly, all the world was mad," say the most refined, and they blink.

One is clever and knows everything that has ever happened: so there is no end of derision. One still quarrels, but one is soon reconciled—else it might spoil the digestion.

One has one's little pleasure for the day and one's little pleasure for the night: but one has a regard for health.

Zarathustra's audience is not horrified by this vision of man at the end of history. When he finishes speaking, he is interrupted "by the clamor and delight of the crowd. 'Give us this last man, O Zarathustra,' they shouted. 'Turn us into these last men!'"[1]

To borrow from Eliot, the Villagers are "hollow men." Or to borrow from C. S. Lewis they are "men without chests." They have no soul and no spirit. They are concerned only with comfort, safety, and satisfaction. They have no ideals, and consider nothing to be worth fighting for. In "Free for All," No. 6 tells the Villagers "I am not a number, I am a person." They laugh at him. Then, when he continues to address them, briefly expounding views which No. 2 characterizes as "individualistic," their faces are blank, uncomprehending. Later in the same episode, No. 6 addresses the Town Council: "Look at them. Brainwashed imbeciles. Can you laugh? Can you cry? Can you think? . . . In your heads must still be a brain. In your hearts must still be the desire to be a human being again." McGoohan's portrayal of modern man might have seemed an exaggeration in 1967, but not today. Contemporary man—thirty-five years on—does not even rise to the level of a Babbitt or a Willy Loman. He is Dilbert. He is Homer Simpson.

All right, we have seen what McGoohan is against, but what is he for? I will offer the following guesses—with apologies to Mr. McGoohan if I happen to misread him.

First and foremost, based on what we know of McGoohan himself, as well as clues internal to the series, I think we can say that he is a theist who believes that man is a creature of God, with an immortal soul, subject to divine law. (Obviously, McGoohan is against materialism in metaphysics and in culture—in "Fall Out" the President states that No. 6 has triumphed "despite materialistic efforts.") He believes that when men no longer turn their souls toward God, they stop being men. He believes that societies have souls too, and that the soul of a society is its spirituality. Again, the most significant fact about the Village is the total lack of any religious or spiritual institutions.

McGoohan also seems to place importance on cultural and ethnic identity. We cannot simply be "citizens of the world." We are English, or Irish, or French, or Estonian, or Japanese. He is against the modern homogenization of the globe (physically embodied in the "internationalism" of the Village) which is rapidly making every place look pretty much like every other.

McGoohan seems also to be for self-reliance and minimal government. He opposes government intrusion into our lives, as well as "cradle to grave" socialism. This is the "libertarian" aspect to *The Prisoner.* McGoohan also would seem to favor somehow limiting what science and technology can meddle with. One supposes that he is a conservationist, who in particular regards human life as sacred and inviolable.

If McGoohan wants us to identify him with his character, then, based on what we learn about No. 6 in the course of seventeen episodes, we can conclude that McGoohan believes in honor, in dignity, in fighting for ideals, in discipline, in self-denial, and in absolute truth. He believes in self-sacrifice and service to others (note how he buys the candy for the old lady in "It's Your Funeral"), not out of duty to "the majority" or to the state, but out of benevolence (note the use of the Beatles' tune "All You Need Is

Love" in "Fall Out"). Quite simply, he is a Christian. Not a mushy "Jesus Freak" sort of Christian, but a tough, muscular C. S. Lewis sort of Christian.

Finally, McGoohan believes in a life that makes room for silence, for thought, for contemplation. He believes in taking life seriously. Is McGoohan a liberal or a conservative? His emphasis on freedom of thought and freedom of expression, and his belief in minimal government seem to make him a classical liberal. But his spirituality, his emphasis on place and culture, his skepticism about "rule by the majority," and his old-fashioned ideals make him look like a conservative (in "A Change of Mind" one Villager accuses him of being "reactionary"). In truth, it is really unimportant where we locate McGoohan on the political spectrum. If we asked him, we can be fairly sure he would eschew all our ready-made labels.

So what does McGoohan propose doing about our plight? Here the answer is simple: he advocates a revolution. In "Dance of The Dead," "Bo Peep" states: "It is the duty of all of us to care for each other, and to see that the rules are obeyed. Without their discipline we should exist in a state of anarchy." No. 6 replies "Here! Here!" In the same episode, he finds a transistor radio on a dead body. When he switches it on, we hear the following: "I have a message for you. . . . The appointment cannot be fulfilled. Other things must be done tonight. If our torment is to end, if liberty is to be restored, we must grasp the nettle even though it makes our hands bleed. Only through pain can tomorrow be assured."

Furthermore, in interviews McGoohan has actually said that he had hoped the protest movement of the 1960s would lead to a revolution. He referred to the action of the final episode of *The Prisoner* as "revolution time." But who are to be the revolutionaries, other than McGoohan? He probably wonders the same thing. In the world of the Last Man, what can one do except cultivate one's own garden? McGoohan has made his impassioned, seventeen-hour speech on behalf of revolution. Now, we hear, he spends his time writing poetry that he may never publish, and acts only occasionally.

4. Patrick McGoohan's Anti-Individualism

Earlier, I said that although No. 6 is clearly portrayed as a hero, he is not perfect. He is misguided in two significant ways. The first I have already discussed: he does not seem to realize that in essential terms his own society and the Village are identical. There is no *physical* escape from them. The second way he is misguided is that he is an individualist. This statement will surely shock many fans of the series.

Several episodes (such as "Free for All") explicitly refer to his individualism. No. 6 continually asserts his individuality. In "Arrival" he tells us that he will not be "pushed, filed, stamped, indexed, briefed, debriefed, or numbered! My life is my own." Fourteen episodes open with his proclaiming "I am not a number! I am a free man!" In "Dance of the Dead," No. 6's costume for Carnival is his own tuxedo, specially delivered for the occasion. "What does that mean?" asks his maid. "That I'm still . . . myself," he answers, dramatically. In the same episode, No. 2 tells him, "If you insist on living a dream you may be taken for mad." "I like my dream," he says. "Then you are mad," she replies.

But the attitude of the series toward individualism is, contrary to appearances, ambivalent. Up to the final episode, one could perhaps be excused for thinking that *The Prisoner* is an unqualifiedly positive portrayal of an individualist hero. But in "Fall Out," when No. 6 addresses the assembly, he begins his first sentence with "I" and the assemblymen drown him out chanting "I! I! I! I! I! I!" The President states that No. 6 has "gloriously vindicated the right of the individual to be individual"—but his unctuous manner suggests that these are merely empty platitudes. When the Prisoner enters No. 1's chamber, he sees himself on a TV screen saying "I will not be pushed, filed, stamped," et cetera, as quoted earlier. Then we hear his voice speeded up, hysterically chanting "I! I! I! I! I! I!" And we see the image that closes almost every episode: iron bars slamming shut over McGoohan's face, this time over and over again. Are we being told here that the ego is a prison?

No. 1 wears a mask like that of the assemblymen: half black, half white. When No. 6 rips it off, underneath is a *monkey mask*. The monkey face gibbers "I! I! I!" along with the soundtrack. When No. 6 rips that mask off we see that No. 1 is McGoohan. He laughs maniacally and disappears through a hatch in the ceiling. All along, the Prisoner has wanted to discover the identity of No. 1, and now he finds out that he has been No. 1 all along. Understanding the meaning of this is the key to understanding the entire series. In the 1977 Troyer interview, the following exchange occurs:

> *McGoohan:* [The audience] thought they'd been cheated. Because it wasn't, you know, a "James Bond" No. 1 guy.
>
> *Troyer:* It was themselves.
>
> *McGoohan:* Yes, well, we'll get into that later, I think. (Knowing laughter from Troyer) Come back to that one, that's a very important one.

That the Prisoner is No. 1 is hinted at throughout the entire series. McGoohan has said that he did not know in advance that things would work out the way they did. However, given his description of how "Fall Out" essentially "wrote itself," we have some grounds for supposing that McGoohan knew the identity of No. 1 all along, subconsciously. The number on the Prisoner's house in London is "1" (the actual address is 1 Buckingham Place). The dwarf butler always bows to him. The large, red phone No. 2 uses to speak with No. 1 in "A, B and C" (and seen again in other episodes) is shaped suspiciously like the number 6. Finally, at times it seems that the Village exists just in order to break No. 6; as if he is at the center of the whole thing.

No. 1 represents man's ego in the bad sense. In an interview that pre-dates *The Prisoner*, McGoohan was quoted as saying, "But what is the greatest evil? If you're going to epitomize evil, what is it? Is it the [atomic] bomb? The greatest evil that one has to fight constantly, every minute of the day until one dies, is the worst part of oneself." In the Troyer interview, the following exchange occurs:

> *Audience member:* No. 1 is the evil side of man's nature?
>
> *McGoohan:* The greatest enemy that we have. No. 1 was depicted as an evil, governing force in this Village. So, who is this No. 1? We just see the No. 2's, the sidekicks. Now this overriding, evil force is at its most powerful

within ourselves and we have constantly to fight it, I think, and that is why I made No. 1 an image of No. 6. His other half, his alter ego.

No. 1 is the embodiment of what I call "Will." See my essay "Knowing the Gods," elsewhere in this issue of *TYR*, for a fuller discussion of this concept. Will is that dark impulse inside all of us which desires to close itself to what is other (including the transcendent, divine other) and to raise itself above all else. No. 1's monkey mask represents this primal, brutish aspect in all of us. (Significantly, the first task No. 2 sets for himself in "Once Upon a Time" is to find the Prisoner's "missing link.") When Warner Troyer asked McGoohan about the monkey mask, McGoohan said:

> Yeah, well, we're supposed to come from these things, you know. It's the same with the penny-farthing bicycle symbol thing. Progress. I don't think we've [truly] progressed much. But the monkey thing was, according to various theories extant today, that we all come from the original ape, so I just used that as a symbol, you know. The bestial thing and then the other bestial face behind it which was laughing, jeering and jabbering like a monkey.

Will manifests itself in more or less sophisticated forms. In "Knowing the Gods" I write that

> In its higher forms, Will manifests itself . . . in (1) the transformation of the given world according to human designs, and (2) the yearning to penetrate and master the world through the instrument of the human mind—through exploration, analysis, dissection, categorization, observation, and theory. In its most refined form, Will becomes what might be called a "Titanic Humanism": a seeking to make man the measure, to exalt man as the be-all and end-all of existence, to bend all things to human desires.

Modernity is the Age of Will, the age of this Titanic Humanism. It is this which *The Prisoner* so brilliantly lays bare and parodies as "the Village."

Why is Will, as "No. 1," the head of the Village? Or: why is Will the true master of modernity? I write, further, in the same essay:

> It is no accident that all the grand schemes and contrivances of modernity (the technological mastery of nature, the global marketplace, socialism, universal health care, etc.) have as their end exactly what [Will in its infantile form] seeks: the satisfaction of desires, and the maintenance of comfort and security.

East and West, communism and capitalism are metaphysically identical because both are run by Will; both are run by an exclusive concern with the values of the Last Man: comfort, security, and satisfaction of (physical) desire. McGoohan has said, "I think progress is the biggest enemy on earth, apart from oneself, and that goes with oneself, a two-handed pair with oneself and progress."

But why does McGoohan confront us with this hard truth by having our hero discover No. 1 in himself? Isn't he the exception? Isn't he the man who has rejected Will and the world it has created? No. 6 has indeed rejected modernity, but he himself exhibits Will in one of its more subtle forms. He does not turn from modernity to anything higher than it, or higher than himself. He turns inward and wills himself as, in effect, an atomic individual. As I have said, the most significant thing about the Village is that it has no church. But perhaps the most significant thing about No. 6 is that he doesn't ask about this. Again, we see him fly a helicopter, build two escape rafts, mix it up with thugs (countless times), box, fence, shoot, play chess, demonstrate his psychic powers, display his knowledge of Shakespeare, do gymnastics, and much else, but we never see him pray. No. 6 is, in effect, a secular humanist who believes that he can stand alone, needing no one, not even God. (In this respect, of course, he is *not* McGoohan, but "Everyman"—or, perhaps, McGoohan in those moments of doubt that all of us have.)

The series presents us with numerous examples of No. 6's hubris. In "Free for All" he shouts "I'm afraid of nothing!" In the same episode, after he is elected the new No. 2, he gets on the Village loudspeaker and cries "I am in command! Obey me and be free!" A psychologist in "Checkmate" expresses the desire to learn

No. 6's "breaking point." "You might make that your life's ambition," he says to her. In "Once Upon a Time," the silent butler obeys No. 6. "He thinks you're the boss!" Leo McKern exclaims. "I am," McGoohan replies. When he sits down on the throne in "Fall Out" he seems quite pleased with himself. No. 6 is a strong man, but he is not introspective. He is a man of action. He lacks self-criticism.

"Many Happy Returns" is an episode that many take to be a straightforward thriller: No. 6 wakes up to find the Village deserted, sails away on a raft, but, predictably, winds up back in the Village by the end of the hour. There is more here than meets the eye, however. Consider what No. 6's behavior in this episode reveals. Finally left alone—a lone wolf, a true individual, an atom in the void at last—he does not look inside himself and take stock. Instead, he promptly goes in search of the world that, in the beginning of the series, he rejected and sought to escape from. *Then*, once back there, he goes in search of the Village! No. 6 is the proverbial rebel without a cause. He is constantly *reacting* against the world. He needs others, he needs the world, in order to reject them, for he can do nothing else. He is sheer negativity—sheer rejection and cancellation of otherness. His constant activity—pacing around his apartment, walking around the village, working out—as well as his acts of violence, are expressions of this.

Now, this life of rebellion and negativity is not a truly human life. It is a kind of Purgatory. It is no accident that there are continual references in the series to No. 6's being *dead*. An undertaker in a top hat, driving an old hearse, is the man who kidnaps him and takes him to the Village. (This lends itself to the irresistible, but wrong-headed speculation that in the beginning McGoohan really dies, and that the Village is Hell, or Purgatory!) In "Dance of the Dead" No. 6 asks No. 2 why he doesn't have a costume for Carnival. "Perhaps because you don't exist," she says. In the same episode, after the Villagers try and kill the Prisoner, No. 2 tells him, "They don't know you're already dead." She tells him that the body he found on the beach will be "amended" to look like him, so that to the outside world No. 6 will be dead. "A small confirmation of a known fact," she says. There are suggestions that the Village is populated by the living dead. Once again, in "Dance of The Dead" (note the title itself!) No. 6 finds the key to the morgue hanging on a hook outside the door. What can this mean, except that the door is locked not to keep people from getting in, but to keep them from getting out? In "Once Upon A Time," No. 2 cries "I'll kill you!" "I'll die," whispers our hero. "You're dead," No. 2 replies. Then there is No. 6's dalliance with "The Girl Who Was Death." And finally, there is the fact that No. 6 almost always appears in black.

The best literary parallel I can think of to No. 6 is the character of Hazel Motes in Flannery O'Connor's *Wise Blood*. Motes is also an atomic individualist who despises society and modern people. Raised in a religious home, he rejects the God that society believes in and founds an atheist "religion": "the Church Without Christ." He buys a disastrous used car (an old Essex), but no matter how many times it breaks down and reveals its frailty, he insists that it's a fine car and will get him wherever he needs to go. "Nobody with a good car needs to be justified," he says. The car represents man's mortal coil, and the Catholic O'Connor is telling us that man cannot stand totally alone; he must turn his soul to something higher. McGoohan is telling us something similar. He is saying, "Fine. Reject society. Reject materialism and the modern world. But if you reject them in the name of your own ego you are buying into that primal, Biblical sin that is at root of modernity itself: the placing of ego and its interests, narrowly conceived, above all else." Without preaching to us, without ever mentioning religion, McGoohan invites us to rise above our No. 1, and turn our souls toward the Real Boss. One need not be a Christian, let alone a Catholic, to understand and sympathize with this message. Indeed, the idea that it is our ego that holds us back from enlightenment or true liberation is a perennial idea. (One of the ironies of the series is that *resignation* is a trait No. 6 is singularly lacking!)

Christian themes are to be found throughout *The Prisoner*. In several episodes we hear a march-version of the hymn "How Great Thou Art." This occurs first in "The General," in which No. 6 destroys a super-computer with the question "Why?" (One is reminded of the old story—probably apocryphal—of President Eisenhower asking Univac if there is a God; "Now there is," the computer is said to have shot back.) In "Once Upon A Time" we hear this theme played on a church organ. In "Fall Out" we are repeatedly bombarded with the old spiritual "Dry Bones." "Them bones, them bones, them dry bones! Now hear the Word of the Lord!"

"Dry Bones" is an old Negro spiritual inspired by the Book of Ezekiel, which is one of the prophetic books of the Old Testament. In Chapter 37, the prophet relates his "vision of the dry bones":

> The hand of the Lord came upon me, and he led me out in the spirit of the Lord and set me in the center of the plain, which was now filled with bones. . . . How dry they were! He asked me: Son of man, can these bones come to life? "Lord God," I answered, "you alone know that." Then he said to me: Prophesy over these bones, and say to them: Dry bones, hear the word of the Lord! Thus says the Lord God to these bones: See! I will bring spirit into you, that you may come to life.

In the Bible, the bones represent the Israelites who have lost hope and faith. In "Fall Out," the dry bones are modern men, who have lost their souls. When the young rebel No. 48 sings "Dry Bones," the members of the assembly (who bear such titles as "Welfare," "Identification," "Therapy," and "Education") go mad: "Them bones, them bones gonna walk around!" They are the dry bones of our world. "The bones is yours, dad!" says No. 48. "They came from you, my daddy."

No. 48 and No. 2 are fastened to metal poles, in a manner that suggests crucifixion. When No. 6 speaks some soothing words to No. 48, the young man says "I'm born all over," suggesting the Christian theme of the second birth. No. 6 also undergoes a Christlike temptation at the hands of the President, who offers him "ultimate power." Then there is the small matter of Leo McKern's "resurrection."

Does No. 6 get the message in the end? Not at all. In the Troyer interview, McGoohan states that his character is "essentially the same" at the end of the series. The final shot of *The Prisoner* is the same as the very first shot: there is a thunderclap, and McGoohan comes speeding toward us in his handbuilt Lotus. He is caught in the circle: an eternal cycle of rebellion, leading nowhere, and certainly not upwards. He is still a prisoner—not of the Village or of society, but of his own ego.

Appendix: What about Rover?

The one thing everyone seems to remember about *The Prisoner* is Rover. Mention the series to someone over 40 and they are likely to say "is that the one where he's chased around by the big, white balloon?" Indeed, Rover is one of the most curious, frightening, and unforgettable aspects of the series. Despite his claim (in "Free for All") that he is afraid of nothing, No. 6 is *clearly* frightened by Rover. Here are some of the odd facts about this strange beast/machine:

1) It is first seen in "Arrival" as a tiny white ball, bobbing on a jet of water at the top of a fountain. It then expands into the size of a weather balloon (which is apparently what the prop man used).

2) It roars.

3) It can stun (several episodes) or kill ("Schizoid Man"). How it does this is not clear, but it involves covering the victim's face.

4) It can understand language ("Schizoid Man").

5) It can divide into small balls in order to move unconscious victims ("Chimes of Big Ben" and "Free for All").

6) It has some connection with the "goop" inside the lava lamps seen throughout the Village.

7) It seems to "live" on the ocean floor, where it is apparently part of a larger body of "goop." When "activated" (by a flick of a switch on No. 2's desk) it separates itself from this goop and rises to the surface.

8) It can move at high speeds.

Now, some of the above suggests that Rover is a living thing—but other things suggest that it is a machine (in "Schizoid Man" No. 2 commands, "Deactivate Rover immediately!"). That it has a mind of its own was implied in the original "Arrival" script, in which Rover is a sort of windowless hovercraft with a police light on top. "Who drives it?" No. 6 was to have said. "*Drives* it?" No. 2 was to have replied, incredulous.

What does Rover mean, if anything? Here there is a danger, for making Rover a balloon was a last-minute inspiration. The original Rover machine—just described—sank in the ocean dur-

FILMING ROVER ON THE SET OF "THE PRISONER."
(INCORPORATED TELEVISION COMPANY, LTD.)

ing filming. But over time, the new form of Rover must have acquired some significance in the minds of McGoohan and the other writers, and so we can ask about its "meaning" nonetheless.

My suggestion is that Rover is supposed to be a hybrid animal-machine. It represents the mysterious, amorphous, chthonic, primal, uncanny element in nature, which modern man tries to factor out, to deny, or to control. It is what Sartre calls "the viscous." But man cannot fully tame the chthonic. Rover's imprisonment in the lava lamp represents man's attempt to do this.[2] Rover's killing "Curtis" in "Schizoid Man" represents man's failure at it. Even the masters of the Village are afraid of their "machine." No. 6's fear-reaction when confronted by Rover has a special quality: he is reacting to the terrible, the uncanny. When not doing man's bidding, Rover sinks to the bottom of the ocean, where it reunites with a much vaster "viscous," the parameters of which we do not see—suggesting our inability to *comprehend* the chthonic. It is our confrontation with the uncanny that is often our first confrontation with something that transcends human knowledge and power. Thoughtful people reflect on this, and eventually turn their gaze upwards.

Sources:

Alain Carrazé and Hélène Oswald, *The Prisoner*, translated by Christine Donougher (London: Virgin Publishing, 1995). The stills illustrating the present article appear in this work.

Six of One: The Prisoner Appreciation Society

In the UK:

Six of One
P.O. Box 66
Ipswich, Suffolk
IP2 9TZ, United Kingdom

In the USA:

Six of One
c/o Bruce Clark
871 Clover Drive
North Wales, PA 19454

website: www.netreach.net/~sixofone/

Notes:

1. Friedrich Nietzsche, *Thus Spoke Zarathustra*, trans. Walter Kaufmann (New York: Viking Press, 1986), pp. 17–18.
2. After writing the above, I purchased a lava lamp to celebrate the completion of this essay. The lamp came with a card from the manufacturer, which included the following statement: "The Lava brand is a philosophy. It stems from the primordial ooze that once ruled our world [and] has now been captured in perpetual motion in our Lava brand wax. . . . The Lava motion lamp is pre-historic and post-modern."

REVIEWS: BOOKS & MUSIC

Book Reviews

The Secret King: Karl Maria Wiligut, Himmler's Lord of the Runes. **Translated with Introduction by Stephen E. Flowers, Ph.D. Edited by Michael Moynihan. Vermont and Texas: Dominion and Rûna-Raven, 2001. Softbound, 164 pages, with appendices, chronology, and bibliography. No index. Illustrated with photographs and drawings. ISBN 1-885972-21-0.**

Much has been written in the last four decades concerning "Nazi occultism," most of it nonsense. Incredibly, no one has published a collection of original texts from the Third Reich dealing with these matters—until now. Michael Moynihan and Stephen E. Flowers have put together a collection of fascinating texts written by and about Karl Maria Wiligut (1866–1946). Called "Himmler's Rasputin" by some, Wiligut came from a prominent Viennese family, and served honorably in the Great War. He delved deeply into the Germanic esoteric tradition, forming ties to Lanz von Liebenfel's *Ordo Novi Templi*, and joining a quasi-Masonic lodge, in which he was called "Lobesam" ("Praiseworthy"). In 1924, while sipping coffee at a Viennese café, Wiligut was forcibly hauled off to a mental hospital, where doctors noted his queer ideas, including his belief that he was descended from "Wodan."

After his release, Wiligut formed ties to the NSDAP, and began contributing articles to a *völkisch* journal called *Hagal*. Wiligut met *Reichsführer*-SS Heinrich Himmler in 1933, and subsequently joined the SS under the name "Weisthor." This was done with Himmler's knowledge and consent, in order to conceal Wiligut's embarrassing past. Within two months, "Weisthor" was made head of the Department for Pre- and Early History within the *Rasse- und Siedlungshauptamt* (Main Office for Race and Settlement). Himmler appears to have seen Wiligut as a guru, and in 1935 made him part of his personal staff. Wiligut sent Himmler a regular stream of memos, purporting to unveil the secrets of Germanic esotericism. Wiligut was also highly influential in helping Himmler develop various aspects of SS ceremony and insignia. It was Wiligut who designed the famous SS ring. He developed a "name-giving rite" to be performed over the newborn children of SS men. Wiligut also contributed greatly to the conceptualization and renovation of the Wewelsburg castle, which Himmler intended as a worldwide headquarters for the "knights" of the SS.

Was Wiligut mad? This question is not relevant when examining the *ideas* of an author or a guru. Sanity is a relevant issue only when we must evaluate a *report* (such as eyewitness testimony in a trial) or a *promise*, in which case the reliability of the reporter or promiser must be assessed. Character and mental state thus become issues. But when a philosophy is expressed, we must evaluate the ideas themselves, not the philosopher. Thus, when we read Wiligut we must ask such questions as: are these ideas coherent (i.e., non-contradictory)? Do they seem to have some basis, or are they merely arbitrary assertions? And (most important of all in the case of ideas such as these): are they truly tied to tradition? To dismiss a thinker's ideas by labeling him "mad" is simply *argumentum ad hominem*. Besides, if the standard of sanity is being well-adjusted to the modern world, then sanity is hardly a desirable condition.

It is my belief that the documents translated in *The Secret King* present a coherent philosophy. Further, they give evidence of profound reflection upon the Germanic tradition. Nevertheless, Wiligut's philosophy is deeply flawed. It is not a *fully* coherent and integrated system of ideas. Further, much of Wiligut's claims in his memos to Himmler do indeed seem like fanciful, arbitrary assertions, without any ties to authentic tradition. And some elements of Wiligut's thought actually *clash* with authentic Germanic lore.

In the remainder of the essay, I will attempt to systematize Wiligut's ideas; to present his thought *as far as possible* as a coherent philosophical system. This is no easy task, as any reader of *The Secret King* will realize. I will structure my account around the very first text presented in the book, "The Nine Commandments of Gôt." It is my belief that these nine statements provide the framework of Wiligut's philosophy, in terms of which most of the other ideas can be understood. First, I will simply present this text in its entirety:

The Nine Commandment of Gôt

1. Gôt is Al-Unity!

2. Gôt is "Spirit and Matter," the dyad. He brings duality, and is nevertheless, unity and purity . . .

3. Gôt is a triad: Spirit, Energy and Matter. Gôt-Spirit, Gôt-Ur, Gôt-Being, or Sun-Light and Waker [*Wekr*], the dyad.

4. Gôt is eternal—as Time, Space, Energy and Matter in his circulating current.

5. Gôt is cause and effect. Therefore, out of Gôt flows right, might, duty and happiness.

6. Gôt is eternally generating. The Matter, Energy and Light of Gôt are that which carry this along.

7. Gôt—beyond the concepts of good and evil—is that which carries the seven epochs of human history.

8. Rulership in the circulation of cause-and-effect carries along the highness—the secret tribunal [*heimliche Acht*].

9. Gôt is beginning without end—the Al. He is completion in Nothingness, and, nevertheless, Al in the three-times-three realization of all things. He closes the circle at N-yule, at Nothingness, out of the conscious into the unconscious, so that this may again become conscious.

These "commandments" were apparently formulated by Wiligut in 1908, and communicated to Himmler in a memo, signed and dated by Himmler "Sommer 1935." To the right of each commandment, Wiligut had drawn complex runic formulas. It is beyond the scope of this essay to attempt an analysis of these formulas.

The fact that there are *nine* commandments is, of course, significant, given the importance of the number nine in Germanic lore. In another text, Wiligut states: "In 'nine' the whole universal form is completed in a circle" (p. 74).

I will now comment on each of the Nine Commandments in turn.

1. Gôt is Al-Unity!

What is suggested here is the perennial mystic theology of *hen kai pan* (one and all). This Greek phrase achieved notoriety in the German-speaking world with the publication of Jacobi's *Über die Lehre des Spinoza in Briefen an der Herrn Moses Mendelssohn* (1785), in which Jacobi quotes Lessing as saying, "The orthodox concepts of the deity are no longer for me. *Hen kai pan*, I know no other." This quotation subsequently exercised a tremendous influence on German intellectuals, among them the young Hölderlin, Schelling, and Hegel, who adopted *hen kai pan* as their personal motto during their school days. *Hen kai pan* implies that God is beyond duality, hence "one," but not one in the since of being "simple," a bare unit. Instead, God is the unity of All. Ordinary experience displays to us not only duality, but a whole chaos of multiplicity. In truth, however, all the world is really one.

Wiligut later tells us (p. 54) that Gôt is Gibor-Othil-Tyr. This should remind us of another trinity of gods: Óðinn-Vili-Vé. Gibor, Wiligut says, is the sun rune (Sowilho) plus the ice rune (Isa) or "Sun-I." The significance of the sun and its relationship to I or ego will shortly become apparent. Othil is the "eternal manifestation of spiritual-material being." Tyr is the "victory of light over Matter [*Stoff*] in the action of Light (eternal cycle)." All this shall become clearer as we proceed.

It follows from the identification of Gôt with Gibor-Othil-Tyr that Gôt means (in Wiligut's words) "Hallowed All-Light of spiritual-material being in an eternal cycle in the circle of the creation in the All." On a cursory reading, this may seem like gibberish, but a careful reading will disclose that this is, in fact, a summary statement of the meaning of Gôt as Gibor-Othil-Tyr. As we shall see, Gôt for Wiligut is the eternal, dynamic realization of Spirit *(Geist)* in matter as part of the cyclical process which defines the whole of creation.

2. Gôt is "Spirit and Matter," the dyad. He brings duality, and is nevertheless, unity and purity . . .

But Gôt, as we have seen, is Unity, so how can he bring duality? Wiligut is no Manichean: he does not oppose a positive unity-principle, to a negative "dual" principle (or principle of multiplicity or indefiniteness). Instead, duality comes from the One. This is a doctrine of emanation, such as we find in Plotinus. Wiligut gives the fullest statement of his cosmogony in a poem entitled "Number," published in *Hagal* in 1934:

N'ul-ni—the unconscious I, ul = Spirit,
Ni = the non-spiritual essence.

In the beginning was a unity of two aspects: Spirit and non-Spiritual essence (proto-Matter). These are not two, but a unity which we must *understand* as two. Ni is the non-spiritual essence of Ul (spirit), *because it is the essence of spirit to become non-spiritual.* It is the end or aim of spirit to become *embodied*, and body is the opposite of spirit. If it is the end of the caterpillar to become a butterfly, then we may speak of the butterfly as the essence or being of the caterpillar. If it is the end of Spirit to become embodied, then the essence or being of Spirit is non-Spirit. Thus, Spirit (Ul) *is* Non-Spirit (Ni). They are not two but one. Furthermore, Non-Spirit only is what it is by participating in Spirit, thus the being (essence, end) of Non-Spirit is Spirit.

It stands beyond time and space,
as "Nothing," which once had been . . .

Again, we are dealing with Gôt as beyond duality. It is, but is no-thing. ("which once had been" implies eternal cycles of creation and destruction). Wiligut represents this initial stage as a circle with a dot in the middle, which is also the astrological and alchemical symbol for the sun:

It is "original-being, Ru" in Spirit and Matter,
which no force penetrated,
Subdued by the Will of Gôt-har
as only a point in the Al—in being—
There rest the commandments of Gôt—his I—
as a point in the circle . . .

The being of Gôt, which is Being-Nothing, One-All, Spirit-Non-Spirit, a unity of *polar tension*, is contracted into a point, and in this point is the incipient universe, from which will unfold the complete essence of Gôt (note "there rest the commandments of Gôt"—we are exploring precisely those commandments; Gôt's law or commandments are akin to the Platonic *eide*, the system of forms that is the Gôt-being).

> ... *it became the "world-egg,"*
> *the Will toward solidification* ...

Wiligut posits that at the root of all being is a striving toward definiteness, concreteness, embodiment. What explains the overflow of existence from the dimensionless point that is the Gôt-being? It is simply the nature of Al to strive for full expression—concrete realization. This is a perennial theme in German mysticism, present in such authors as Schwenkfeld, Böhme, and Oetinger. It also carried over into philosophers like Schelling and Hegel. In Oetinger's terms, it is called *Geistleiblichkeit*, "spiritual corporeality." Oetinger sees God as coming to progressively greater concreteness or embodiment *through* the world. God is not some sort of wispy wraith. His true nature is to be the most concrete, specific, fully-realized individual being of all, while at the same time not existing merely as one being among others, but as *Being-as-such* (Aristotle's Unmoved Mover fits this description, although Aristotle does not see his God as developing or evolving through time and through the world).

And from this "egg" duality comes into being:

> *Duality: Spirit in Matter formed by Energy*
> *in order to complete,*
> *It becomes the Eye of Gôt in a ring—*
> *"Drehauge"—to turn itself,*
> *And from Two arises*
> *the "Three" we certainly all know*
> *And which we call the Tri-unity as Gotos' form* ...

Another piece by Wiligut, "The Creative Spiral of the 'World-Egg'!" (*Hagal* 11, 1934) seems to expand upon these ideas. It opens, "Primal law: 'Above as below, below as above!" This is, of course, the famous maxim of Hermes Trismegistus, usually stated as "As above, so below." Wiligut reminds us in this text that "from *two* comes *one (ans)*." The unity of Gôt in His original state as unity of Spirit-Non-Spirit gives rise to the "World Egg": Spirit in its "striving" to be concrete (non-Spirit) and Non-Spirit in its "striving" to be in-formed (Spirit) exist in tension, and this tension, as an equilibrium of primordial forces, produces an excrescence on the "physical plane" (or, more properly speaking, this tension *creates* the physical plane). The "two" that is the Ur-Gôt gives birth to one (the "egg") which then must become two ("hatch" or "divide") and from this two comes other ones, and other twos until there is a proliferation of ultimate dualities within each of the primary "regions" of Being: definite/indefinite, one/multiple, positive/negative, straight/round, passive/active, rest/motion, systole/diastole, light/darkness, cold/hot, dry/moist, love/hate, sky/earth, male/female, good/evil, etc. Each pair is a pair of "ones" which only are what they in relation to another, and whose relation-connection "gives birth to" other *ones*, which then exist in further dual relationships.

Wiligut invokes the principle of "As above, so below" because of the replication of this pattern (the primordial creation process) on all levels of existence, high and low, above and below. Wiligut states (p. 80): "I recognize that in the 'spiral unity' the 'dyad' (duality) becomes a 'unity' in humanity through 'man and woman.' Man 'giving' and therefore 'Above,' woman taking him, therefore receiving and so 'Below.' And by means of this 'unification to unity' (World-Egg) in generation . . ." And (p. 81): "We are moreover Nordic, i.e., polarized from above. We—as Gôt-seed—impregnate 'Erda' [Earth] according to the Will of Gôt . . ."

3. Gôt is a triad: Spirit, Energy and Matter. Gôt-Spirit, Gôt-Ur, Gôt-Being, or Sun-Light and Waker [*Wekr*], the dyad.

"Energy" *(Kraft)* is now mentioned in addition to Spirit and Matter. Matter becomes inspirited (and spirit enmattered) through Energy. Energy is the Greek *energeia* which means function, act, or actualization. It is *matter doing*. All things are what they do, or how they function, act, or react to other things. This is Aristotle's conception of form: form = function. It is through having a characteristic function or doing (Energy, *energeia*) that Matter has a form or nature. Without *energeia*, matter is dead, dis-spirited. This is why Aristotle says that a severed hand is, in a real sense, no longer a hand at all (*Metaphysics* 1036b30).

"Sun-light" is to the Waker as Spirit is to Matter. The Waker *rises* to greet the sunlight as Matter must "rise" and do, act, *work* in order to have an essence or nature, in order to be inspirited (recall Wiligut's use of the sun symbol—circle with central dot—

to represent the Ur-Gôt, Gôt-in-Himself). This is the primordial dyad: Spirit and Matter yearning for each other, joined through a middle which is Energy. The working of the thing (its Energy) is Spirit coming to be in it. All the acts of a being are directed toward the realization of Spirit (form), whether the actor is aware of it or not (this is, again, similar to Aristotle: all beings are, in all their acts or functions, "striving" to be like God). Through Energy, Spirit realizes itself in Matter, which is *its* ultimate aim.

Wiligut offers the following helpful diagram:

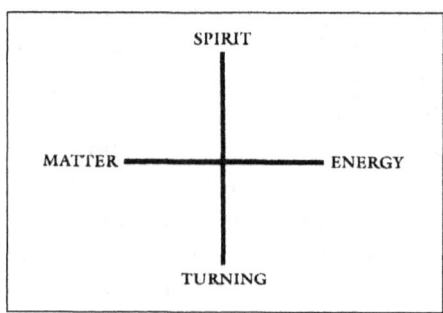

My interpretation of "Energy" is confirmed by other Wiligut texts. In "The Cosmos in the Conception of Our Ancestors" (*Hagal* 12, 1935), Wiligut disciple Gabriele Dechend offers several diagrams made up of combinations of triangles. She writes of one: "The upper triangle represents Spirit becoming conscious in Matter, and this actually by means of the current of Energy" (p. 119).

In the same text, Dechend writes: "When the Spirit, in eternal circulation, approaches the Energy-Matter Plane, which is set for release as a potential 'plan'—then the 'Will to Become' is awakened in this plane" (pp. 120–121). Incidentally, there is a "lower triangle" opposed to the "upper triangle" mentioned in the first quote. It contains a figure that is a combination of the Elhaz and Thurisaz runes:

This was apparently a very significant figure for Wiligut. In his Introduction, Flowers mentions that Wiligut disciple Richard Anders stated to an interviewer, "This is all I learned from Wiligut," and drew the following:

ᛉ + ᚦ = ᛤ

Of this figure (placed within the "lower triangle"), Dechend remarks, "The lower triangle becomes the image of the 'crucified,' or in the Wotan-cult that of 'Odhinn hanging on the world tree'" (p. 119). This is as good a place as any to mention one of the most puzzling and disappointing aspects of Wiligut: his belief in an *Irmin-Kristianity*. Wiligut believed that this, and not "Wotanism," was the original religion of the Germanic people. Not only does this seem absurd (for all sorts of reasons, the least of them historical) but it is very difficult for us today to understand why Wiligut, and some other German *völkisch* thinkers, were so keen to save Christianity. (One is reminded, for example, of Chamberlain and Rosenberg's silly attempts to prove that Christ was really an Aryan.) Not able to imagine the complete dissolution of the faith in which they were raised, these men wanted to create (or re-discover) a virile, German Christianity—a Christianity with a K! This is reflected in Wiligut's bind rune depicting "the crucified." The Elhaz rune is commonly referred to as the "life rune": it is positive; life-affirming in Nietzsche's sense (and opposed, therefore, to a life-denying "semitic" Christianity). The Thurisaz rune is (among other things) a symbol of virile male power. Its "thorn" is a clear phallic image (note how it can be inserted into Berkano [ᛒ], the rune of the "Great Mother"). Wiligut's Christ (Krist?) is a virile, life-affirming God. Christ as Dionysus.

4. Gôt is eternal—as Time, Space, Energy and Matter in his circulating current.

Matter awakens to Spirit as Energy *(energeia)* and produces Space and Time. Time can only be perceived if there is motion (e.g., the position of the sun overhead, the hands on the clock, the sand in the hour glass, etc.). Motion is *energeia*, and *energeia* exists only if there is Matter. (Aristotle wrote: "Time is just this: a measure of motion with respect to the before and the after," *Physics* 219b2.) Space only exists relative to material objects. Thus, Matter and Energy actualize Time and Space. "Gôt is eternal ... in his circulating current" means: the cycle of matter "awakening" to Spirit through Energy is eternal. Spirit and Matter are *both* actual only in their relationship to each other (see above). Gôt is not Spirit, nor is He Matter or Energy. He is the dynamic interrelation of these three. Gôt *just is* the awakening.

5. Gôt is cause and effect. Therefore, out of Gôt flows right, might, duty and happiness.

Might, right, duty, and happiness map onto the three Indo-European "functions" identified by Georges Dumézil:

1st Function (priestly/juridical): Right

2nd Function (war/protection): Might (power), & Duty (control/discipline)

3rd Function (trade/sustenance): Happiness (pleasure)

This fourfold division appears to be Wiligut's description of the primary aspects of human life, and is reminiscent of the Hindu division of Virtue, Success, Pleasure, and Liberation. But why do right, might, duty, and happiness flow from Gôt *because* Gôt is "cause and effect"? We can answer this by looking, again, toward Hinduism: right, might, duty, and happiness flow from cause and effect, which means from *action (karma)*. If this seems far removed from Wiligut's Germanic milieu, think again. In "Whispering of Gotos—Rune Knowledge" (*Hagal* 11, 1934) Wiligut writes:

As Spirit submerges to the depths
it is set free from the restraint of both!
"Life aware of Spirit," mindful of Energy and Matter—
Is awakened to its Garma—in a circular pattern . . .
And becomes a child of Gotos, a Spirit in the son of man . . .
And thus Gotos himself is able to recognize—
Gôt-Spirit on the throne . . .

In a footnote, Flowers reminds us that "Garma" was Guido von List's version of *karma*.

Incidentally, the above quote confirms my earlier claim that Gôt for Wiligut just is the "awakening" of Matter to Spirit in Energy, and takes it a step further. Wiligut is here speaking specifically of the awakening of Gôt/Gotos in *man*, and he is saying that through man Gôt comes to consciousness of himself ("Gotos himself is able to recognize—Gôt-Spirit on the throne . . ."). Recall Wiligut's description of "N'ul-ni" as "the unconscious I," where ul=Spirit, and Ni=the non-spiritual essence. Gôt-in-Himself, as Al-Unity, before his unfolding in/as the world is "the unconscious I" (a union of Spirit and non-Spirit, Proto-Matter). Through His unfolding, Gôt becomes Conscious I.

This is a perennial mystical teaching. Eckhart states that "The eye with which God sees me is the same eye by which I see Him, my eye and His eye are one and the same. In righteousness I am weighed in God and He in me. If God did not exist nor would I; if I did not exist nor would He." In the Kabbalah, *Ein-Sof*, the Infinite, is held to be identical to *Ayin*, Nothing. The telos of *Ein-Sof/Ayin* is to develop into *Ani*, "I" (*Ayin le-Ani*, "Nothing changes into I"). This is also found in the "mainstream" philosophical tradition in the person of Hegel. The three primary divisions of Hegel's philosophy (*Logik*, *Natur*, *Geist*) are modeled on the Trinity: Father, Son, Holy Spirit. The reference to "Spirit in the son of man" and to "Gôt-Spirit on the throne" certainly call Hegel to mind. (Meister Eckhart, incidentally, also identified "the Son" with Nature.)

6. Gôt is eternally generating. The Matter, Energy and Light of Gôt are that which carry this along.

The awakening (Gôt) of Spirit in Matter through Energy is not a once-only process, or one which takes place outside space and time. It is perpetual, it is everywhere (even if, as suggested above, its *chief* or highest expression might be in man), it is without end. Gôt is the eternal fecundity of the world—or fecundity itself. Wiligut mentions Light here, making a triad of Matter, Energy, and Light. What are we to make of this?

These are the primary categories introduced thus far in Wiligut's Commandments:

(Metaphysical Categories)

Al-Unity (N'ul-ni—the unconscious I) =
Spirit (ul) + Non-Spiritual essence (Proto-Matter) (Ni)
(tension gives rise to:)

(Natural Categories)

"World Egg"

(in which are incipient:)

Energy
Matter
Space
Time
Light
"Turning"

("Human" Categories)

Right
Might
Duty
Happiness

(Note that while Wiligut clearly has a cosmogony and a doctrine of emanations, there is no explanation for why "the human" comes to be in nature—except, perhaps, that it *must* come to be so that Gôt can recognize Himself.)

Wiligut puts Light together with Matter and Energy, suggesting a connection. The relation of Light to Energy is obvious: the display of energy frequently produces light (e.g., electrical phenomena), particularly when extreme heat is involved. Light is the apex of energy. It is the moment where matter becomes so energized that it gives rise to a phenomenon which *reveals* itself and others. It reveals itself to itself and/or to others, and/or reveals others to itself. In this Light, the Spirit, the Form of things is unveiled. Thus, when Wiligut links Energy and Light, he is linking Energy/Functioning with Manifestation or Revealing as such (Hegel held light to be "pure manifestation, and nothing but manifestation"). The natural or proper working or functioning of something leads, in the interaction of one thing with another, to the opening up and unveiling of the being of things. Being is "illuminated." In sum, Energy/Functioning, the actualization of Spirit in Matter, is the shining forth of Spirit in Matter, which in turn illuminates the Spirit in Matter elsewhere. (In truth, the revealing of a thing's being could not happen apart from the revealing of the being of others, since the being of something consists ultimately in its not being anything else.)

7. Gôt—beyond the concepts of good and evil—is that which carries the seven epochs of human history.

The idea that Gôt—and higher consciousness—is beyond good and evil is, of course, a perennial idea. What are "the seven epochs of human history"? Wiligut describes them in an SS document written June 17, 1936 and marked read by "H. H." (Heinrich Himmler). Wiligut claims that an account of the seven epochs "was recorded on seven Runo-wooden tablets (of oak) in ancient Aryan linear script supplemented by images" (pp. 98–99). These were destroyed, he further claims, when his grandfather's house burned down in 1848. There is no point in going into an account of the seven epochs, for here we encounter Wiligut at his worst. The seven epochs are a fanciful, wholly invented account of pre-history. I make this claim for two reasons: (1) there are no independent (traditional) sources that confirm Wiligut's account; and (2) there is no compelling reason to believe Wiligut's story about the "Runo-wooden tablets." Even mystics, or followers of mystics, cannot take things "on faith"; i.e., without either experiential evidence, or compelling reasons to believe. Wiligut tells us, among other things, that in the third epoch human beings "could fly and partly lived in the water, partly on land and had three eyes. The third one supposedly in the middle of their foreheads" (p. 100). The whole thing has the same ring of the arbitrary that we find in similar accounts from Blavatsky and Steiner.

Elsewhere, Wiligut has some interesting things to say about human origins and history. He seems to endorse the belief in an original, Arctic homeland for the Aryans (p. 56). His "Runic Exhortation" (pp. 76–77) gives a poetic account of the dispersion of the Aryans and the gradual forgetting of runic wisdom.

8. Rulership in the circulation of cause-and-effect carries along the highness—the secret tribunal [heimliche Acht].

I have little to say about this baffling statement. Does it refer to the characteristics of kingship? Is it claiming that rule (or true authority) consists in mastery of the "Gôt power"?

9. Gôt is beginning without end—the Al. He is completion in Nothingness, and, nevertheless, Al in the three-times-three realization of all things. He closes the circle at N-yule, at Nothingness, out of the conscious into the unconscious, so that this may again become conscious.

The ninth "commandment" seems almost a kind of summation of the others. We are being told here, again, that God is an eternally generating cycle in which Matter is united with Spirit. "He is completion in Nothingness, and, nevertheless, Al . . . ." God is All and Nothing is a perennial mystic doctrine (found, for example, in Böhme). God is nothing (no-thing; no-one-thing) precisely because he is All. But Wiligut says He is Al "in the three-times-three realization of all things." Flowers is translating *Erkenntniss* as "realization." I prefer the more traditional translation, "knowledge": "Al in the three-times-three knowledge of all things." 3 x 3 = 9. Nine commandments? Nine worlds? Is Wiligut saying that our nine-fold knowledge of Gôt in some sense completes or realizes Gôt as the Al-Nothing? Recall my remarks about the fifth commandment. Wiligut seems to be saying that originally Gôt is "unconscious I," who comes to consciousness through man. Recall these lines: "'Life aware of Spirit' . . . becomes a child of Gotos, a Spirit in the son of man . . . And thus Gotos himself is able to recognize—Gôt-Spirit on the throne . . ."

Note the final line of the ninth commandment: "He closes the circle at N-yule, at Nothingness, out of the conscious into the unconscious, so that this may again become conscious." Wiligut's use of "N-yule" is fascinating. "N-yule" is a play on German *null*, zero, nothingness, and Yuletide, the end of the year, a time of winter and death. The year ends with *null/Yule*. Life goes within itself: trees "die," animals hibernate, humans spend time huddled indoors, etc. This "within," is the implicit, the "in-itself" (to use the Hegelian term), which is the unconscious. But life arises out of this unconscious. It blooms and displays itself to itself: it becomes explicit, "conscious." The eternal cycle of generation is "unconscious," "dead" Matter *awakening* to "conscious," "living" Spirit through Energy. But Spirit in-itself, Idea, is only implicitly conscious. Spirit becomes *real* only when embodied in a reflective, material being who becomes conscious of its Spirit. Thus, Spirit goes over into Matter so that it may truly realize itself as Objective Spirit, or: "out of the conscious into the unconscious, so that this may again become conscious."

Gabriele Dechend also speaks of the "N-Yule": "Life as movement contains in itself a compelling drive, it comes to an 'eternal' generation, which is for its own part prevented, because 'without essence' Spirit, Energy and Matter tend to sink down into Nothing, into N-yule, into the Al. So here it becomes clear to us why the drive to reproduce is necessary. It turns the Need around: the sinking back into 'Nothing'" (p. 121). This passage does not seem to directly contradict the interpretation I have given above, but it is puzzling. What does "without essence" mean? Spirit, Energy, and Matter have a tendency to entropy, to sinking down into Nothing, into the dark and death, and inwardness of winter: the winter of the year, and the winter of one's life. In another essay I have written:

> Living things are different from inanimate objects in being dynamic forms which actively maintain themselves in what they are by regenerating and repairing their structure, thus holding themselves in the arms of Verthandi, and resisting the going over to Urth [passing out of the present, into the past; i.e., dying]. If the being is complex enough, it possesses some amount of versatility in taking action to evade this dissolution. It seeks finally to cheat Urth by passing its being on in the shape of another, by duplicating itself in another like itself, like a blazing log throwing off embers. This is the "immortality" of subhuman life.

Always knowing that there will be a final winter, the winter of one's life, we pass on life (we reproduce) and thus the cycle continues.

Obviously, there is more to Wiligut than I have presented here, and my interpretations have been, of necessity, highly speculative. As I have said, Wiligut's philosophy is confused, often arbitrary, and frequently hard to reconcile with what we know of the Germanic tradition from other sources. Nevertheless, I hope this review has demonstrated that Wiligut's writings are highly thought-provoking, and worthy of some study. Michael Moynihan and Stephen E. Flowers are to be commended for making these writings finally available to the public. To top it off, the book is extremely attractive, and contains numerous interesting illustrations.

Collin Cleary

The Only Tradition by William W. Quinn, Jr. Hardbound, 384 pages, with bibliography and index. Albany: SUNY Press. 1997. ISBN 0-7914-3214-9.

Ever since the "first shots" were fired in the Industrial Revolution, critiques of modernity have issued from every quarter: from William Blake to Jacques Ellul, to neo-Luddites like the anarchist-primitivist John Zerzan and the Unabomber. As the modern ethos has permeated every level of society, however, these attempts to grapple with modernity assume many of the characteristics of Scholastic negative theology. Modernity is so pervasive that it becomes simpler to describe what modernity is not, than what it is. More problematic, though, is the inability of modernity's critics to describe just what an anti-modern ideology might consist of. This is the work of Traditionalist philosophy.

Actually, to speak of Traditionalist "philosophy" is itself misleading. The Traditionalists distinguished themselves from the rational, analytical methodology characteristic of the Western philosophical tradition, at least since Bacon and Descartes. If Tradition can lay claim to a precursor within Western intellectual history, then that precursor would be Plato. Plato's concept of *anamnesis* (recollection) closely resembles Traditional formulas for the attainment of gnosis. Traditional knowledge is intuitive knowledge, which descends a hierarchical axis from essential, first principles down to the quantitative world of substantial physical forms (rather than vice-versa). These first principles cannot be arrived at using conventional, rational means: knowledge of qualitative essences can only be achieved by way of a total identification with those essences. René Guénon's "crisis of the modern world" is the result of the West's total domination by inductive scientism, which, by its very nature is incapable of unlocking these immutable truths. Lacking first principles in the Traditional sense, and subject to the tyranny of materialist ideologies (e.g., Marxism and psychoanalysis), the chaotic disintegration of Western culture stands in marked contrast to the holism of Traditional societies.

The Traditional society is one in which, in Ananda K. Coomaraswamy's words, "the politics of the heavenly, social, and individual communities are governed by one and the same law." Since Traditional man has access to first principles, his every act assumes the significance of a rite, having an archetypal or mythical referent. Primitive societies, by their very nature, are

Traditional societies, but both Coomaraswamy and Guénon have also provided descriptions of "developed" Traditional cultures, such as the Hindu and Medieval Christian. In terms of social organization, the Traditional society is a highly ordered society: each individual fulfills a specific function within a clearly defined hierarchy, which in turn reflects the hierarchy of essences itself. (It might also be noted that, in practical terms, the social hierarchy described by Traditionalism's chief proponents conforms in almost every detail to the tripartite division Georges Dumézil has identified within the mythical and social structures of the Indo-Europeans.)

But what are Tradition's first principles? Here Quinn's study takes a series of detours, first situating the "only Tradition" within the more generalized notion of perennial philosophy, and second by considering Tradition in terms of theosophy. This includes the theosophy formulated by Porphyry (and later exemplified by the writings of Jacob Böhme and Giordano Bruno), as well as that propounded by Madame Blavatsky's Theosophical Society (Quinn's insistence that Tradition and Theosophy have more in common than either would like to admit, however, seems strained and unconvincing). These digressions are necessary, we are told, to establish the recurrent themes that constitute the first principles: the Absolute and the One, *aeviternity* (the Tradition stands outside time), periodicity (the doctrine of the ages or Yugas), polarity and duality, cause and effect, and Traditional gnoseology (the intuitive method). But one might have hoped for a more detailed explanation as to how these themes are actually applied, and it is the primary weakness of Quinn's book that this is never forthcoming.

Most of Quinn's discussion is limited to the works of Guénon and Coomaraswamy, which seems reasonable enough, since they were the first to speak of Tradition per se. Unfortunately, only passing mention is made of Julius Evola, the greatest Italian expositor of the movement, in whom Tradition's anti-egalitarian, anti-democratic tendencies found their most extreme expression. Huston Smith is given far more consideration, although Evola would seem to be the more profound thinker—but perhaps this can be explained by the fact that Evola's ideas have only recently begun to receive attention in the English-speaking world.

Another complaint I can't help voicing (and I do think *The Only Tradition* is a useful book overall), concerns Quinn's fanciful final chapter, "The Solution to the Vicissitudes of Modernity."

Here Quinn diverges completely from simply describing the Traditional worldview of Guénon and Coomaraswamy, to voicing his own humanistic hopes for the future. Although its adherents view the tenets of Tradition as universal, Guenon and others were quick to point out the "inevitable diversity" of forms in which the Tradition must be expressed in actual, living societies. Quinn, however, is so optimistic about the emergence of what he calls "planetary consciousness," that he neatly dispenses with these objections, calling for a universally applicable, "planetary" Traditional culture. That the entire process of globalization—which is strip-mining the few remaining Traditional cultures from the earth at an ever accelerating rate—might be the solution to modernity rather than one of its most damning consequences seems unlikely, at best.

Though unpalatable to most, the Traditional perspective regarding the modern world was one of almost total pessimism: the Kali Yuga is drawing to a close, and it would be sheer folly to believe human beings can ameliorate its effects.

Joshua Buckley

An Orthodox Voice by John Michell. Softbound, 56 pages, no bibliography or index. Middlesex: Jam Publications, 1995. ISBN 0-9527305-0-2.

Ronald Hutton once described John Michell as a "reincarnation of the free-thinking English gentleman-scholars of the eighteenth century," and it would seem to be the case: Michell is both a gentleman and a true eccentric in the finest British tradition. The author of *The View Over Atlantis*, which achieved cult-status amongst the counter-culture in the 1960s and elevated Michell to guru stature with both the Rolling Stones and the Grateful Dead, Michell has never used his prodigious intellectual abilities to curry favor with the academic establishment. The author of *Megalithomania*, *At the Center of the World*, and *The City of Revelation*, Michell is a traditionalist who contrasts the "principles of true spiritual science" with "the history of our era . . . of continuous defeat for those groups or individuals who have attempted to reverse the flowing tide of ignorance, superstition, and arbitrary violence." In addition to writing books, Michell has contributed to numerous journals and magazines, as well as editing *The Cereologist*, a publication chronicling the crop circle phenomenon. A steady stream of pamphlets has also carried forth his personal crusades, most notably against Metrication. Michell's columns, like his weekly "Mysteries" segment in the *Daily Mirror*, serve as yet another forum for disseminating his message.

Edited and introduced by Deborah James, *An Orthodox Voice* contains twenty-four selections from Michell's column in *The Oldie*, short, pithy commentaries which, like his pieces in *The Mirror*, are surprisingly non-esoteric, yet filled with genuine insight and wisdom. With constant recourse to Plato and an eye on his "Golden Age" (which Michell identifies with the Bronze and Middle Ages in Britain, when a cultivated nobility presided over peasants celebrating an endless round of seasonal festivals), Michell's essays are jewels of crystalline common sense. Here you will find sound opinions on evolution, hunting, modern art, drugs, education, and sex, delivered in a friendly, down-home tone, wholeheartedly sincere, but never degenerating into smarmy sentimentality. This is the sort of sage advice your grandparents might have given, had they spent more time reading Plotinus (and perhaps Charles Fort), and less time watching Lawrence Welk.

"If you observe a decline in standards," writes Michell, "the perversion of values, vices presented as virtues, ignorance extolled above learning; if you see these things and do not speak out, calling a spade a spade, you are a coward and a traitor. If, on the other hand, you harp on about it, you are a bore. In either case you are ineffectual. The problem is, how to speak the truth in such a way that younger people will listen to you."

For his part at least, John Michell has done just that.

Joshua Buckley

Running on Emptiness: The Pathology of Civilization **by John Zerzan. Introduction by Theresa Kintz. Softbound, 215 pages, with bibliography, no index. Los Angeles: Feral House, 2002. ISBN: 0-922915-75-X.**

It may sound like a contradiction, but anarchy is gaining power these days. Considering the state of the world, with governments barely able to maintain order despite omnipresent high-tech surveillance methods and a vanished boundary between the police and the military, is it really any wonder? And while the old image of the sinister, bomb-throwing anarchist may have been somewhat defused over the last half-century, a new and more volatile breed of anti-authoritarian activist is on the rise. Certainly the continuing popularity of punk rock—which turned the circle-A sign into a cultural commodity to be worn like a badge by angry teenagers—may have partly encouraged this development. But there is something deeper going on, and the writings of John Zerzan can help us to understand it.

Zerzan is one of the few modern thinkers who could be called a genuine anarchist philosopher. He does not, however, expend too much effort on exposing the errors or crimes of government—these are assumed from the outset to be an intrinsic by-product of any ruling system. His vision of anarchy also goes beyond a mere desire to simply undo the current ruling system. To Zerzan, *any* form of domination must be rooted out and dissolved, regardless of whether this is on a social or even a more abstract level. Merely attacking the government is insufficient when there are countless other levels of social control that equally ache to be eradicated. Zerzan's position is that the only way to truly find freedom is through a return to the origins: the primitive origins that existed for human beings before the advent of technology and its co-extension, civilization. He is therefore a radical in the most literal sense of the word (deriving from the Latin *radix*, "root"), and his outlook is uncompromising and extreme in its implications. In past collections of writings such as *The Elements of Refusal* (Seattle: Left Bank, 1988), he trained a harshly critical eye not just on political forces and ideologies, but on the actual foundations of modern life and thought. He has relentlessly exposed what he believes to be the intrinsic authoritarian impulses that lurk in the very nature of our symbolic consciousness and in the meanings assigned to categories like time, art, and the use of agriculture: in short, the cornerstones of civilization.

In subsequent writings he has employed recent anthropological evidence to bolster his case against civilization. Zerzan's ideal social arrangement is apparently a "hunter-gatherer" society: small, completely decentralized, and exhibiting no domination between the sexes. According to the material he cites, human beings existed this way for immense periods of time with no need for codified laws or hierarchical divisions of labor. Having to work only minimally to feed themselves, they enjoyed a wealth of leisure time. His aversion to religion notwithstanding, Zerzan's descriptions of such social arrangements call to mind the myth of the Garden, and nostalgic romanticism for the "Golden Age."

Future Primitive (Brooklyn: Autonomedia, 1994) expands upon his earlier premises, bringing the attack right up against more recent intellectual and cultural trends, especially in "The Catastrophe of Post-Modernism." Here Zerzan exhibits a genuine free-spiritedness and healthy refusal to tolerate the perpetuation of self-serving academic fashions—not least of which those that loudly proclaim themselves as "liberating." Zerzan deftly lays bare their hollow premises and shallow limitations, and a decade after it was written this essay remains a valuable antidote to postmodernist nonsense. And surely the irony was not lost on Zerzan that *Future Primitive* was published by the same crowd who have worked overtime to promulgate much of the sort of gibberish that he despises.

Zerzan has also edited anthologies of anti-technology writings by others; most notable is *Against Civilization: Readings and Reflections* (Eugene, Oregon: Uncivilized Books, 1999). As a succinct compendium of thinkers who have expressed serious misgivings about the worth of technological and civilizational advancement, the book has its merits, although there is little to be found here that is unexpected. Zerzan often alludes to being ideologically neither of the left nor right, yet his pedigree is certainly of the former (which he would not deny) and this inevitably limits his perspective to somewhat predictable sources, Freud and the Frankfurt School among them. Thus he seems unaware of—or unwilling to acknowledge—other figures who ought to at least be mentioned in a compilation of this nature, such as Ralph Borsodi (author of the 1929 book *This Ugly Civilization*, which asked the question "Is man a manufacturing animal—or is he a human being?"), Pentti Linkola (the uncompromising Finnish advocate of the biosphere who lives his life as a solitary fisherman), or José Argüelles (the visionary author of a number of works concerning deleterious time conceptions and their direct relation to technology). On the other hand, it must be noted that Zerzan does continue to vocally support the ideas of the "Unabomber," Ted Kaczynski, a man whose position *is* neither left nor right, and whose commentaries are incisive and persuasive.

This brings us to Zerzan's latest collection of writings, *Running on Emptiness*. It may seem odd that it emanates from an *outré* imprint like Feral House (in contrast to the more typically left-wing collectivist publishers that have issued his previous books), but in fact Zerzan has a long-standing relationship of sorts with the company. An essay of his ("The Case Against Art") was included in the original edition of the Feral House underground bestseller *Apocalypse Culture* in 1986. This was at a time when Zerzan's ideas were otherwise only being circulated (and often vehemently debated or criticized) in obscure anarchist journals. And while the weighty sequel *Apocalypse Culture II* (2000) contained no texts by Zerzan himself, he did help to arrange for Ted Kaczynski's parable "Ship of Fools" to appear as the dire and biting conclusion to the volume.

In the last few years, Zerzan's ideas have been reaching a much wider audience. This has mainly occurred in the wake of dramatic anti-globalization protests, such as in Seattle where some journalists tried to paint Zerzan as the mentor to the "black block" factions that caused an inordinate share of the destruction. His friendship with Ted Kaczynski has also contributed to his notoriety; likewise the endorsement of his ideas by more widely read authors such as Derrick Jensen (whose interview with Zerzan, entitled "Enemy of the State," is also included in the new book).

Running on Emptiness presents an assortment of texts ranging from short broadsides (some titles of which are illustrative: "We Have to Dismantle All This," "Whose Unabomber?," "We All Live in Waco," or "How Ruinous Does it Have to Get?") to more extended ruminations on the totalitarian nature of time conceptions ("Time and its Discontents"), the use of symbols ("Running on Emptiness: The Failure of Symbolic Thought"), and the reification or objectification of all aspects of life ("That Thing We Do"). Zerzan is at his most effective in these longer essays. He is one of the few commentators coming from the left who dares to question the holy writ otherwise known as "progress," and in this regard he has more in common with voices from the so-called extreme right. Unlike most anti-modernists, however, he wants to uproot any inkling of "patriarchy" or social-intellectual "domination." (Whether he would be equally as antagonistic to "matriarchy" is never indicated, but I suspect the answer might be no.) Looking at the matter from a metaphysical perspective, one might even view a thinker like Zerzan as working for a return to a more chthonic, primordial world of the "Mothers," in contrast to a traditionalist such as Julius Evola who desired a return to a primordial masculine, solar culture. Despite this fundamental difference, the two writers are not dissimilar in the forcefulness of their critique against the modern world and their wish to shatter its very foundations, in order that something more noble might be recovered.

While he can undoubtedly be situated in the larger history of anarchist philosophy, Zerzan seems in many ways to be a direct product of the 1960s, a fact which becomes evident in the essay "So... How Did You Become an Anarchist?" where he recounts various key episodes in his life. For a reader already familiar with Zerzan's ideological positions, this piece offers an interesting sidelight as he discusses real-world personal situations amid the politicized subcultures of Northern California and Oregon.

Getting his start in the radical political milieu of the late '60s, it's no wonder that Zerzan has rubbed shoulders with Marxists and communists over the years. Unfortunately, he still seems to share vestiges of their outlook. This left-leaning tendency is also quite apparent in the newspaper *Green Anarchy*, which Zerzan is associated with. While claiming to be opposed to any and every form of "domination" under the sun, the paper cuts quite a bit of slack for various communist or Marxist initiatives, although claiming not to fully support their goals. They apparently don't extend the same courtesy to revolutionary groups or individuals without the proper leftist credentials, and this indicates a fundamental lack of pragmatic balance. When the paper recently printed an article by Ted Kaczynski, the "Green Anarchy Collective" felt obliged to follow it up with a ludicrous editorial statement declaring their opposition to Ted's "homophobia" (supposedly evidenced by his negative use of the word "pink"—actually an old-fashioned term for communist—as an adjective in the phrase "pink reformers" describing Green Party leaders) and alleged sexism. We thus find in the "Green Anarchy Collective" the usual Marxian predilection for excruciatingly tedious debate over the very, very small points of ideology—in other words, the type of behavior that tends to lead to the witch-hunting and suppression of anyone who doesn't pay full lip-service to that ideology in its "correct" formulation. Despite the anarchists' sensible dismissal of democracy as a corrupt form of government, one wonders: how do they arrive at their own position(s), and what happens to the dissenting voices drowned out by the more vocal factions?

We now arrive at a looming, unanswered question with regard to Zerzan and his fellow anarchists: are they genuinely dedicated to the cultivation of "freedom" (which in intellectual terms also must mean "free thought"), or only to the varieties of it which tow the party line and elicit their personal stamp of "enlightened" approval? If civilization is ever actively "undone"—for, as Zerzan rightly notes, the chances are it will undo itself in an even more appalling way if passively allowed to run its present course—and people do revert to a prehistoric level of hunter-gatherer tribal formulations, will there really be no rules in the new society? For example, what if certain hunter-gatherer tribes voluntarily elected to follow a patriarchal arrangement? Would this be acceptable—or must they all adhere to a prescribed ideology that has been approved point-for-point by the "green anarchists"? What would stop a tyrannical association of "correct-thinking" anarchists from wiping out anyone they consider as harboring the wrong ideas? Even if the former might be opposed to wiping out the latter through literal violence, are soft techniques of mental coercion any less repugnant? Are these people really going to accept differences of opinion as long as everyone minds their own business?

None of these issues are addressed by Zerzan, and perhaps in light of the present situation they are not so important. Yet considering the fact that his cohorts are already espousing an agenda bearing more than a trace of strident Marxist dogmatism, one has to wonder how truly free a society composed of the new breed of anarchists would be.

Another trait that Zerzan shares with the Marxist continuum left is materialism. He seems to view any form of religion as a tool that inherently functions to enslave the minds of some human beings for the benefit of others. Even primordial traditions like shamanism are suspect to him, although his assessments in this regard are based on a limited understanding of the subject. Ironically, his materialistic view of life and nature is a wholly modern one—a fact that doesn't jibe well with a projected return to a pre-civilized existence. Thus, no matter how clever his arguments, anyone who does not share Zerzan's materialistic frame-of-mind will never be able to completely follow him. Ironically, the primitive tribes whose mode of existence Zerzan often extols would have little use either for his brand of materialism, or his brand of ideological hairsplitting.

TYR: Myth—Culture—Tradition

It is also questionable whether certain of Zerzan's assumptions can be taken entirely at face value. The opening sentence of the essay "He Means It—Do You?" (a reference to the Unabomber) states "Today's opposition is anarchist or it is non-existent. This is the barest minimum coherence in the struggle against an engulfing totality." And later: "Anarchism, if not yet anarchy, is the only scene going, even if the blackout on the subject is still in effect." Here Zerzan falls into the hubristic trap of the ideologue who is convinced of the rightness of his own position above all others, certain that if the message were ever to reach the masses, the revelation of the new truth will set them free. Although today's society is more locked-down than ever, there is definitely opposition seething under the surface—but, contra Zerzan, not all of it is anarchist.

For Zerzan and his colleagues, another overriding assumption is that any form of hierarchy and inegalitarianism is inherently bad, presumably because these equate with "domination." This is asserted (or rather assumed) dogmatically. No justification is offered for this position, or for the counterposed ideal of peace, love, and the absence of hierarchy. The arbitrary division of labor may indeed inflict unjust duties to individuals, but what is wrong with the division of labor according to natural skill? Or have the new breed of anarchists convinced themselves that there is no such thing as a distribution of unequal talents among different members of the same species? A similar sort of dogmatism is present in Zerzan's belief that all forms of agriculture or domestication inevitably produce violence and oppression. Needless to say, many readers who might agree with some of his positions—especially those living in a rural environment—are probably going to have a hard time swallowing, let alone rallying behind, premises such as these.

John Zerzan's words are undoubtedly sincere, but they also emanate from a place of contradiction. His position is entirely theoretical, and the mundane details of his own life offer little proof for the viability of the ideas espoused. He lives in a modern city (Eugene, Oregon) and interacts with the disgruntled and frustrated offspring of civilization as they formulate their worldviews and try to take greater control of their lives. He rightly points the finger at technology and civilization as being two primary causes for the lack of real human experience in this modern and increasingly "virtual" world. His sense of despair is palpable, and when he states that "The unprecedented reality of the present is one of enormous sorrow and cynicism," there can be no doubt that he feels this to the core of his being. He yearns for direct and sincere human interaction, yet his activity as an intellectual—reading, cataloging, and critiquing ideas and historical abstractions—is about as far as one can get from an existence where reality is experienced in the most full and immediate way. In this respect, a thinker like Pentti Linkola (or Ted Kacynzski, before he was apprehended) is a lot closer than John Zerzan toward closing the gap between ideology and real life.

Zerzan's writings on the catastrophic state of the modern world are powerful and few people could deny that his assessment is largely accurate, at least in terms of its descriptions. This aspect alone makes his writings worth exploring, regardless of whether or not one agrees with his entire ideology or his proposed solution. He has invested years of time, effort, and intelligent thought to elucidate both the problems of civilization as well as to propose a utopian alternative. While there is much to agree with in his diagnosis of symptoms and causes, he offers little advice on how people are supposed to get from point Z back to point A. Nor does he ever explain why the whole process wouldn't immediately start over again, even if humans could undo everything they have created. If a hunter-gatherer future for humanity is realized, the leisure time available would likely allow the mind to wander, but also to hone itself by observing nature, and then we are back at the first step to agriculture, which is the beginning of one creature dominating another, man dominating nature, and on and on. And these are just the contradictions that become apparent on a physical-material level. From an intellectual standpoint, the ascension of those who agree with John Zerzan might not ultimately be any more liberating than the present malaise—unless your mind is already dominated by the same belief system as theirs, that is.

Michael Moynihan

Team Rodent: How Disney Devours the World by **Carl Hiassen**. Softbound, 83 pages, no bibliography or index. New York: Ballantine Library of Contemporary Thought, 1998. ISBN 0-345-42280-5.

One of my favorite passages in Jerry Mander's *In The Absence of the Sacred* is his description of Disney's EPCOT Center. Built with the financial backing of multi-national corporations like Kraft Foods and Exxon, EPCOT's "vision of Tomorrow" is the corporate philosophy now dictating the course of Western Civilization: unlimited growth and "progress." Mander summarizes the EPCOT ethos: "We don't need to maintain our charming but hindering bonds to such anomalies as land, family farms, or community or the natural world. All we need do now is relax, float in our little cars, and be awed with the skill, thoughtfulness, imagination, and devotion of these can-do visionary corporations and their astounding new tools. We can all look forward to a future of very little work, total comfort and complete technological control of the environment, the weather, nature and *us*." In other words, the Disney "world" is the world at the end of history.

When Disney agents bought up forty-five acres of Florida woodlands and swamps in the 1960s, they quickly set about to transform them into the more manageable marketing environment that is Disney World. Lakes were drained, paved, and refilled with dyed, more "real" looking water. Native animals were removed and replaced by plastic replicas. Should someone step out of line in this perfectly orchestrated, clockwork alternate reality, they are quickly, quietly dealt with by Draconian Disney security personnel. Walt himself understood that the one essential ingredient necessary to maintaining the illusion of perfection—the "magic" in the Magic Kingdom—is total control. Wild nature must be made harmless and cuddly. Real human beings, with their neuroses and poor personal hygiene, must be refashioned into smiling, happy-go-lucky man-children.

New Yorkers couldn't have been happier when Disney arrived in Times Square, long a Mecca for whores, dope-peddlers, and pornographers. Disney opened a massive retail outlet, restored the New Amsterdam Theatre, and began "cleaning up" the neighborhood. Today, Times Square is a world transformed—a safe place for children and old folks to shop for the latest Disney DVD or Mickey doll. But while few would eulogize the now-vanquished sleaze merchants, fewer still have stopped to consider the cost of this happy transformation. The "new" Times Square is a Times Square without a soul: sanitized, homogenized, and micro-managed to the extent that the only surprises are those that Disney's "imagineers" have planned. There are even fewer surprises in Orlando's "Celebration," the Disney Corporation's most ambitious foray into suburban development. Described as Disney's first functioning "tomorrowland," Celebration consists of row upon row of cookie-cutter houses, deliberately reminiscent of good old days no one can remember. But in true Disney fashion, life in Celebration comes with the stipulation that residents follow certain rules. The Celebration handbook includes regulations governing everything from the proper maintenance of shrubbery to the appropriate colors for house paint. Everything is subject to Disney veto. Everything is under control.

But Celebration really isn't all that different from the suburbs that now encircle most American major cities. For the most part, the suburbanite lives in Disney World all year round. He has traded freedom for security and personal choice for uniformity. His lawn is a masterpiece of human manipulation and chemical engineering, where wild nature will never intrude. His family life and personal relationships could have been scripted by a sitcom writer. He looks like his neighbors, drives the same car as his neighbors, and watches the same television programs as his neighbors. Like Disney World, the modern world is a giant marketing environment built by corporations to ensure maximum profitability. Real tradition and spirituality, not to mention local and national distinctions, have been dismantled and replaced by a crass consumer culture that panders to the lowest common denominator. Like the song says: "It's a small world, after all."

Scathing, witty, and filled with amusing anecdotes, Carl Hiaasen's *Team Rodent* goes after Disney for all the right reasons. The problem is figuring out what can be done about it.

Joshua Buckley

Hermann Hendrich: Leben und Werk by Elke Rohling. Hardbound, 104 pages, with numerous color and black and white illustrations. Billerbeck: Selbstverlag Werdandi, 2001. ISBN 3-00-008228-X.

This remarkable book is a labor of love, a work by an enthusiastic lay person. A few years ago, Elke Rohling had the idea to found a non-profit organization that would provide information on Hermann Hendrich's work as well as financial support and initiative for the task of preserving his remarkable total-art temples for future generations. The result is the *Nibelungenhort* cultural association, and this book and the benefit CD of the same title are the first efforts towards raising awareness of Hendrich's art.

Together with Fidus, Franz Stassen, and Ludwig Fahrenkrog, Hermann Hendrich was part of a loose grouping of visual artists who were heavily inspired by Wagner's ideas of the *Gesamtkunstwerk*, or total work of art. They shared a passion for the German heritage of fairy tales, the older traditions preserved in the *Eddas* as well as for other kindred mystical currents of the time. In their own way, they were the Symbolists of Germany, taking cues from the literary nature-mystical school, reformist movements, and even attempts to create a new paganism. In contrast to Stassen's precise Art Nouveau lines, Hendrich chose a sombre palette, sometimes using expressionistic brushwork to create hauntingly simple narratives and mystical landscapes. Often, the figures blend into the surroundings and form an inseparable totality. His portrait of Odin at the onset of the twilight of the gods shows the god alone, shrouded in darkness, while the fires of *ragnarök* loom in the distance. And in contrast to both Fidus and Fahrenkrog, who had grandiose yet never realized ideas for temple architecture, Hendrich was successful in his quest to create fitting homes for his noble work, the Nibelungenhalle and the Walpurgishalle being the best known examples.

In order to reach the largest possible audience, the text is included in both German and English. Separate chapters deal with each of the architectural projects that Hendrich was involved in and the excellent color and black and white reproductions give an impressive overview of Hendrich's works. In addition, the 102-page book includes a time line of Hendrich's life, an interesting autobiographical sketch by Hendrich, a list of works, and a thorough biography. Be forewarned: once one owns this unique book, it might prove hard to resist the *Wanderlust* to pay homage to Hendrich's temples in person.

Markus Wolff

Mythos Tier: Geschichte und Mythologie einer ewigen Verbindung, Sven Henkler. Softbound, 112 pages, with illustrations. Dresden: Verlag Zeitenwende, 2001. ISBN 3-934291-09-0.

Sven Henkler, who has already authored a short work on the Wild Hunt, returns with a 104-page treatise on the sacred role of animals in Northern European consciousness, as seen through the eyes of myth and folklore. The first part explores the lore of animals in faith and ritual, the significance of male and female animals, as well as the role of animals in fairy tales. The second part consists of separate sections exploring individual animals: horse, dog, cat, pig, goat, sheep, stag, and bear. Henkler sees the animal as an essential companion of man and as an innate part of the *folk-soul*, seen in the frequent references to animals as travelers between the worlds.

Significantly, Henkler pleads for a complete revision of our relationship with animals, for a return to the sacred dimension. Such a transformation might even someday supersede today's protective environmental measures, which Henkler calls "one of the biggest unnecessary necessities." While that day might be far off in the future, his argument is a good one, and the book is an excellent introduction to the world of animal lore.

The author plans a second volume that will deal with the wolf, the serpent, and various birds. The Verlag Zeitenwende has further published such works as Oliver Ritter's *Magische Männlichkeit: Mann-Sein aus initiatischer Sicht*, a traditionalist work on the real essence of maleness and masculinity; *Raido: Ein Handbuch der Tradition*, edited by the noted Evola scholar Martin Schwarz; and other works on Germanic folklore and tradition are also available.

Markus Wolff

Urbock: Bier Jenseits von Hopfen und Malz **by Christian Rätsch. Hardbound, 223 pages, bibliography, index. Aarau, Switzerland: AT Verlag, 1996. ISBN 3-85502-553-3.**

Beer has long played an integral part in cultures across time and throughout the world. The first beer was brewed more than ten thousand years ago. Rätsch's book begins by simply asking, "what is beer, what was beer?" Beer is the most popular alcoholic beverage on the planet. The book is divided into four parts, beginning with "The Fruit of the Earth." This section deals with the foundation of beer—nature and all her bounty. The grains, minerals, secret plants, and that mysterious creature, the yeast. The next section, "The Drink of the Gods," provides a history of the production and use of sacred beer throughout the world, from

Mesopotamia through Egypt, Africa, the Himalayas, Ireland, Germany, and Scandinavia. The final two sections concern the modern era and are called "The Age of Hops" and "The Age of Hemp."

The author points out that although there are thousands of different kinds of beer available today, they are really all based on the same boring recipe of grain, water, and hops. Hops is a soothing and sedative herb and lends beer its bitter taste, making a beer which is refreshing and calming, ultimately lulling the drinker to sleep.

"But beer wasn't always such a boring drink. In ancient times, beer was enlivened by the addition of certain herbs. Beer had magic: the spirit of a god or goddess lived within it. It contained the power of the sacred plants and was created through the mystical metamorphosis of nature. It was food, drink and sacrament at the same time. ... There are scarcely any known psychedelic, narcotic, or intoxicating plants which have not been added to beer at some time during the history of mankind. A beer made more potent in this way was not used as a daily sedative but as a ritual drink intended to bring humans, gods and ancestors into connection with one another. ... Such a beer was consciousness-expanding, stimulating, and sexually arousing. It blessed the humans with heavenly visions, divine ecstasy and unshakable strength. ... The drink was the medium between man and god; it connected the visible with the invisible world. Beer was honored as a gift from the gods, valued as miraculous medicine, and used during magical practices." (pp. 6–7)

The most detailed sections of the book are devoted to the history of beer in northern Europe. Stories of sacred brews in the Celtic lands are recounted—including the story of Gwion Bach, who drank from his mother Ceridwen's secret and forbidden brew, underwent a transformation from human to grain, was eaten by Ceridwen, and traveled through her body to be reborn as Taliesin. Rätsch suggests that this story and others like it correspond to the matrix of psychedelic experience and shamanic initiation; this includes transformation of the human shape, experiencing a violent death such as being chewed up, and the rebirth into a new existence with expanded consciousness. He wonders if the brew in Ceridwen's kettle contained psychoactive plants, such as those in the Nightshade family, known to cause the same effects that Taliesin experienced.

The history of beer in Germany is rich and Rätsch gives it the attention it deserves. From the mysterious "beer runes" A:L:U, to remarks by Tacitus about how easy it will be to conquer the Germans with beer instead of weapons, there is a wide variety of information about the sacred plants of Germany and their use in beer. The title of the book, *Urbock*, refers to a particularly strong German beer. *Ur* means "primordial" or "original" and *Bock* means "billy-goat" or "buck." There are a number of traces of the practice of sacrificing beer and goats, particularly in honor of Thor at his most important festival in the spring, thus the "Urbock" was a part of the ritual beginning of spring. As late as 1854 in one area of Germany they still drank particularly strong beer at the slaughtering of a goat. A popular additive in northern Europe was the widely distributed plant mugwort (this English common name reveals its use as a beer additive as well). There is evidence that mugwort *(Artemisia vulgaris)* has been utilized since antiquity to enhance fertility, as medicine for female reproductive problems, and as an aphrodisiac. There were many other plants used as beer adjuncts in Germany with stimulant, aphrodisiac, and even hallucinogenic properties. This brings us to the plant whose effects are exactly the opposite, a plant that causes drowsiness and slumber, and which currently enjoys almost exclusive popularity in beer brewing: hops.

"The history of beer is the history of the descent from a sacred drink of the gods to a profane swill of the masses." (p. 7) The history of how it came to be that only hops are allowed in beer in Germany parallels the rising strength of the Christian Church and the period during which the final vestiges of heathen Europe were destroyed. The famous "Bavarian purity laws," which later became the more general "German purity laws," were signed on April 24, 1516 and included the following words regarding what was permissible to use in beer: "on the markets and in the countryside ... nothing more than yeast, hops, and water shall be bought or used." The effects of some of the old herbs—aphrodisiac, abortive, stimulant, mystical—were decidedly *un*-Christian. The German purity laws were the first drug laws, in other words, laws in which the use of consciousness-expanding and consciousness-changing plants were explicitly forbidden. "In the end, our modern drug laws are Christian attacks against the sacred healing plants of our ancestors." (p. 171)

The medicinal effects of hops *(Humulus lupulus)* are anaphrodisiac and sedative—quite the opposite of what were previously favored effects. In addition, hops contain lupiline which prohibits ejaculation in men. Hops also contain traces of estrogen, the female hormone, and men who drink too much beer sometimes develop "beer breasts" (Rätsch bluntly calls these *Biertitten*) and a softer, more rounded feminine physique because of it. Although hops were known in the Middle Ages, they were not used medicinally because their effects were thought to be ill-suited for human use, making them melancholic and sad. Perhaps this is why hopped beer is so popular in our over-stimulated modern culture.

The last chapter of the book is dedicated to the "Age of Hemp" which, according to the author, began over ten-thousand years ago. From a botanical perspective, hemp is the closest plant cousin to hops. Next to beer, hemp is the most popular drug in the world. Hemp was among the herbs used in beer in Europe during the Middle Ages, and Rätsch laments the passing of its use but says that there is a new dawn rising and the art of hemp beer is being rediscovered. The author offers three recipes for sacred beers at the end of this chapter, for mandrake beer, henbane beer (the original "Pilsner"), and hemp beer.

The author is one of the greatest living authorities in the discipline of ethnobotany. He has written a number of outstanding books on the interaction between man, religion, and sacred plants. There are a few of his books available in English: *Marijuana Medicine* (Rochester, Vermont: Inner Traditions 2000), *Plants of Love* (Berkeley: Ten Speed Press, 1997), as well as the seminal work about sacred plants by Schultes and Hoffman, *Plants of the Gods*, which been recently updated and revised by Rätsch (Inner Traditions, 2001). The fall of 2002 will see the publication in English of *Shamanism and Tantra in the Himalayas* (also Inner Traditions), written by Rätsch along with his wife Claudia Müller-Ebeling, the thangka artist Surendra Bahadur Shahi, and the cooperation of five shamans from the region.

Although *Urbock* is only presently available in German, the lavish illustrations of unusual beer paraphernalia from the author's personal collection make it a worthwhile purchase for anyone interested in the history of the relationship between beer, man, and plants.

Annabel Lee

RÛNA = RAVEN PRESS

RECENT RÛNA=RAVEN TITLES INCLUDE:

THE SECRET KING: KARL MARIA WILIGUT: HIMMLER'S LORD OF THE RUNES
TRANSLATED AND INTRODUCED BY
STEPHEN E. FLOWERS
EDITED BY MICHAEL MOYNIHAN

There is much speculation about the "occult roots of National Socialism," yet very little concrete documentation has ever been uncovered about the actual occult practices of the Nazis themselves. Of the materials that do exist, almost nothing has been translated into English – until now. This book contains the entire corpus of occult writings by Karl Maria Wiligut, who was a runic initiate and shadowy "Secret King" of Germany. Wiligut was commissioned by the SS to write rituals and private reports on runes, secret Germanic traditions and pre-history. It was through this position within the SS that he came to be known after his death as "Himmler's Rasputin." This book contains a vast amount of never-before translated and published primary evidence that shows the extent of Nazi involvement with Runic esotericism.

THIS BOOK IS CO-PUBLISHED WITH DOMINION
$18.00

BLUE-RÛNA: EDRED'S SHORTER WORKS VOL. III

This seminal volume contains four of the most important articles by Edred: *The Way of Woden,*

How to be a Heathen, *The Secret of the Gothick God of Darkness*, and *The Alchemy of Yggdrasil*. These are among the most influential works by Edred and should be read by all serious students.

$11.00

Johannes Bureus and the Adalruna

The first extensive treatment of the esoteric runology of Johan Bure, the 17th century runologist and Rosicrucian rune-mystic of Sweden to appear in English. This includes a biography of Bure and a systematic presentation of his ideas on esoteric runology, called by him "Adalruna."

$10.00

Wendish Mythology: Divinities and Religious Practices of the Western Slavs

This is an exploration of the myths and divinities of the tribes of Slavs known as the Wends or Sorbians. These tribes were among the most difficult for the Christians to conquer and their lore is often closely related to the Germanic lore of their neighbors. Today the Sorbians are a Slavic-speaking minority in eastern Germany.

$7.00

Witchdom of the True: A Study of the Vana-Troth and the Practice of Seidr

This is the long-awaited and much anticipated study of the history, lore, religion and magic of the Vanir branch of the Germanic way. Its contents will prove of extreme interest to those of the Wiccan path or modern witchcraft, for it is in the way of the Vanir, or Wanes, that their roots are to be found. From a manuscript originally titled "True Wicca."

$15.00

Strange Tales
by Hanns Heinz Ewers
Edited and introduced by
Stephen E. Flowers
Foreword by Don Webb

Hanns Heinz Ewers is a vastly ignored and misunderstood master of the horror and fantasy genre of literature. He was an associate of Guido von List, Lanz von Liebenfels, and Aleister Crowley and later a member of the NSDAP, but also a nudist, pioneer of sexology and decadent poet, film-maker, playwright, and cabaret performer. This volume contains most of Ewers's stories which had been previously translated and also includes two newly translated tales: *The Water-Corpse* and *From The Diary of an Orange Tree*. There is also an extensive 22-page introduction that makes the reader familiar with the facts of Ewers's life and his sometimes overtly Satanic ideas and philosophies, to an extent never before discussed in the English language.

$25.00

=

Rûna=Raven also carries all other titles by Stephen Flowers / Edred Thorsson currently in print, as well as an extensive collection of other titles relevant to the Germanic tradition. US residents add $4.00 shipping and handling for the first item and $1.00 for each additional item. Foreign orders should include $5.00 shipping and handling for each item ordered. Texas residents include 7% sales tax.

RÛNA-RAVEN PRESS
PO Box 557
Smithville, TX
78957
USA
(512) 237 4283
runa@texas.net

=

INFORMATION ON THE RUNE GILD

The Rune-Gild is a school of esoteric knowledge based on the Odian system of the Runes. The Gild is a world-wide organization with Halls in North America, England, and Australia. Within the Gild there are works, such as the Gildisbok, which are otherwise unavailable to the general public. If you are interested in joining the Gild, write a letter of application to:

The Rune-Gild
PO Box 7622
Austin, TX
78713
USA

The letter should contain your legal name, address and any information on your background in Runic studies, areas of special interest, and any other information you think the Gild should know about you as an applicant for sponsorship. Include a fee of $50.00 (USA) or $60.00 (foreign). If for any reason you can not be sponsored you will receive the fee back along with an explanation. The fee entitles you to one year's membership in the Gild, a copy of the Gildisbok, and four numbers of the Gild's official insider publication, Rune-Kevels.

The Red Brook **by Herman Löns. Translated by Markus Wolff. Booklet, 20 pages, no bibliography or index. Ohio: Europa, 2001. Illustrations by Erich Feyerabend. No ISBN.**

An avid outdoorsman and keen observer of wildlife, Hermann Löns (1866–1914) is best remembered for his animal stories. But Löns was also a fierce anti-Cleric, an early critic of industrialization, and a devoted student of Germanic folklore and mythology. To date, only *Harm Wulf: A Peasant Chronicle* (New York, 1931) has been translated into English.

The Red Brook is Löns's fictionalized account of the Massacre at Verden, where Charlemagne (Karl the Butcher) treacherously slaughtered thousands of pagan Saxons—"four thousand five hundred just ones who would rather bow their heads and accept the axe than submit to Frankish justice and foreign ways." Löns's prose is crisp and concise, yet still exudes his deep love of wild nature and his heathen Saxon forebears, men who "hung Karl's administrators from the willows, sacrificed the Christian priests by the megaliths, mounted the red cock on the houses of usury, leveled the houses of prayer and threw the Rolands into the village ponds. Free men they wanted to be in a free land." Löns's tale is brought to life by his rich descriptions of the living environment, and stirs and seethes with the rustle of leaves, the humming of insects, and the howling of wolves. Hopefully, this small sampling will inspire further examination of his work in the English-speaking world.

Joshua Buckley

Epitaph for a Desert Anarchist **by James Bishop, Jr. Hardbound, 254 pages, with bibliography and index. New York: Atheneum, 1994. ISBN 0-689-12195-2.**

Edward Abbey (1927–1989) now lies buried—illegally—under a pile of black rocks somewhere in the vast Southwestern desert. It was undoubtedly what he would have wanted. More than anything else, Abbey was the 20th century's greatest champion of the American West.

Abbey's love for the West wasn't motivated solely by environmental concerns, although he *was* an environmentalist. Abbey loved the West because it was *wild*, perhaps the last great expanse of untouched wilderness left in the United States. But Abbey was much else besides. Author, ranger, college professor, desert rat—Abbey was a protean character even his friends found enigmatic.

Abbey's most famous novel, *The Monkey Wrench Gang*, is the story of four unlikely companions possessed of Abbey's "visceral hostility for the kind of modern industrialism that would mar and scar the silent, natural world." Blazing across the desert, the Gang cuts power-lines, hacks down billboards and attempts to dynamite a bridge. Although Abbey claims it would have happened anyway, *The Monkey Wrench Gang* helped inspire the "epidemic" of monkey wrenching waged by lone wolf *eco-tuers* ever since the books publication. Abbey also contributed a "Foreward!" to Dave Foreman's *Ecodefense*, a handbook with tips on disabling construction equipment, tree-spiking, and other assorted mischief. Despite his prolific output as a writer, Abbey was a firm believer that the deed was more important than the word.

Be that as it may, Abbey's words were a consistent source of trouble. He irked liberals by being a staunch advocate of private gun ownership, a critic of feminism, and a proponent of immigration reform. Abbey's comment that America didn't need any more "hungry, ignorant, unskilled, culturally, generally impoverished people" brought hysterical charges of racism and "xenophobia." But Abbey the man was as wild as the untamed landscapes he loved, and said what he thought regardless of the consequences.

Epitaph is more a tribute than a definitive biography, although Bishop does provide significant insights into Abbey's literary output and life. In the end, it may be hard to predict which will outlast the other. Abbey was the archetypal rugged individualist, a living anachronism in an age of smooth-cheeked conformists. If and when the modern world jumps the tracks, it will be men like Abbey, the "redneck environmentalist," who will endure.

Joshua Buckley

The Triumph of the Moon: A History of Modern Pagan Witchcraft by **Ronald Hutton.** Softbound, 486 pages, with index. New York: Oxford University Press, 1999. No illustrations. ISBN 0-19-285449-6.

British historian Ronald Hutton's *Pagan Religions of the British Isles*, *The Rise and Fall of Merry England* and its "sequel," the magisterial *Stations of the Sun*, should be familiar to many readers. Though thoroughly academic in his own approach, Hutton is unique in acknowledging fringe perspectives usually ignored by other serious writers. In his discussions of Neolithic mound-building for instance, Hutton takes into account not only the available scholarly literature, but also the alternate histories propounded by the Earth Mysteries sub-cult. Though unwilling to follow these "alternative archaeologists" in their at times wildly fanciful speculations, Hutton's open-mindedness is no less a foil to the intellectual snobbery indulged in by so many of his colleagues.

In this sweeping history of modern pagan witchcraft in Britain, Hutton remains skeptical about the supposed lineage of the contemporary witch-cult, while finding much to sympathize with in the contemporary witches themselves. While I've seen his study attacked on a number of Wiccan and other heathen internet sites, Hutton for his part appears more than willing to engage the pagan community in a dialogue which, it seems to me, could only be beneficial for all sides concerned. But meaningful discussion has never been the province of fundamentalists, be they Christian or pagan.

Even more so than Margot Adler's partisan *Drawing Down the Moon*, *Triumph* might justly be considered the definitive study of the modern witch phenomenon. Of particular interest is the extensive historical background Hutton provides to illuminate the context in which Gerald Gardner (foremost amongst others) first formulated his (new) Old Religion. Hutton traces many of the currents contributing to the Wiccan belief system back nearly two hundred years, weaving together trends in literature, folklore studies, popular superstition, history, and what Antoine Faivre would call the "Western Esoteric Tradition." What emerges is a surprisingly coherent chronology of the idea that the Gods of Nature, exemplified by the "Great God Pan," have never left, an idea which, Hutton contends, seemed to gain force in direct response to the spread of Industrial modernity. The willingness of Victorian folklorists to equate local customs and peasant superstitions with pagan survivals, the Romantic inclination towards a nature-worshipping pantheism, and the unbounded popularity of anthropological works like Frazier's *Golden Bough*, can all be viewed as indicative of this tendency. Its culmination came with popular phenomena like the Woodcraft movement, which developed in Britain between 1900 and the opening of World War II.

As with the *völkisch* subculture in Germany, many of those involved in Woodcraft (like Aleister Crowley's ex-lover Victor Neuberg) were also practicing pagans.

By far the most distressing aspect of Hutton's history for neo-pagans, though, is the thoroughness with which he dismantles so many of Wicca's treasured shibboleths. Margaret Murray has been skewered elsewhere; here she receives equally unsparing treatment. An entire chapter is devoted to the "cunning folk" who latter-day Wiccans have often claimed as transmitters of ancestral witch traditions. Hutton demonstrates that what can be reconstructed as to the actual practices of these nineteenth-century peasant healers, indicates that they trafficked more in Christian superstition than ancient pagan lore. Robert Graves's *White Goddess* is shown to be more a work of fantasy than history or anthropology denounced, not least of all, by its own author. More problematic is Hutton's scrutiny of Gerald Gardner's claim that he was initiated into a coven practicing traditional witchcraft. Hutton unmasks "Old Dorothy" Clutterbuck, who supposedly provided Gardner with access to this tradition, as a thoroughly unexceptional person who—if indeed a practicing witch—led "one of the most remarkable double lives in history."

Despite Gardner's dubious claims (are there any occultists who haven't engaged in similar dissimulations?), he nevertheless comes across as a remarkably appealing, even dashing figure. Finding less to sympathize with in the contemporary Wiccan community (and particularly its American variants) than Hutton himself, I can't help but read his post-Gardnerian history of the movement in terms of the progressive dismantling of Gardner's original vision. A staunch conservative despite his eccentricities, Gardner would no doubt find the extreme liberalism of his successors appalling—not to mention the rabidly feminist bent Wicca has assumed since the 1970s. Largely the work of anti-sex feminists like Mary Daly and Andrea Dworkin, who proffered the notion that the suppression of witchcraft was synonymous with the suppression of female power (and that the latter might be reinvigorated by the resurrection of the former), this view was championed in turn by the widely-read Jewish witch Starhawk. That Gardner's Craft, which he viewed largely as a fertility cult in the Frazierian mode, could be co-opted by Lesbians and radical feminists seems supremely ironic. The individualism and syncretism inherent in modern Wicca likewise seem incompatible with the Gardnerian model. Forgetting for a moment that Gardner's "tradition" was largely imagined, it was still firmly situated in a European, tribal context.

This is a highly readable, utterly engrossing study, as entertaining and rich in fascinating detail as it is useful, particularly for those of heathen disposition. I cannot recommend it highly enough.

Joshua Buckley

Journal of Indo-European Studies Monograph No. 3: Homage to Georges Dumézil. Edited by Edgar C. Polomé. Washington D.C.: Institute For the Study of Man, 1982. Softbound, 143 pages. No ISBN.

Most of the essays here were composed shortly after Georges Dumézil's reception by the French Academy, and represent an American tribute to Dumézil by many of his former students. Ranging broadly over much of the territory Dumézil traversed in his extensive *ouvre* of books and articles, this is also an ideal introduction to the various directions Indo-European studies have taken under Dumézil's guidance.

Of particular interest are Jaan Puhvel and Udo Strutynski's complementary examinations of the hero motif in the Indo-European tradition. According to Dumézil, the Indo-European hero is the stakes in a conflict between the gods of the first and second functions. Puhvel has expanded on this by suggesting that what is really at stake here is the precarious balance between nature (in its chthonic aspect) and culture. The first function god is manifest in his demonic aspect (e.g., Odin) and the second function god is the Culture God (e.g., Thor). This is a fairly profound conception. In a very real sense, the warrior is in the paradoxical position of defending the culture that his own war-like tendencies threaten to engulf. Strutynski develops this theme further in his examination of Sir Gawain, whose "three sins" place him well within the province of the Indo-European hero typology.

C. Scott Littleton weighs in with a possible source for the sword-in-the-stone motif in the Arthurian legends. Littleton contends that the cultic significance of the sword, as well as many other aspects of the Arthurian legends, may have arrived in Britain with Sarmatian auxiliaries in the 2nd century C.E. One especially fascinating tidbit—which I'd love to see developed elsewhere—is Littleton's speculation that this Alano-Sarmation and Scythian sword-cult may have penetrated as far as Japan, and that the cultic features of Japanese swordsmanship might ultimately have an Indo-European origin.

In "Places Outside Space, Moments Outside Time," Bruce Lincoln discusses the mythological function of interstitial phenomena—i.e., those that exist outside pat taxonomic concepts. These are the source of both great danger and great possibility. Lincoln writes: "An obvious case in point is the proto-Indo-European analysis of dawn: neither day nor night, often dangerous, it is yet more often a time of recreation and victory."

Other articles include "Comparative Mythology and Comparative Philology" (Jean Haudry), "Brothers, Friends, and Charioteers: Parallel Episodes in the Irish and Indian Epics" (Alf Hiltebeitel), "Katla and Her Distaff: An Episode of Tri-Functional Magic in the Eyrbyggja Saga?" (Francois-Xavier Dillman), "A Folk-Tale: The Three Counsels" (J. C. Riviere), "The Cosmology of Lear and His Daughters" (T. L. Markey), and "Beowulf 2863a ces [g]" (Eric Hamp).

Joshua Buckley

Studia Germanica Volume 1, Stephen Edred Flowers. Texas: Rûna-Raven Press, 2000. Softbound, 75 pages, with bibliography. Some charts and illustrations. ISBN 1-885972-18-0.

Blue Rûna: Edred's Shorter Works Vol. III, Edred Thorsson. Texas: Rûna-Raven Press, 2001. Booklet, 45 pages, with charts and tables. ISBN 1-885972-16-4.

These two small collections encompass some of the best of Stephen Flowers's (Edred Thorsson's) shorter essays, and represent the two poles at which he operates as a writer. *Studia Germanica* features a sampling of Flowers's more academic work, while *Blue Runa* is the third in a series to present the more interdisciplinary, speculative ruminations that have established his "popular" reputation. Of course these poles invariably meet, and it is to Flowers's great advantage that his career as an esoteric writer has been developed against a solid academic background. Conversely, his academic writing has never been hemmed in by scholarly conventionality.

Studia Germanica is divided into four sections: Runic Studies, Old Norse Studies, Old English Studies, and Middle High German Studies. Of particular interest is Flowers's "Socio-Cultic Aspects of the Runes During the Migration Ages." Originally penned over twenty years ago, shortly after the formation of the Rune-Gild, this essay provides the justification for his controversial thesis that the runic tradition was disseminated and maintained by "an institutional network of runemasters and apprentices throughout the Germanic territory." This is, of course, the model upon which the Gild structure is based, and receives its traditional mandate. The remaining pieces deal with the ideological subtexts found in the Germanic literature composed during the periods concerned. Flowers's examines the initiatory structure of Ulrich von Zatzikhoven's *Lanzelet*, and delineates the idea of intergenerational rebirth in the Sagas. In his meditation on Walther's "Do der summer komen was?" he illuminates the attitude of pagan immanentism (joy in this world) underlying the poem's outwardly dualist piety. That similarly heathen concepts persisted under the "mask" of Christianity is another support for Flowers's contention that paganism can be revived in the modern era. The Gods have never left, but simply been driven underground.

This is expressed more radically in Flowers's famous (infamous?) "The Secret of the Gothick God of Darkness," which was originally published in *Fringeware Review*, but should now be more widely available as one of the four essays in *Blue Rûna*. The spirit of Woden is the Gothick spirit, the nightside shadow behind the Appolonian sun of Western Classicism. This spirit can be found in writers like Byron, Novalis, and Poe, painters like Doré, and in even more contemporary figures like Lovecraft and Anne Rice. But "the mystery and the secret of Woden is not that 'knowledge' of him is passed along through clandestine cults or even through books and texts—but rather that such knowledge is actually encoded in the genetic material of those who are descended from him. . . . Runic (mysterious) information is stored in the blood, where it lies dormant until the right stimulus is applied." The essay "How to be a Heathen," based on a talk delivered to the Pagan Student Alliance of The University of Texas, picks up a similar thread with Flowers's assertion that the decision to be a pagan cannot be an arbitrary, subjective one, but must acknowledge the "culture grid"—and one's own ethnicity in particular.

"The Alchemy of Yggdrasill" is a brief description of Germanic cosmogonic myth, as rich in complexity as any Hermetic doctrine. "The Way of Woden" is a concise—but fairly elementary—introduction to the Odinic archetype.

Joshua Buckley

The Myths and Gods of India by Alain Danielou. Rochester, Vermont: Inner Traditions, 1991. (Originally published as *Hindu Polytheism* by Bollingen Foundation, New York, 1964.) Softbound, 441 pages, with bibliography and index. Illustrated with 32 black and white photographic plates, and 17 drawings or charts. ISBN 0-89281-354-7.

Typically, those who profess an interest in what might be called "Indo-European spirituality" gravitate toward either the Celtic or Germanic traditions. The Indian tradition tends to be ignored. In part, this is because present-day Indians seem so different from us. We think of their culture and philosophy as "Eastern," as alien. Physically, the Indians look very different from those of European descent (though higher caste Indians tend to look very European, right down to lighter skin and hair, and sometimes blue eyes). But if we wish to rediscover the religion and traditions of our ancestors, what better place is there to begin than with India? The oldest Indo-European texts are the Vedas, after all. To be sure, it is hard to separate what comes from the ancient Aryans in Indian religion, myth, and mysticism, and what was contributed by the indigenous peoples conquered by the Aryans. But the same problem exists with respect to the Celtic and Germanic traditions. In addition, we know far more about the culture and religion of the ancient Aryans who invaded India, than we do about the culture and religion of the Celts and the Vikings. For one thing, more ancient texts survive in India. Therefore, anyone wishing to re-construct the "old ways" must become deeply immersed in all things Indian.

It is a cliché to state this in a review, but I write the following with total sincerity: if you read only one book on Hinduism, it must be Danielou's *Myths and Gods of India*. Indeed, it is hard to imagine why one would need to read any other. Danielou's account of Hinduism is exhaustive, profound, and detailed. The book contains, first of all, cogent arguments on behalf of polytheism. It details the Indian cosmogony and cosmology; the nature of Space, Time, and Thought; the nature of Brahman and Maya. Danielou gives a complete description of every major Hindu divinity in terms of his or her function, myths, and symbolism. He details the minor gods and genii. He discusses the theory behind Mantras and Yantras. There is even extensive coverage of ritual, and the manner in which the gods must be worshiped.

Alain Danielou was born in 1907 in Paris. He was a true Renaissance man, trained in music, painting, and dance. He gave recitals and exhibited his paintings. Danielou was also an avid sportsman: a canoeing champion, and an expert race-car driver. He was also homosexual. Danielou and his gay lover ventured to India, traveling around in a deluxe, Silverstream camper imported from southern California, photographing erotic sculpture. They later settled down in a Maharajah's estate on the banks of the Ganges and devoted themselves to Sanskrit, Hinduism, music, and entertaining. Danielou gradually "went native" and stayed in India many years. In time, he became known throughout the world as an authority on Indian music and culture. He published works dealing with Hindu religion, society, music, sculpture, architecture, and other topics. It was Danielou, more than anyone else, who was responsible for popularizing Indian music in the West (among other things, he was the "discoverer" of Ravi Shankar). Danielou died in 1994.

The Myths and Gods of India is a delight to read, but it can also be treated as a reference work for those needing a clear and accurate account of various gods or Hindu religious concepts. For the student of Indo-European culture, the book is a treasure trove. Indeed, those who are familiar with the Indo-European comparativist school of Georges Dumézil, Jaan Puhvel, and others, will get the most out of this book. I will offer a few brief examples here.

Danielou writes on page 27 that "Human beings, according to their nature and stage of development, are inclined toward ... different aspects of the Cosmic Being. Those in whom consciousness is predominant worship the gods (deva); those in whom action or existence predominates worship genii (yaksha) and antigods (asura); and those in whom enjoyment or sensation predominates worship ghosts and spirits (bhuta and preta)." This suggests, of course, the Indo-European tripartition identified by Dumézil.

On page 66 we learn that Soma was "brought to earth by a large hawk," just as Odin, in the form of an eagle, brought mead to the Æsir. On page 87 we are told that "The earth is also represented as a goddess, or as a cow that feeds everyone with her milk. She is the mother of life, the substance of all things." What can this remind us of, except the Norse Audumla?

There also seem to be parallels between Agni (the god of fire) and Loki. Like Loki, Agni is an outcast among the gods. Danielou tells us further that, "The fire of destruction, Agni's most fearful form, was born of the primeval waters and remains hidden under the sea, ever ready to destroy the world" (p. 89). This is reminiscent of the Midgard Serpent, the progeny of Loki. Page 151: "When Vishnu sleeps, the universe dissolves into its formless state, represented as the causal ocean. The remnants of manifestation are represented as the serpent Remainder (Sesa) coiled upon itself and floating upon the abysmal waters."

Danielou tells us (p. 92) that "the sun . . . is envisaged [by the Hindus] under two aspects. As one of the spheres, one of the Vasus, the physical sun is the celestial form of fire, of agni. As the source of light, of warmth, of life, of knowledge, the solar energy is the source of all life, represented in the twelve sons-of-the-Primordial-Vastness (Adityas), the twelve sovereign principles." In *Futhark* (pp. 51–52), Edred Thorsson tells us that "The sun was known by two special names in the North. . . . Sol represents the phenomenon, while sunna is the *noumenon*, the spiritual power residing in the concept." Also, the "twelve sons-of-the-Primordial-Vastness" immanent within the solar energy must remind us of the twelve sig-runes that make up the Wewelsburg "sun-wheel" of Karl Maria Wiligut.

Page 99: "When the gods were receiving the ambrosia of immortality, the Moon [Soma; equivalent to Mead] detected the antigod Rahu disguised as a god. Because of the Moon Rahu had to die, but although his head was severed from his body, he could not truly die, for he had tasted the ambrosia. His head remained alive." Mimir?

Page 103: "Rudra, the lord of tears, is said to have sprung from the forehead of the Immense-Being (Brahma) and, at the command of that god, to have divided himself into a male form and a female form . . ." Athena?

Page 103: "The Maruts (immortals) are a restless, warlike troupe of flashy young men, transposition in space of the hordes of young warriors called the marya (mortals). . . . They are the embodiment of moral and heroic deeds and of the exuberance of youth." Maruts=Einherjar; Marya=Indo-European *Männerbünde*.

Page 104: "The Maruts are the friends of Indra, the wielder of the thunderbolt . . ." Thor? Page 110: Indra's thunderbolt is "shaped like a mace . . ." Page 111: "Indra had been the deity worshiped among the pastoral people of Vraja." Again, just as Thor was.

Page 118: Varuna "is the ruler of the 'other side,' of the invisible world." He is "said to be an antigod, a magician." Odin? Page 119: "He catches the evildoers and binds them with his noose." Criminals sacrificed to Odin were hung. Varuna also "knows the track of birds in the sky," just as Odin knows the track of Huginn and Muninn.

Page 132: The god of death is named Yama, which means "Twin" (Ymir). "Yama's brother is the lawgiver, Manu, who shares with him the title of progenitor of mankind." Yama "owns two four-eyed dogs with wide nostrils . . . They watch the path of the dead." What can this remind us of except the Greek hellhound, Cerberus?

Page 138: "In contrast to the gods, the antigods [asura] are the inclinations of the senses which, by their nature, belong to the obscuring tendency, and which delight in life, that is, in the activities of the life energies in all the fields of sensation." This is an accurate description of the Norse Vanir. Asura is cognate with Æsir, so, oddly enough, the term shifts meaning either in the Norse or the Indian tradition.

Page 159: The four ages (yugas) are represented as white (the golden age), red, yellow, and black (the dark age). The stages of the alchemical process (as represented in the West) are black, white, yellow, and red.

Pages 243–245 detail the Upanishadic account of creation out of the primal man Purusha: "He desired a second. He became as large as a woman and man in close embrace. He divided himself into two. From him arose a husband and a wife. Hence it is that everyone is but half a being. The vacant space is filled by a wife." This is extraordinarily similar to the account of the creation of men and woman given by Aristophanes in Plato's *Symposium*. The world is then created out of Purusha's body—just as the world is created out of Ymir's body in Norse myth. "The virile member was separated; from this virile member came forth semen and from semen the earthly waters." This is identical to the account of the creation of the ocean in the Greek myth of the sacrifice of Ouranos by Kronos.

The account of the hero Kumara/Skana (pp. 297–300) is strikingly like the saga of Sigurd, and also similar in some respects to the *Parzival* of Wolfram von Eschenbach.

The "essences" (apsaras; pp. 304–305) are "water nymphs, eternally young women who are the courtesans and dancers of heaven." Rhine Maidens? "They are depicted as uncommonly beautiful, with lotus eyes, slender waists, and large hips. By their languid postures and sweet words they rob those who see them of their wisdom and their intellect." Sirens? "One can master them by stealing their clothes while they bathe. They choose lovers among the dead fallen on the battlefield." Valkyries?

The above merely scratches the surface of this immensely rich text, which demands careful study and multiple readings.

Collin Cleary

Virtue, Success, Pleasure, and Liberation: The Four Aims of Life in Ancient India, **Alain Danielou. Introduction by Robert Lawlor. Rochester, Vermont: Inner Traditions, 1993. Softbound, 182 pages, including sources and index. ISBN 0-89281-218-4.**

One hears a great deal today about "multiculturalism," and the multicultural society. We (i.e., we Americans) are told that ours is a multicultural society. But, curiously, multiculturalism is also spoken of as a goal. What this reveals is that multiculturalism is not simply the recognition and affirmation of the fact that the U.S.A. is made up of different people from different cultural backgrounds. Instead, multiculturalism is an ideology which is predicated on cultural relativism. Its proponents want to convince people that (a) all cultures are equally good, rich, interesting, and wholesome, and that (b) a multicultural society can exist in which no one culture is dominant. The first idea is absurd, the second is impossible.

The apostles of multiculturalism are moved less by a genuine desire to "celebrate diversity" than by a hatred for Northern European culture, which is the semi-official, dominant culture of America. Indeed, multiculturalists generally nurture the most naive and simplistic ideas of what a culture is. Their conception of "culture" is fixated at the perceptual level: culture is costume, music, dance, decoration, food. What is essential to culture, however, is a certain *Weltanschauung:* a view of the world, and of human nature. It is in their response to these *Weltanschauungen* that multiculturalists reveal their true colors, for they tolerate and permit only those elements of a culture's *Weltanschauung* that do not conflict with liberal ideology.

Out of one side of their mouths, the multiculturalists tell us that one cannot judge a culture, that morality is culturally relative, that cultures are not better or worse, just "different," and that we must revel in these differences. Thus, the English do not drive on the "wrong" side of the road, merely the left side. But when it's not a matter of traffic laws, but a matter of severed clitorises, then the other, louder side of the multiculturalists' mouths open, and they tell us that this sort of thing isn't just different, it's evil.

In addition to this, one also sees that multiculturalism involves a relentless trivialization of important cultural differences. Thus, college students are encouraged to see religion almost as a matter of "local color." Isn't it wonderful that the Indians cook such spicy food, and worship such colorful gods! Isn't it all terribly charming? They are further encouraged to view religion as a thoroughly irrational affair. Rather than encouraging an appreciation for different faiths, what this produces is a condescending attitude, and resistance to taking the claims of religion seriously when they conflict with the "rational" agenda of modern liberalism.

Indeed, multiculturalism is so anti-cultural that one is tempted to see behind it an even deeper, more sinister agenda. Perhaps the whole idea is to deliberately gut the world's cultures, reducing their differences to matters of dress and cuisine, and to replace those earthborn guts with a plastic, Naugahyde culture of secularism, scientism, and egalitarianism. Why? Because real, significant cultural differences make it very hard for our corporations to do business overseas and to sell their wares. Solution: homogenization masquerading as "celebration of diversity."

The multiculturalists are right when they declare that *de facto,* the United States is a multicultural society. But there has never been a multicultural society in the history of the world in which there was not one dominant culture which provided a framework allowing the others to co-exist. To the multiculturalist, the unacknowledged framework is modern liberalism. I will assume that I do not have to rehearse for my readers the many arguments for why modern liberalism is untenable as a long-term societal framework.

Where should we look, then, for a framework for a multicultural society? Why not look to the Indian caste system? It was the caste system that allowed Aryan and non-Aryan to co-exist peacefully in India for centuries.

The liberals will immediately object that the caste system is oppressive and unjust. In *Virtue, Success, Pleasure and Liberation*, however, Alain Danielou argues that the caste system is actually a supremely just and peaceful arrangement. It is just because it is built on a recognition of real human difference; a "celebration of diversity," if you will. Aristotle held that justice is treating equals equally, and unequals unequally. If people are not the same, then it is a mistake to treat them as if they are. The caste system is built on the idea that some human beings are born to work, others to fight and lead, and others to pray. The caste system gives to each human being a place, a community, a code of ethics, and a sense of identity and pride. Danielou points out that although the system involves hierarchy, each level of the hierarchy is regarded as intrinsically valuable and as essential. Each plays a role that is regarded as important and indispensable. Thus, it is the caste system which truly affirms that different groups are merely different, not better or worse.

Is Danielou whitewashing the caste system? Consider the words he quotes from the *Mahabharata*: "There is no superior caste. The Universe is the work of the Immense Being. The beings created by him were only divided into castes according to their aptitude." But what of individuals born to the wrong caste? For example, what of a child born to the merchant class who shows aptitude to be a priest or scholar? Such things happen. Danielou tells us that exceptional individuals are allowed to live "outside" the caste system, and are accepted as valuable members of the society as a whole. Modern society is structured on the premise that everyone is exceptional and can make up his mind what he wants to do. Given that sort of freedom, most people get lost—as witness the modern phenomenon of the "slacker," or the flotsam and jetsam going in and out of psychiatrists' offices every day.

Despite what I have said, this book is not a treatise on the caste system, but on the four things that all human lives must possess or achieve in order to be complete. In discussing virtue, success, pleasure, and liberation, Danielou quotes extensively from ancient Indian texts, offering us an abundance of excellent advice about how to understand life and to live well. Indeed, this is really a book about how to lead a truly human life.

Danielou places the four aims in a cosmic context, showing how the same fourfold division is present in all levels of reality. It is present, of course, in the four castes (worker/artisan, producer/merchant, warrior/aristocrat, priest/scholar), and in the four stages of biological development (childhood, youth, maturity, old age), the four seasons, the four elements, the four races of humanity (black, yellow, red, white), the cycle of ages (yugas), the four bodily functions (digestion, assimilation, circulation, excretion), and the four points of the compass (in this order, significantly: south, east, west, north).

This is an excellent companion volume to Danielou's *Myths and Gods of India*.

Collin Cleary

Getica—Jordanes's History of the Goths. **Presented at www.harbornet.com/folks/theedrich/hive/ (viewable on the Mediævalia menu).**

A millennium and a half ago, the mighty western Roman Empire, one of the two deep taproots of the modern West, collapsed in agony, exhaustion, and gore. The primary reason for this collapse was economic: the people were no longer willing to foot the bill for the vast bureaucracy and military needed to keep the Empire going. Taxes were so oppressive that, even in a system in which the majority were slaves, it came to a point where the taxpayers had nothing more to give.

Into this moribund system came the Germanic warriors from the north and east. In the beginning they were used as cheap mercenaries. Julius Caesar (100–44 B.C.E.) conquered Gaul with their help, laying the foundations for modern France. There are many reports handed down from antiquity concerning their relationships with the Romans, both hostile and friendly.

The most powerful and threatening of all these peoples were the Goths, who called themselves the Gut-þiuda, the "Gothic people." The "h" in the word "Goth" is a result of the fact that the preceding "t" was aspirated (pronounced with a puff of air, exactly as in modern English or German), whereas the Latin "t" was unaspirated.

From about 200 to 370, the Goths ruled over a vast empire in the area of what is today western Russia and Ukraine. But in the 370s of the current era, the Huns, a mixed Turkic-Mongol people, broke in from the East with a new, highly effective mode of warfare: the mounted archer. With extreme cruelty they subjected all the peoples of northeastern Europe to their sway, including the Goths, who by this time had become divided into western (Tervingians/*Tairwingos*—"Forest dwellers"—later Visigoths) and eastern (*Greutungos* —"Plains dwellers"—later Ostrogoths). The Visigoths escaped to the Roman Empire, eventually ending up in Spain, while the Ostrogoths remained and fought under the Huns until after the death of Attila and the Huns' defeat by a coalition of their formerly subject tribes led by the Gepidi *(Gibidos)*. Those Ostrogoths who remained outside of the Roman Empire or returned to the north became the source of the great Germanic lays, sagas, and epics such as the *Niebelungenlied, The Battle of the Goths and the Huns*, and many others. Those who moved south eventually set up a kingdom in the 490s in northern Italy under their king, Theodoric (Þiudareik), but were in the end destroyed by the forces of the Byzantine Empire under Justinian and subsequent emperors in the 550s.

In the year 551 a Roman Catholic (but probably originally Arian-Christian) cleric named Jordanes undertook to write a history of the Goths in the Latin language. Jordanes himself, probably a half-Goth with an Alan mother ("Jordanes" is not a Gothic name), was not very well versed in Latin and his text is tortured, to say the least. There is scarcely a single sentence in his writings which is not replete with every possible kind of orthographical, lexical, and grammatical error.

To begin with, the title normally bestowed on his Gothic history, "*Getica,*" is itself an error. Jordanes, as also many earlier historians, confused the Goths with a much earlier people of the area north of the Black Sea known as the *Getae*. So the work should actually have been termed "*Gothica.*" An alternative title, *De Origine Actibusque Getarum* (On the Origin and Deeds of the *Getae*) suffers from this same confusion: its last word should be "*Gothorum.*"

The author was mainly concerned to show how all of the works of man are ultimately futile and only God could provide peace and stability to the human soul. To this end he also wrote another history of the Roman Empire (the *Romana*). He interrupted the writing of this work to write the *Getica*, then returned to finish the *Romana* after he was through with the Gothic history.

Despite Jordanes's botched Latin, and the partly mythological history and geographical excursus with which he prefixes the *Getica*, his work contains a great deal about the early Goths which can be found nowhere else. He wrote his history in Constantinople at a time when the Gothic kingdom of Theodoric/Þiudareik was long past and the Goths were in disrepute. His source for much of the narrative was a much longer, twelve-volume work by a senator named Cassiodorus, *On the Origin and Deeds of the Goths from Long Ago and Descending through Generations and Kings to Now*. But this work disappeared, very likely destroyed by Cassiodorus himself in order to avoid suspicion of being pro-Gothic, which in the Constantinople of that time was politically incorrect and could even have led to his death.

Jordanes tells tales of unceasing battle, beginning from the egress of the Goths from Scandinavia to the final warfare of the Ostrogothic armies against the Eastern Roman Empire up to 551. The eight-decade period under Hun domination was especially violent. To a modern American living in relative peace, these stories of repeated mass slaughters are almost unbelievable. Yet it all happened.

Since Jordanes's history is generally difficult to obtain, I have placed it on my website, the Latin and modern English side-by-side. I have also converted the Latinized names back into their Gothic forms, adding translations of the names. The reader will notice that perhaps ninety percent of the Germanic names have to do with warfare or power. This faithfully reflects the situation of those bloodthirsty times. For those who can read Latin, I have also polished the Latin up a bit by correcting some of Jordanes's more egregious linguistic errors. But not too much. His language reflects the disintegrating popular Latin of the sixth century, when the foundations of the Romance languages were beginning to form. In some respects, the Latin seems to me to be leaning in a "proto-Spanish" direction (e.g., "brother" and "sister" are rendered with *"germanus"* and *"germana,"* not the standard *"frater"* and *"soror"*—cf. Spanish *"hermano"* and *"hermana"*).

Although the Goths went down to bloody defeat, they so weakened the western Roman Empire that their kinsmen—the Lombards, the Franks, the Angles and Saxons—were able to move into its depleted territories and set up nations which combine the best of Mediterranean and Germanic cultures. Perhaps one of the more interesting legacies is the ancient Gothic name Amala-reik "Amal ruler," which has come down to us in the modern form we know as America.

Þeedrich

Women in Old Norse Society by Jenny Jochens. Hardbound, 266 pages, with bibliography and index. Ithaca: Cornell University Press, 1995. ISBN 0-8014-3165-4.

The status of women in pre-Christian and early Christian Europe has been a source of considerable debate. Drawing on source material from the late 9th and mid-13th centuries in Iceland and Norway, *Women in Old Norse Society* sheds considerable light on the issue, providing an intimate glimpse into the lives of women in this period of cultural and religious transformation. By focusing on the day-to-day domestic concerns of these communities (and the women who ensured their smooth functioning), Jochens has crafted a work of cultural history unique both in focus and in its at times unorthodox (and, presumably, feminist) perspective.

Perhaps one of the most notable benefits women derived from Christianity was the right of consent regarding marriage. Prior to the conversion, pagan marriages were primarily economic affairs in which the prospective bride had little or no say. Of all the pre-Christian marriage customs celebrated in the North, only two were incorporated into the Christian marriage ceremony: engagement (the period during which the "bride price" was negotiated), and the "giving away" of the bride. Needless to say, both are vestiges of a system in which the woman was viewed as an economic commodity, and the orderly transfer of familial property was paramount. But while on first glance the institutionalization of female consent might seem an advance, the reality was more ambiguous. Divorce was common before the conversion, and easy to obtain. While women might not have been able to choose their marriage partners, they could dissolve a marriage for any number of reasons—male violence and even mutual incompatibility are commonly cited. Heathen marriage never had the binding character of Christian marriage, and illegitimacy was common. It was typical for men to take a number of mistresses. To a lesser extent, female infidelity was not unusual.

One of Jochens's more interesting claims is that sexual promiscuity has been downplayed in the sagas, due to the Christianizing influence of the saga writers. For women, one of the more negative ramifications of Christianity involved the Church's efforts to curb this untamed sexuality. Whereas the heathen Scandinavians had always placed the blame in cases of sexual aggression with the male, Christianity increasingly emphasized the culpability of women in instances where Christian morality failed to hamper passions. Though the Church proclaimed "gender equality and the extension of the Christian family beyond inherited tribal and social restrictions," the reality was that women came to be viewed as unclean vessels of lustfulness and sin.

In Iceland, the Christians were forced to grant two concessions to the heathen population: the maintenance of the horse sacrifice, and the continued acceptance of infanticide. The latter is perhaps one of the more troubling aspects of old Germanic society, and Jochens provides an ample explication of the varying rationales and social conventions surrounding the practice. Exposure was often employed in cases of physical weakness or deformity (which may have reached epidemic proportions in Norway, due to inbreeding), but could ultimately be carried out for any number of reasons. The life or death of the child was entirely the prerogative of the father. Presented with the newborn, he could accept or reject it at will. As is often the case, female children were rejected more frequently than males. In certain respects, the (eventual) abolition of infanticide could be viewed as an advantage for women. In a broader perspective, however, the Christian emphasis on caring for the unfit (the severely handicapped, etc.), as well as the elimination of other eugenic measures (the castration of beggars, limitations on the number of children allowed to poor families) probably helped to undermine a society forced to survive in a less charitably-minded physical environment.

Many of the social aspects of women's lives remained unchanged despite the conversion, of course, and Jochens emphasizes the continuity in the everyday routines of female existence. Her detailed descriptions of women's working lives, leisure activities, and sexual proclivities make for fascinating reading. Particularly detailed is her discussion of "homespun." Produced in surplus quantities during the Middle Ages in Iceland, homespun eventually became the standard medium of exchange.

Though ultimately controlled by men, the central role of women in producing this essential economic asset is used to highlight the important role of women in sustaining the Old Norse world.

An excellent resource concerning aspects of Old Norse life typically neglected elsewhere.

Joshua Buckley

The Old World Kitchen: The Rich Tradition of European Peasant Cooking by Elizabeth Luard. Softcover, 538 pages, with some illustrations. New York: Akadine Press, 2000. ISBN 1-888173-50-5.

This amazing, recently re-issued text should not rightfully be called a cookbook, as its instructive value lends it the quality of a reference work as much as a collection of recipes. From the earliest and simplest of peasant meals to the most elaborate, the author will teach you things about your European heritage that you might never read elsewhere. I rarely pick it up without being delighted at learning some new item of trivia. To cite one example, Luard's family is French—Huguenots who fled to London after the Edict of Nantes. Having little money, the Huguenot population lived frugally, and one of their habits was to make a soup of the unwanted oxtails that accompanied the hides sent to the tanners. In a strange twist of fate, Oxtail Soup caught on with the Anglo-Saxons and is now known as a quintessentially English soup.

Peasant cookery, by its very nature, revolved around self-sufficiency and deep knowledge of the land and its fruits. Rural folk in early times had few possessions. Most homes would have three cooking implements: a boiling pot, a frying pan, and a kettle, along with a communal bowl for eating, wooden spoons, perhaps a single cup and single knife, shared. There would be a single heat source, and initially there was no access to imported food or spices. Children often ate standing up. But what they managed to do with this limited equipment would astound a modern housewife. And the chronicles of early travelers attest to the excellent health of these hardworking folk. The author cites F. P. Armitage in his description of the classic peasant diet of the long-lived Georgians: "black bread, rice, wheat cakes, beans, raw green vegetables, cheese, milk both fresh and soured, and fish—salted, smoked and dried."

These foods more or less characterize the type of recipes you will find in this collection. But don't be misled. Along with the bone-marrow broths and vegetable stews you will find Danish pastries, classic treatments of meat such as roast beef with Yorkshire pudding, fancy *paellas*, rich strudels, sturdy breads (currently resurrected as "artisan breads" in yuppie bakeries), flaky turnovers, casseroles . . . many, many old favorites in their most authentic form, and many traditional dishes you probably haven't ever heard of.

But these are not, for the most part, low-calorie, so be warned. Sibiu-Saxon Soup—or *Eintopfgericht*, a Saxon recipe from Rumania—contains cabbage, onions, herbs, knockwurst, heavy cream, and egg yolks, poured over day-old bread. Faithfully represented are both the garlic-and-oil cultures of Southern Europe and the butter-and-dumpling cultures of the North, as well as everything in between. Luard does not turn a blind eye to distinctive national characteristics; rather, she celebrates them here in the most joyful way. The Bulgarians are the best vegetable gardeners, she asserts, while rural Finns do not like the oatmeal the Scots have raised to an art form.

In fact, what may strike you most about this collection is that it is an excellent demonstration of bioregionalism. It indirectly shows the culinary ethnic evolutionary pattern as a function of native natural resources. For example, polenta is thought by most to be a cornmeal pudding, but the original polenta was made from chestnut flour. In olden times, before the blight, there were plantations of chestnut trees growing in the hills of Italy. When corn was introduced from the New World, it was found to grow so well that it replaced the chestnut as a peasant staple, leading to pellagra (a protein-deficiency disease) among the poor. For those interested in the effects which geographic diversity exerts on the human inhabitants of various eco-niches and their resulting cultures, this book is a gift from the gods. My own theory is that the edibles available in a given area may influence the physical make-up (such as metabolism) of a population in addition to contributing to their unique repertoire of dishes. Wilson's Syndrome and other thyroid disorders seem to be rife, and the problem appears to be getting worse. Some medical authorities attribute thyroid problems to a lack of iodine in the diet. Perhaps adding

Sloke as a side dish to the main meal would reverse this strange trend, given that some European peoples may have initially evolved on a diet rich in seaweed.

Nor does Luard neglect the Celts. She includes a recipe for Haggis, the classic Scots dish cooked in the stomach of a sheep, quoting T. F. Henderson in his 1893 book *Old World Scotland:* "In the peasant's home it was set in the center of the table, all gathering round with their horn spoons, and it was *'deil tak'* the hindmost." And there are *Boxty* and *Colcannon*, Celtic Samhain dishes having their roots in bonfire traditions. The famous Scottish *Cock-a-leekie*, related to the ancient English dishes *Malachi* and *Gallimawfrey*, is featured as well. Originally this soup was made using only bone stock and leeks. In later centuries chicken was added as poultry became more affordable, and "the loser in a cockfight used to be recommended, since its sinews would be firm and give body to the soup".

Some dishes reveal an interesting functionality underlying the choice of components or design. In the recipe for the Belgian dish *paling in't groen* (green eel stew), Luard reveals that the "green" comes from the 1½ lbs. of green herbs, with a large proportion of sorrel to flavor and color the concoction. Why so much sorrel? It has a high content of oxalic acid, which dissolves the small bones. Cornish pasties were originally fashioned with a "handle" on one end, so that the fieldworker or miner could stick his thumb through it and carry it around. They were sometimes baked with a savory filling at one end and a sweet one at the other, so you could have your meal and dessert all in one easy piece.

The wealth of historical trivia is worth the price of the book alone. *Bouillabaisse*, the famous fish soup from Marseille, has the key ingredient saffron, which some maintain is a soporific. Alexander the Great once complained that he found his army dozing on a crocus-covered hillside (saffron is extracted from that flower). Take that one with a grain of salt, but this item a few chapters earlier sounds more likely: popular myth cites Marco Polo as having brought pasta back from China and introduced it to the Italians in or around 1271. But the Italians were actually making macaroni and ravioli long before then, as Boccaccio describes in his *Decameron*. In fact, Luard suggests that it may have been the Italian adventurer who taught the Chinese how to refine their own noodle-making methods! The earliest European pastas were variations on *trahana* (Bulgaria and Greece) or *tarhonya* (Hungary) a grated or rolled-dough noodle which the author suggests is "the most primitive noodle dough in the world." It is made by kneading flour and eggs into little pellets, drying them in the sun, then storing them indefinitely, later to be thrown into a soup or stew or simply boiled as a starchy accompaniment.

Luard even discusses hunting and slaughtering methods, and rightfully so: in rural communities hunting and sustenance could not be separated as they can in the more sterile, industrialized society we live in today. Andalusian peasant boys, for example, caught birds with bait that they hung on slip-knotted threads attached to kites. They would fly the kites, the birds would take the bait on the wing, stick their heads in the noose, and the boys would pull the drawstring and yank the bird out of the air, "like reeling in trout." And how to catch frogs in the traditional way for *Grenouilles sautés au beurre?* A cane rod, line, lead weight, and hook baited with a scrap of red rag.

Luard includes suggestions for accompaniments, carefully thought-out as to regional and seasonal appropriateness, as well as historical and cultural correctness. Nevertheless, she is not a total stickler and will suggest more creative treatments if the result is delightful enough. In true peasant tradition, she even indicates which dishes will taste better the next day! She dissects the various influences on European cuisine, discussing the culinary remnants from the Ottoman occupation and other cultural aftereffects. Rhubarb, for one, is a native of Tibet, but was so suited to the cold climate that it was adopted by Northern Europeans. And there she inserts a recipe for a lovely rhubarb dumpling with custard (English).

The book is also an adventure in material culture. Luard goes into great detail regarding specialized implements employed to make certain foods, such as the beautifully patterned irons with extra-long handles used to make Scandinavian fire-baked *goro* (cardamom crackers). For the benefit of the purists, she explains how to make everything from scratch—yogurt, sausages, noodles, you name it. She details the different regional breeds of food animals, and the areas that gave rise to them. There is an entire section on shepherd's meats, with recipes for lamb and mutton stews.

At the end, Luard has a chapter on the rustic kitchen: herbs, spices, mushrooms and fungi, various types of ethnic meats and cheeses, salted and cured fish and the methods used, origins of names, etc. One small drawback is that there are only a few scattered black-and-white drawings and sketches for illustration, but no color photos. So the home cook has no actual idea of what the dish is supposed to look like when preparing a recipe for the first time.

In summary, you may not have access to a peat fire or fresh goat milk, but many of these recipes can be recreated in our own homes with whatever ingredients we can obtain, until such a day arrives that we return to a lifestyle more in tune with the ways of our ancestors and in closer harmony with natural cycles. Elisabeth Luard's *Old World Kitchen* may have taken 20 years to write, but as an addition to the literature of Western cuisine, it is timeless.

Elizabeth Griffin

Woodcut by Albrecht Dürer, 1514.

Music Reviews

Waterson: Carthy—*Broken Ground* (Topic)

Originally dubbed the Mariners, then the Folksons, the group the world would eventually know as the Watersons was formed in the early 1960s by Norma, Mike, and Lal Waterson, along with cousin John Harrison (unlike the Ramones, for example, the Watersons really *were* family). Perhaps more than any other outfit in the genre, the Watersons represented the best of the folk revival that swept the British Isles in the late '60s and early '70s— mindful of tradition, but brimming with youthful enthusiasm and a willingness to innovate. Their debut, *Frost and Fire*—which featured a collection of ritual songs based on the heathen calendar— proved an instant sensation when it debuted in 1965, and two subsequent recordings followed. But then, perhaps exhausted after three years of touring the burgeoning club circuit, the group disbanded. In 1972 the hiatus came to an end with *Bright Phoebus*, an album that must have come as a surprise to former fans. Like contemporaries Steeleye Span and Fairport Convention, *Bright Phoebus* seemed to indicate a shift away from tradition in favor of new material and rock 'n' roll arrangements. Nevertheless, 1975's *For Pence and Spicy Ale* saw the family returning to their roots with a line-up consisting entirely of traditional songs, performed *a cap - pella*. Several more records materialized throughout the ensuing years, along with a slew of solo projects and collaborative efforts.

When Norma Waterson and Martin Carthy married, a sort of first family of English traditional music was inaugurated. Carthy was himself one of the pioneers of the traditional scene. Recently awarded an M.B.E. for "services to English music," his style has been emulated by Bob Dylan and Simon and Garfunkel (whose "Scarborough Fair" is based on Carthy's version). Some time after John Harrison's departure, Carthy joined the Waterson line-up as a permanent addition. When Mike and Lal left the fold, Waterson: Carthy was born.

Perhaps the most notable addition to this new folk "super group" has been Martin and Norma's pulchritudinous daughter, Eliza. With her day-glow hair and body piercings, Eliza has established herself as a solo performer in her own right. Her latest album, *Angels and Cigarettes*, is an audacious blend of traditional and contemporary styles (not to mention erotically-charged lyrics) calculated to appeal to an alt-rock audience.

But as a collective, Waterson: Carthy has remained true to tradition. Released via the British label Topic (who, with 60+ years of recordings to their credit, are something of a "tradition" themselves), *Broken Ground* is as lively and vital as anything produced during the salad days of the revival. Most of the pieces here were culled from local singers, as well as the collections of folklorists like Cecil Sharp and folk-traditional luminary Ewan MacColl. Reels and waltzes—including the Quebecois "Waltz Clog"—also figure prominently. Perhaps the most unexpected number is the albums final cut, "The Bald-Headed End of the Broom." Prefaced with a morris tune entitled "The Royal Forrester," this is a rousing marching song performed with great fanfare to the accompaniment of The Phoenix New Orleans Parade Band.

Hopefully, the Waterson: Carthy legacy will march on well into the new millennium.

Joshua Buckley

Various Artists—*Anthology of Indian Classical Music: A Tribute to Alain Danielou* (The Unesco Collection: Auvidis Music)

This three-CD set is a re-issue of recordings made in India in the early 1960s by Alain Danielou, under the patronage of UNESCO. This was the first anthology released in the West to present Indian music as "serious" music rather than as "folklore" or "exotica." (In other words, this is not your Dad's Martin Denny collection.) For more information on Alain Danielou, see the review of his book *Myths and Gods of India* elsewhere in this issue. Suffice it to say here that it was Danielou, more than any other person, who awakened the world to the beauty and mystery of Indian music. It was Alain Danielou who discovered Ravi Shankar, and who introduced the West to Bismillah Khan, Ali Akbar Kahn, and the Dagar brothers.

Danielou's book *Music and the Power of Sound: The Influence of Tuning and Interval on Consciousness* (Inner Traditions, 1995) compares the basic scales of India, China, and classical Greece. He argues that modern, western music is decadent because it derives from the confused Greek scale. His conclusion, not surprisingly, is that Indian music is superior.

Danielou was a Breton. Could there have been something in his Celtic soul which responded to the sounds of Indian music? This may seem a strange question, but consider the following. Today, in County Kerry, Ireland, historian Bryan McMahon plays an unusual game with any Indians who happen to visit his neck of the woods. He hums or whistles a bit of traditional Irish music and asks them to finish the tune in any way they please. McMahon says that they usually finish the tune as if they knew it already (source: *Hinduism Today*, "Common Ground of European Celts and Indian Vedic Hindus").

This CD set is divided into "North" (CD 1 and half of CD 2) and "South" (the remainder of CD 2, and CD 3). Listeners will immediately notice a difference between the music of the two regions. The music of the North is what we typically think of as "Indian music." Sitars, flutes, and sarangis abound. The sound is elegant, cool, noble, and controlled. The music of the South is heavily vocal. It is ecstatic, repetitive, hot, and passionate. One would expect a heavier influence of European sounds on the music of the North, since it was into the North that the ancient Aryan invaders first entered. The strongest parallels between Indian and traditional Celtic and Scandinavian music can therefore be found in northern India.

We suggest that the listener try the following experiment. Find a CD player that can accommodate several (say five or more) CDs at a time. Place CD Number One of this set in the player, along with several CDs of traditional Celtic, Scandinavian, and other Indo-European music. Activate the "scramble" function, and press "play." Most CD players have this "scramble" function. It will randomly play tracks on the CDs, moving from one CD to another, to another. In this way, one will begin to see the common melodic threads to Indo-European music. An identity will come to display itself in the manifold, and repeated listening will give one a sensuous glimpse into the *ur*-forms that emerged when our ancestors spontaneously and naïvely expressed themselves in sound.

The recordings on these CDs are of the very best quality, as are the performances. The notes on each track, written by Danielou himself, are extremely helpful. They provide a miniature lesson in Indian music, and will teach one to tell the sitar from the *vina*, and the *shahnai* from the Bengali bamboo flute. The artists include Ravi Shankar, Ali Akbar Khan, and Mohin ud din and Amin ud din Dagar. The sixth track on CD One features Svami D. R. Parvatikar playing a vina. A wandering monk born in 1915, Parvatikar observed a vow of silence, never speaking. Bala Sarasvati, the most famous dancer of Southern India, performs track five on CD Two. The collection also boasts a performance by D. K. Pattamal, the most famous classical singer of Southern India.

For anyone interested in learning to appreciate Indian music, there is no better place to begin.

Collin Cleary

Blood Axis & Les Joyaux De La Princesse—*Absinthe: La Folie Verte* (Athanor)

One legend has it that wormwood—the essential ingredient in absinthe, and the source of absinthe's special intoxicating qualities—grew along the path the serpent used to depart the Garden of Eden. Yet despite its sinister reputation, wormwood has long been extolled as an elixir for all sorts of ailments, both of the body and soul. Pythagoras prescribed it as a cure for labor pains. Galen and Hippocrates praised its fortifying virtues. Roman charioteers would quaff a cup of absinthe-spiked wine before a tournament. According to Apuleius's Herbarium, absinthe was discovered by the goddess Diana, who "delivered (its) power and leechdom to Chiron the Centaur."

Yet despite its longstanding inclusion in any European herbal worth its salt, absinthe was better known as the beverage of choice of Baudelaire, Oscar Wilde, Toulouse-Lautrec, Huysmans, Van Gogh, and Harry Crosby—seers and visionaries all. In France, the "Green Hour" (so named for absinthe's emerald color) was an essential part of Parisian life for decades. Then, shortly before the outbreak of World War I, absinthe was banned by the French authorities. Like the criminalization of marijuana in the United States, the ban was motivated more by the ravings of yellow journalists and teetotalers than by any hard evidence of absinthe's "madness inducing" properties. Now, after nearly a century, the European Union has opted for legalization. The "Green Fairy" flies free.

Reviews: Books & Music

Blood Axis and Les Joyaux De La Princesse have collaborated to commemorate the absinthe culture of turn-of-the-century Paris with a musical homage as sensual as absinthe itself. Though joined by Annabel Lee on violin, *La Folie Verte* consists primarily of electronic manipulations of period recordings and keyboard-driven ambiance. Poetry and excerpts from absinthe-inspired literary works waft in and out of these aural collages. "Absinthia Taetra (Opaline)," the fourth track on the CD, is perhaps the best example of this fusion of spoken and synthetic sound. French label Athanor are also to be commended for the remarkable digipack design and accompanying booklet. Filled with absinthe imagery, including old labels, illustrations, and sheet music for absinthe-themed music, each page is a miniature lesson in an otherwise-neglected history.

Absinthe and other wormwood concoctions were once a viable part of the European tradition—as were many other mind-altering herbs and potions. That these substances have been forgotten by modern Westerners—their rightful place usurped by the often inferior substitute of ordinary beer and liquor—is one of the many misfortunes of our age. Perhaps releases such as this will help usher in the Restoration.

Joshua Buckley

Boyd Rice and Fiends—*Wolf Pact* (NEROZ)

Boyd Rice seems to delight in his ability to confound friends and enemies alike. A key player in the creation of industrial music, Rice's first few albums were characterized by massive noise collages, many of them emanating from Duchamp-inspired machines. His other interests range from forgotten kitsch music and films (like his friend the late Anton LaVey, though, Rice's real interest seems to be in investing these with new, more magical meanings) to recreational bowling. But Rice's various affronts to political correctness have done far more to establish his reputation. A self-professed misanthrope and "social Darwinist," Rice's various musical incarnations over the past decade and a half have been characterized by his denunciations of "the weak" and his waxing romantic over "men across the sea / who settle scores by deeds of war / just like they used to be." All this as Rice continues to extol the virtues of bubblegum-pop girl groups, Bobby Sherman, and the Partridge Family.

The "Fiends" alluded to in the title are Death In June's Douglas Pierce and Der Blutharsch's Albin Julius. As with recent DIJ releases, the inclusion of Julius has added tremendously to Pierce's by-now formulaic acoustic minimalism. A fuller, noisier sound is the norm here, laden with samples and snippets of dialogue, the majority of which I don't recognize. Luckily, the lyrics are also somewhat more adventurous (we're even spared the usual excerpts from Ragnar Redbeard's *Might Is Right*). With allusions that call to mind the sleeping King Frederick Barbarossa, "Rex Mundi" is an invocation of a "Lord of the Earth" "before Alexander, before Caesar, before Hiram of Tyre . . . remembered by some as a God, by others—the Devil." This mysterious entity is summoned again on "The Forgotten Father" and its companion-piece "The Tomb of the Forgotten Father." Marshalling strange, dream-like imagery, Rice describes his encounter with this long-lost patriarch, whose doctrine is "the unknown tradition from which all known to the West are derived" and whose "temple is in the blood, where his memory lives." Shades, perhaps, of the "Gothick God of Darkness"? Other tracks here, many of them simply atmospheric soundscapes, include "The Orchid and the Death's Head," "Joe Liked to Go (To the Cemetery)," and "The Reign Song."

Joshua Buckley

Tom Russell—*The Man From God Knows Where* (Hightone Records)

Tom Russell spent his childhood on a ranch in Topanga Canyon, California listening to Merle Travis, Spade Cooley, and Tex Williams, and began his musical career playing cowboy songs on a Tijuana gut string guitar. When he discovered Bob Dylan and Ian and Sylvia in the sixties, however, Russell was inspired to branch out into more adventurous territory, and has been doing so ever since. Since his early days "backing topless dancers, strippers, female impersonators, dog acts, and sword-swallowers," Russell has recorded several progressive country albums, a banner collection of cowboy songs (1987's *Cowboy Real*), an homage to

Merle Haggard, and two collaborative albums with R & B singer Barrence Whitfield. Russell's songs have been recorded by a number of other artists, most notably Nanci Griffith and Johnny Cash. The latter may be the greatest tribute of all.

Russell's family came from Templemore, Ireland and Bergen, Norway, and "The Man From God Knows Where" is Russell's attempt to "summon his ancestors from their graves, and bid them tell their stories." Juxtaposing folk music from Ireland and Norway with Americana, the album is a remarkable demonstration of the continuity between these traditions, and the extent to which the style and spirit of the cowboy music of Russell's youth derives from a common European source. The 26 songs presented here recount the Norwegian and Irish immigration experience, the trials and tribulations of the pioneers, as well as more personal material based on Russell's immediate family. The album's title "Man From God Knows Where," is taken from a poem based on Russell's namesake Thomas Russell, who was hanged in 1798 for his part in the United Irish Rebellion.

But perhaps the most ambitious aspect of the project is the number of guest performers. Many portray Russell's ancestors. Kari Bremnes is Anna Olsen in "Anna Olsen's Letter Home" and "Anna Olsen," Irish legend Dolores Keane is Mary Clare Molloy, and Sondre Bratland is Ambrose Larsen on a song of the same name. This opens with the traditional Norwegian tune "Eg veit I himmerik ei borg," performed by NorthSide recording artist Annbjørg Lien. "Eg er framand," another Norwegian traditional piece, is also included. For his part, Russell "plays" Patrick Russell, who arrived in the United States in the nineteenth-century:

> *At night we heard the wolves howl on our newly purchased farm*
> *And starving lads from the Civil War took shelter in our barn*
> *The Larsens and the Cooneys, the Russells and Malloys*
> *We tilled the soil of Iowa, grew a spate of girls and boys.*

This was a different America from the one we know today: slack-jawed, tough and resilient. "Chickasaw County Jail" and "Throwin' Horseshoes at the Moon" are both about Russell's father Charlie, a man who was himself no stranger to hard times, a "horsetrader, gambler, bankruptee, prisoner, recovered alcoholic, survivor." Iris DeMent contributes to eight of the songs

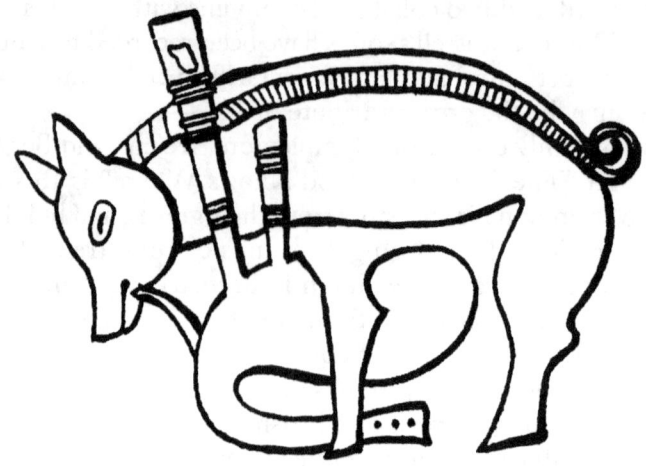

here, the best being her spine-tingling rendition of "Poor Wayfarin' Stranger." Not being a huge fan of Bluegrass music, I wasn't familiar with DeMent before. But I was impressed enough to pick up several of her other records, which I've found myself listening to again and again. With a voice that rivals Allison Krauss or Nanci Griffith—though in many ways more distinct—DeMent's music is an ideal introduction to the American folk tradition. Like a soundtrack to Ole Edvart Rolvaag's *Giants In The Earth*, *The Man From God Knows Where* is a rich depiction of the European-American experience. Recommended.

Joshua Buckley

Ragnarök—*Domgeorn* (Eldethorn Records)

When this CD arrived unbidden for review, I was a little unsure as to whether I was the right person to deal with it. It is a very long time since my musical tastes were considered "cutting edge" and I confess to being personally unable to carry a tune in a bucket. However, always willing to expose myself to new kinds of experience (if only once!) I duly sat back to hear what Ragnarök have to offer.

In practice the CD falls well within the remit of the Anglo-Saxonist, as it is that rare thing: a musical journey performed in Old English! Ragnarök, the musicians behind the project, supply an astonishingly mixed bag of musical virtuosity on the CD, which consists of thirteen tracks. Some are very much in the tradition of English folk music—"John Barleycorn" is a well-known part of any folk-singer's repertoire, but not many begin their rendition with the "Erce" invocation from the *Æcerbot!* The haunting "I Hear The Mountain" stands up well as a fine example of a melodic and atmospheric piece which refuses to descend into New Age pan-pipes and didgeridoos.

Many of the tracks are what I would describe as "thrash metal," i.e., high-speed guitar riffs and gruff, screaming vocals, all well handled and likely to appeal to devotees of the genre. These are in Modern English although on Anglo-Saxon and Norse themes—"Legion of Death" reminded me very much of Black Sabbath in the mid-70's. "Samhain" even manages to cut abruptly from metal to a traditional jig and back again several times in six minutes.

For my money, though, the showstopper is "To Wælhealle"— a Norse warrior sailing to Maldon in 991 and meeting his fate there, followed by his transition to Valholl. This superb piece deserves a very wide audience, with its vivid sound-picture and Old English lyrics, adapted from both "The Battle of Maldon" and Snorri's "Hattatal."

The CD comes with a manuscript-style booklet which includes all the lyrics. My one quibble was with the illustrations for this—a band of Einherjar attacking some monks on the front, and a helmeted figure carrying a naked woman into the sea on his back. I felt the rather adolescent imagery used here—which may be de rigueur in Black Metal circles—really let the product down. It would certainly have put me off as a prospective purchaser and that would have been a great shame as the content of the CD is entertaining and deserving of support.

While probably not to everyone's musical taste, the CD is well worth a listen and not just from an Old English perspective. Musicians and creative people working with Anglo-Saxon themes need to be encouraged in their endeavours; this CD should provoke a dozen others. (A version of this review will appear in *Wipowinde*, the periodical of The English Companions: www.kami.demon.co.uk/gesithas)

Steve Pollington

"An authentic traditional feel of *völkisch* folk music... you may be hard-pressed to guess that this was recorded in the 21st Century."

COMPULSION ONLINE
(www.compulsiononline.com)

"If there was an album that we were waiting for, then this is it... **Superb!**"

CYNFEIRDD MAGAZINE (France)

Waldteufel
Heimliches Deutschland

The much-anticipated full-length CD from Markus Wolff (Crash Worship) and Annabel Lee (Alraune, Blood Axis), *Heimliches Deutschland* also features contributions from Michael Moynihan and B'eirth (In Gowan Ring). A stirring invocation of heathen power, *Heimliches Deutschland* is unlike anything else you've heard.

Available for $15 ppd. in the United States. A $3 discount is available for customers who order both HEIMLICHES DEUTSCHLAND and TYR. (Total price for both items: $28 postpaid.) Georgia residents please include 7% sales tax. European inquiries should be directed to Dark Vinyl (Germany).

Ultra! • PO Box 11736 • Atlanta, GA • 30355 USA • e-mail: Ultrdisc@AOL.com

Sigur Rós—*Ágaetis byrjun* (Krunk/Smekkleysa/PIAS)
Sigur Rós—*Svefn-g-englar* E.P. (Krunk/Smekkleysa/PIAS)

Iceland's Sigur Rós ("victory rose") have been receiving scads of positive attention from listeners and critics around the world, and even found themselves prominently featured in the *New York Times Magazine* last year. The scenario is all the more surprising and unprecedented considering they are an obscure group that eschews typical pop sensibilities, avoids singing in English, and whose latest record was until very recently not even available domestically (their last two releases have since been issued here).

But the band—comprised of singer Jonsi Birgisson, bassist Georg Holm, organist Kjartan Sveinsson, and drummer Orri Pall Dyrason—is that rare exception: one that does deserve to be noticed.

The *NYT Magazine* article told of the journalist being taken to an out-of-the-way tavern in Reykjavik by Sigur Rós's singer in order to hear the traditional *rímnamenn* recite Old Icelandic ballads, or *rímur*. Word has it that Sigur Rós even planned to take one of the elder poetry-singers along with them on tour to perform as part of their concerts. Despite their acknowledgment of their native arts of their homeland, though, the sounds of Sigur Rós are not intrinsically folkloric. They owe far more to dynamic European prog rock of the '70s than to any traditional forms. Nevertheless Sigur Rós deftly transport the listener to a place full of imaginative wonder and emotional intensity, transcending time and space. Their music has a style and class all of its own, existing outside of, but simultaneously overlapping with established sources and genres.

Music critics—thoroughly enchanted but usually at a loss how to describe the band's output—often tend to start drawing abstract parallels with the unusual and dramatic geography of Iceland. But rather than equating it with static frozen vistas or rocky crags, the sound of Sigur Rós might be more accurately described in terms of its seismic vibrational qualities. This is conjured up through a dense wall of instruments that gel together at a slow, driving pace, underpinned by bowed electric guitars and sometimes augmented with swirling brass or string sections. Birgisson's vocals are delivered in an eerie androgynous falsetto and lately he has taken to using his voice as a pure instrument, with words and syllables chosen as much for tonal qualities as for meaning.

Sigur Rós released a previous album titled *Von* (Hope) in 1997, but unfortunately this is only available in Iceland. It shows a rawer side, less accessible and nowhere near as fully-forged as the vision which became evident with their subsequent 1999 work *Ágaetis byrjun* (A Fine Start; the related E.P. *Svefn-g-englar* features two album tracks and two live songs recorded at the Icelandic Opera House). To call this ambient music would be to downplay its capacity for swelling, wrenching passages that will cause your walls to quiver when played at the correct volume. To call it rock would be to overlook its disregard for traditional song structures and its circumventing of traditional playing methods and limitations. By the same token, to call it experimental would be to ignore its consistent employment of classic melodic hooks. These melodies often sound distantly familiar, which only adds to the dreamlike effect of the music as well as to its ability to pull you into an alternate and soaring universe. These epic songs build quietly and naturally, gaining in layered intensity before ultimately discharging and fading away, having mutated in the process according to their own internal logic. The result, as the foregoing description would tend to imply, is organic music of the highest order. Make no mistake, it is also psychedelic music—forged of swirling, churning and often indeterminable elements that leave you little choice but to be enveloped in their contemplative midst until the undulations resolve, releasing you back to a less heightened realm.

Michael Moynihan

Sonnwin—*Fehu* (Lichtbringer)

From the relatively new German label Lichtbringer, the bringer of light, comes a release that does just that, illuminating us with a forceful, emphatic performance that borders on the brilliant. Sonnwin are four young musicians from former East Germany, an area brimming with notable heathen musical groups such as Forseti, Orplid, and Sonne Hagal. On *Fehu* they attempt a difficult undertaking, taking key texts from Karl Simrock's premiere German translation of the *Poetic Edda* and setting them to music. The effort is spearheaded by Hagen Lehmann's powerful recitative vocals, while a spirited and dynamic musical setting is provided by Stefanie Bandel on flute, Ulrike Stegemann on cello, and Steven Beil on percussion, keyboard, and sampling.

A frequent inspiration for the new German music scene is responsible for the text of the "Intro": Friedrich Nietzsche. Three excerpts from the "Völuspa" follow, featuring simple repetitive motifs and beautiful melodies that build up and change with the flow of the language. "Odins Runenlied" is an interpretation of the last part of the "Havamal," commonly known as Odin's Rune Poem. Propelled by drums and a hypnotic cello line, the Rune stanzas also feature Stegemann vocalizing the corresponding Runic *Galdr*. The whole piece achieves a rare and uplifting atmosphere of archaic nobility. The CD concludes with a rendition of an old poem called "Die Nornen," a sombre meditation on the Germanic ideas of time: "What is once woven by fate / Is up to us to complete."

Because of the excellent enunciation and clarity of Hagen's performance, this CD would be a welcome and pleasant learning aid for those learning German and interested in German literature and the old lore. However, the overall beauty and excellence of the music, which could best be described as a new kind of folk-influenced neo-Classical chamber music also makes this release a worthy purchase for the non-German speaker.

Markus Wolff

Changes—*Legends* (Taproot Productions)

Along with Steve McNallen and Else Christensen, Robert N. Taylor was one of the founders of the modern-day Odinist (or Ásatrú) movement in North America. He is also a published poet, artist, and all-around Renaissance man. In the late-'60s and early-'70s, Taylor and his cousin Nicholas Tesluk were traveling around the country playing music under the name Changes. They gigged in coffeehouses, nightclubs, and Renaissance Festivals, and were for a time associated with the infamous but little understood Process Church of the Final Judgement (Taylor has recounted his experiences with the Process in Feral House's *Apocalypse Culture* anthology, and in a series of articles in the underground magazine *Esoterra*). But it would be over a quarter of a century before Changes' original reel-to-reel tapes would see the light of day.

In the early 1990s, prodded on by Blood Axis front man Michael Moynihan, Taylor and friends worked meticulously to salvage these dusty old recordings. Finally re-mastered and restored, they were released as the album *Fire of Life* by the German label Cthulhu, in collaboration with Moynihan's Storm imprint. Although stylistically similar to the folk music being produced by contemporaries like Pete Seeger and Joan Baez, Changes' music was thematically unique. Having immersed himself in the works of Nietzsche, Spengler, and Francis Parker Yockey, Taylor shared the hippies' disillusionment with modern life, and had long since "dropped out" to pursue a lifestyle more conducive to his own nature. But while the hippies had sought enlightenment in various cults imported from the East—as well as the political "enlightenment" promised by the radical Left—Taylor was seeking inspiration in the European heroic tradition. The Weather Underground could look to Che Guevara for a revolutionary role model, but Taylor was looking all the way back to Starkaðr and CúChulainn.

Released independently on Taylor's own Taproot label, *Legends* merits a review nearly four years after its original release as a worthy musical project that might have escaped many readers' attention. Originally composed in the winter of 1969 (when the "Summer of Love" had given way to an icier season), Taylor and Tesluk regrouped in 1997 with production maestro Robert Ferbrache to give the "Legends" cycle an updated re-working. The result is a miniature masterpiece. Reflecting Taylor's conviction that the album should serve as "a mirror in which our contemporaries might measure their own Selves, as well as the base and banal age that we live in," *Legends* is an ambitious distillation of the European saga tradition. Divided into six sections, this includes the Greek (Homeric), Roman (The Aeneid), Germanic (Eddaic), Russian (The Song of Igor), Celtic (Arthurian), and Spanish (El Cid). The music is accentuated by Taylor's soulful vocal delivery, not to mention Tesluk's adept picking style. The release is further embellished by Taylor's original artwork, and a lyric-booklet transcribed entirely in Tesluk's hand-rendered calligraphy.

Although Changes' music might have been an anomaly thirty years ago, one would hope that there is finally a niche for it. A new generation of alienated and disillusioned young people would be well-served by heeding Taylor's refrain that "the answers lie there hidden, in the legends that we know." For ordering information, contact: <wulfing1@AOL.com>.

Joshua Buckley

Belborn—*3-Drei-Three* (World Serpent)

Belborn are one of numerous new outfits playing heathen music in Germany, where the pagan music scene seems to have set down some of its deepest roots (as evidenced by the phenomenal growth of the Eislicht stable of artists). Named after the god Bel (the solar fire deity, also called Balor, Belenos, and Baldur), Belborn's music is inspired in part by the stunning Bavarian countryside where the group has made their home. Consisting of Holger F. and Susanne H., and joined by their daughter Skadi-Lilja, Belborn has described the subject matter of their songs as: "pride, honesty, love of the homeland, individuality, and paganism." As for their music, Belborn manage to create some very listenable, musically accomplished tunes, which are a tribute both to themselves and to the heathen music subculture in Germany.

As you might have guessed, *3-Drei-Three* is Belborn's third studio recording. One of the strongest elements here is the incorporation of keyboards, an element no doubt derived from Holger's professed admiration for '80s New Wave music. In fact, *3-Drei-Three* features a cover version of the *Neue Deutsche Welle* hit "Ich Liebe Sie" by NDW artists Grauzone. Other original compositions include "Heiliger Hain" (Holy Grove), "Neue Dämmerung" (New Dawn), and "Die Ewige Schlacht" (The Eternal Battle). In keeping with the couple's contempt for the "Anglicization" of their native tongue, all lyrics are in German. The CD is attractively packaged with a number of interesting illustrations, my favorite being the whimsical Alraunes on the booklet's cover. Holger is also something of an artist, as visitors to Belborn's web site will see: www.belborn.de

Joshua Buckley

Various Artists—*The Pact Vol. II* (Asafoetida)

For those who enjoyed *The Pact I: Flying in the Face*, which came out a few years ago, this is the long-awaited sequel. Compiled by Ian Read and Michael Moynihan, the compilation is dedicated to the late Robert Williams and features a glossy 14-page booklet showcasing each artist. Naturally, a host of different names appear this time around, along with some new performances from those who appeared on the previous one.

After a brief and somewhat incongruous intro by beatnik author William S. Burroughs, things begin in straightforward, bare bones fashion with Changes' acoustic commencement "Waiting for the Fall." Following that is an untitled piece of rich, drum-ridden orchestration from Austria's Der Blutharsch. Fire + Ice, who appeared on the first CD, are accompanied by Michael Moynihan and Annabel Lee for "Harry The Sun," one of the most charming and memorable songs the group has ever done. The track features Ian Read's trademark vocal style along with acoustic guitar, bodhrán, and violin. Hailing from Vienna, Allerseelen contribute loops of rhythmic electronic percussion and violin with Kadmon's brooding voice on "Spiegellied." Germans' Forseti remain in familiar territory with the characteristic folk number "Heilige Welt," which features flute, drums, violin and accordion. Italy's Ataraxia and Camerata Mediolanense are responsible for some of the most amazing moments on the CD. Inspired by the verse of Edgar Allen Poe, Ataraxia demonstrate their prowess with a beautiful melody on their acoustic rendition of "Zelia (The City in the Sea)." Camerata Mediolanense, on the other hand, deliver an infectious and rabble-rousing live version of the old European anthem, "L'Homme Armé."

Flying in the Face also contains a number of tracks that stray far from the norm, usually in top-notch fashion. Blood Axis exhibit one of their strangest recordings yet with an unsettling combination of violin and theremin, backing a reading from "Der Gefallene Engel" courtesy of Stephen Edred Flowers. B'eirth's In Gowan Ring contribute a soft-spoken rendition of the traditional "The Rolling of the Stones" that culminates in an exciting upbeat finale. Although Death In June didn't make it this time around, member John Murphy holds his own as Shining Vril with the synth-driven "Son; Blessed of the Fire." Mee makes the most of minimalism with female vocals and sparse keyboard meanderings in a piece titled "O." Waldteufel's adrenaline-charged

"Wolfsstund" boasts tribal drum beats, violin and chants, summoning up the Germanic spirit of the hunt. Ostara, formerly Strength Through Joy, voice their own proclamations about the precarious state of Europe. Despite their talent, Ostara's musical style has evolved into second-rate alternative rock which weakens their impact. It's as if their studio engineer duped them into believing that a new sound would perhaps make them more marketable.

Rounding out this CD is a short, dramatic reading by Dave Lee called "Celestial Dragon," along with a closing track by the cleverly-named Beastianity. *The Pact II* maintains high standards, unpredictability, and outdoes its predecessor. Highly recommended.

Aaron Garland

Lutz Kirchhof—*Lute Music for Witches and Alchemists* (Sony Classical)

In pre-modern societies, the magical properties of music are almost universally attested. Athanasius Kircher's theory that music affects the soul by causing subtle vibrations in the "animal spirits" may seem far-fetched to scientifically-minded moderns, but anyone who is open enough to the transports of a Debussy or Ravel knows just what Kircher was talking about. One needn't be schooled in Pythagorean mathematics to intuit that good music—properly executed—somehow points us toward higher planes. For Lutz Kirchhof, the lute has always had this quality.

In the Middle Ages, lute music was ubiquitous—both in the Court and on the streets among the common people. But the lute was eventually eclipsed by other instruments, and has since been consigned to the dustbin of Western cultural history. Kirchhof, a graduate of the Frankfurter Musikhochschule, has campaigned tirelessly to see that the lute is restored to its rightful place in the traditional musician's repertoire. The creator of the Society of Lute Researchers, as well as an annual International Lute Festival in his native Frankfurt, Kirchhof also performs with Liuto Concertato, an ensemble featuring voice, transverse flute, viola da gamba and lute. His many other accomplishments aside, however, *Lute Music For Witches and Alchemists* is without a doubt Kirchhof's most unusual venture thus far.

In the Hermetic philosopher Robert Fludd's *Temple of Music* (1617) the lute is given special distinction as an instrument endowed with particularly magical properties. In Thomas Mace's *Musickes Monument* (1676), Mace proposes that lute music can be used to "transform human consciousness by alchemistic means." According to Kirchhof's notes, Athanasius Kircher's own "Tarantella" has the amazing distinction of being the only tune ever composed as a "musical remedy against the venom of the tarantula." Some of Kirchhof's claims about the lute's magical qualities are more speculative, such as his assertion that the lute was favored by alchemists for its meditative qualities, and as an antidote against the solitude of a lonely profession. His argument that it played a part in a medieval witch-cult rests on shakier ground. Following Margaret Murray, Kirchhof reports "witches—a term that originally was applied to women possessed of wisdom and versed in both medicinal and herbal arts—also used (lute) music for medicinal purposes." Whether or not any of this is true, it certainly provides a romantic atmosphere in which to enjoy Kirchhof's performance. The lute does have an intimate, contemplative quality, and one wonders why it failed to survive the advent of orchestral music. An intriguing release which deserves as much notice as Sequentia and other "breakthrough" medieval musicians.

Joshua Buckley

Sorten Muld—*III* (NorthSide)

Though incorporating a number of traditional instruments—including viola, violin, hurdy-gurdy, and even bagpipes—Danish trio Sorten Muld's music could not rightly be called "traditional" by any stretch of the imagination. That's because the most prominent aspect of the Sorten Muld sound is provided by Henrik Munch and Martin Ottosen's slick electronic manipulations. *III*, the group's latest studio release, would sound more appropriate in a modern dance club (or perhaps thumping over a high-fashion runway) than in 11th or 12th century Denmark.

Yet with two exceptions, Sorten Muld's modern techno arrangements are structured around traditional Danish and Norwegian folk ballads. Lifted from Landsted and Berggen's collections, and sung with Ulla Bendixen's rapturous, soaring vocals, the pieces chosen for the album are among the strangest one could hope for. "Lørdagskvæld" is the story of a young girl who finds her lover in bed with her mother. "Don't be angry with me my daughter so true," the latter explains. "I just wanted to make sure that he was good for you." The Danish tune "Ulver" is grim enough to satisfy any devotee of Gothic or Black Metal music. Venturing out alone with her beloved, Vænelil discovers that his intentions are not quite what she expected. "Eight virgins have I loved before," he tells her, "and I have separated them all from this life." After casting the runes for protection, the maiden distracts Ulver with a ruse, and then hacks him into pieces. "Ramund," another tune involving magical themes, is about a "dwarf daughter" who utilizes rune magic to seduce the hunter Ramund. Though inspired by the Eddic poem "Vølvens Spådom," "Vølven" is one of Ottosen's original compositions:

> *Nothing is the same here*
> *Yet the sun still shines upon the earth*
> *Tamed are the wolves*
> *The night is bathed in light*
>
> *The Gods are all gone now*
> *Yet the sun still shines upon the earth*
> *The barrows are all plowed in*
> *And no one knows what to believe.*

This ends on a more optimistic note, with Ottosen's refrain that when one looks within one's own heart, one finds that—despite outward appearances—nothing has really changed after all. Perhaps this is the justification for Sorten Muld's music. Combining modern and traditional elements in a way few might have imagined, Sorten Muld demonstrate how tradition can persist even within the most modern of frameworks. Though it probably won't sit well with hard-core traditionalists, *III* is nevertheless an interesting (and enjoyable) release, guaranteed to stimulate and provoke.

Joshua Buckley

Väsen: *Live at the Nordic Roots Festival* **(NorthSide)**

Held annually in Minneapolis, the Nordic Roots Festival is the "New Nordic Roots" label NorthSide's gala celebration of Scandinavian folk music and dance. The 2000 Festival featured over 70 performers from Sweden, Finland, and Norway, including JPP, Loituma, Garmarna, and Chateau Neuf. Whereas many of the artists associated with the British and Irish folk revivals ended up playing lame-brained new age or "adult contemporary" muzak twenty years down the line, the Nordic folk scene is young and dynamic. Väsen are no exception. Captured in their element as onstage performers, *Live at Nordic Roots* has more than enough enthusiasm and vitality to go around.

While 1999's *Gront* had the melancholic sound characteristic of so much of Scandinavian music, *Live* spotlights Väsen's lighter side, whipping up the crowd with up-tempo arrangements, suspense-building improvisations and the group's noted sense of humor and showmanship. Väsen consists of Olov Johansson on nyckelharpa (Swedish keyed fiddle), André Ferrari on percussion, Roger Tallroth on guitars, and Michael Marin, who in the liner-notes describes his twin passions as "gathering mushrooms and playing the viola." The quartet are joined here by members of Harv, as well as Annbjørg Lien, who is fast establishing herself as the world's pre-eminent hardanger fiddler. If you are a newcomer to Nordic music, this would be a fine place to get started. For information on upcoming festivals, releases and other news and information about this exciting new genre, visit: www.noside.com

Joshua Buckley

Sinikka Langeland—*Lille Rosa* (Grappa)

Sinikka Langeland was born in 1961 of a Finnish mother and a Norwegian father, and her music reflects this dual heritage. A resident of Finnskogen, the "Finnish forest of Norway," these mixed allegiances become even more apparent. Situated on the northeast borderlands of Oslo and populated largely by Finns who settled there in the 17th century, Finnskogen's rich folk culture is deeply rooted in the mythology and traditions of these early Finnish immigrants.

On past outings (some might recall Langeland's contribution to NorthSide's excellent *Devil's Tune* compilation), Langeland has dealt in both the traditional dances and ballads of Finnskogen, as well as composing original tunes set to Norwegian poetry. "Lille Rosa," her latest, consists of twelve ballads from Østlandet in southeastern Norway. Penned sometime in the early Middle Ages, these are tales of love and longing typically ending in tragedy. Frustrated in their efforts to be together in this life, and often at odds with supernatural forces, Langeland's protagonists find fulfillment only in death.

Langeland sings in the traditional *kveder* style, bringing both warmth and foreboding to the pieces presented here. Accompanied only by the 39-stringed chromatic kantele, or Finno-Ugric table-harp (which, Thomas DuBois has suggested, might once have been a part of the Finnish shaman's repertoire), these are beautiful, haunting renditions that should linger in the imagination long after the music itself is only a memory.

Joshua Buckley

Various Artists—*Hermann Hendrich* (Nibelungenhort)

Hermann Hendrich (1854–1931) was a *völkisch* painter who worked extensively in Norse-Germanic themes. Perhaps his most famous creation was the Walpurgishalle. Located on the *Hexentanzplatz* ("the site of the witches sabbat") above the Bode valley, the Hall was built by Bernhard Sehring in accord with Hendrich's plans. A masterpiece of late Art Nouveau design, it also houses many of Hendrich's paintings. These include "Rhinegold," "The Death of Siegfried," "The Norns," and a number of others, all in a similarly Wagnerian vein.

One of several recent musical releases to honor a cultural figure prominent during the first wave of the Germanic Revival, this twelve-track compilation is also notable in that it includes numerous reproductions of Hendrich's paintings. The music spans a variety of different styles, but thematically at least, each piece would no doubt meet with Hendrich's approval. To name a few, "Fafnir," "Siegfried's Tod," and "Kinder des Nordens" are fairly representative. The music is more of a mixed bag, ranging from folk (Belborn), to atmospherics (Gandolfs Gedanken) and even heavy metal (Freiheitsgeist). Two of John Murphy's projects are featured, Shining Vril and The Sword Volcano Complex. Some may remember Murphy as a founding member of the seminal industrial "band" SPK (variously said to stand for SePpuKku, Systems Planning Korporation, or Surgical Penis Klinik). In the last few years Murphy has resurfaced as a collaborator with Death in June's Douglas P. Perhaps one of my favorite numbers here is Carpe Diem's "Children of the North." A quick perusal of the group's website reveals all manner of strange involvements. Articles defending German nationalist youth, anti-Masonic conspiracy theories, and a section extolling the virtues of organic foods are among the subjects covered. Carpe Diem's music is a powerhouse melding of metal and folk-traditional elements delivered with soaring anthemic bombast. The compilation is nicely rounded out with two more subdued pieces, Waldteufel's "Leben" and Elke Rohling's "Die Traurige Weise." Appropriately, the latter features lyrics excerpted from the prologue to "Tristan and Isolde." (For information on Elke Rohling's monograph on Hendrich, which serves as a companion-piece to the CD, see the book review section elsewhere in this issue.)

Joshua Buckley

Susana Seivane—*Susana Seivane* (Green Linnet)

Like contemporaries Milladoiro, Susana Seivane plays Celtic music in the Galician tradition, a distinctive variant incorporating Middle Eastern elements and a variety of different instruments. Bouzouki, guitar, oboe, clarinet, and violin are all part of the mix. Foremost, however, is Seivane's *gaita*, or Galician bagpipe. Although I've heard the gaita's "nasal moan" described as an acquired taste elsewhere, I found that it quickly grew on me, thanks in no small measure to Seivane's infectious playing. Like her father and grandfather before her, Seivane has been piping since the age of three, and her dexterity is apparent. The pieces here range from *jotas* (dance tunes), waltzes, and rumbas, with Sonia Lebedynski lending vocals to a handful of tracks. There is something spirited about this music—Seivane's exuberant playing and the sheer energy of the style are an interesting contrast to the melancholy often underlying even more upbeat Celtic fare. A welcome diversion for fans of Irish, Scottish, and Anglo traditional music.

Joshua Buckley

Various Artists—*Thousands are Sailing: Irish Songs of Immigration* (Shanachie)

Here is a wonderful anthology of songs that capture the full range of feelings associated with the Irish diaspora—hope, regret, expectation, and sadness. It is also a fantastic showcase for some of the finest Celtic performers currently on the circuit.

First up is Karan Casey, whose solo career has taken off considerably since leaving Solas several years ago. "Shamrock Shore" captures Casey's beautiful singing style. Dolores Keane is one of the more established singers in the Irish traditional genre, and "Galway Bay" (Keane's family hails from Catherlistrane in East Galway) shows why. Keane's voice—rich, deep, and mature—conveys a tremendous breadth of emotion. She is far and away my favorite Celtic female vocalist. Planxty are next with "Thousands Are Sailing" and "Green Fields of America." Planxty were a seminal force in the Irish music revival several decades ago, but I must admit that Johnny Moynihan's vocals here are not quite to my liking. One of the real standouts is De Danann's "Rambling Irishman," a classic cut featuring Dolores Keane. Recorded at the outset of Keane's career, it again confirms why she remains such an important commodity in the world of Irish music. Liam Clancy, another great, contributes "Fare Thee Well," a bittersweet tale of Wanderlust and its cost—the memory of those left behind. Other participants include Boys of the Lough, Cathy Ryan, Arcady, Voice Squad (with the album's only *a cappella* tune), and the Wolfe Tones. If you're an American, this release should be of particular interest, since there is a significant chance that many of your own ancestors set sail from the Shamrock Shore, "On the raging foam / To seek a home / On the shores of America."

Joshua Buckley

Various Artists—*Seven Broken Windows On Our World* (Cynfeirdd)

This seven-song compilation arrived in my mail unsolicited as an insert in the fifteenth issue of the French magazine *Cynfeirdd*. Consisting almost entirely of reviews, *Cynfeirdd* appears to cater to connoisseurs of "darkwave" music in all of its many manifestations—devotees of the genre might distinguish one group as "folk noir," another as "dark ambient." The problem with all of this pigeonholing is that it's so easy to do—most darkwave bands fit their respective categories like a hand to a black velvet glove. A few groups stand out as genuine creative talents, while the rest of the field is cluttered with lackluster imitators.

It was with pleasant surprise, then, that I slipped *Broken Windows* into my CD player, expecting some mildly diverting background noise, but not much more. Instead, *Cynfeirdd* have managed to assemble a collection of tracks that highlight everything the darkwave scene should be. The emphasis seems to be less on contrived melancholia and "spookiness." Though tinged with a hint of sadness, there is a prevailing air of sensuality and even warmth pulsing through each of the pieces presented here. Norwegian Eridu Arcane's soaring vocals are a fine example; icily crisp and seductive, she stands up to repeated listenings with ease. French Am' Ganesha'n contribute their bizarre (but enticing) brand of Franco-Indian fusion. By far the most exciting track, though, is Seven Pines' "Berceuse." Featuring Eric Roger and Gaë Bolg, Seven Pines sound unlike just about anything else I've heard. Jaunty and rousing, with an unforgettable electronic backing loop, this might plausibly be described as medieval Space Rock. For ordering information, check the *Cynfeirdd* website: http://cynfeirdd.free.fr

Joshua Buckley

About the Editors

Joshua Buckley was born in 1974 in Sharon, Connecticut. He has been an occasional contributor to several heathen and music-related periodicals, including *Vor Tru*. Currently he lives and works in Atlanta, Georgia. At the moment, areas of interest include Iyengar yoga, the use of psychotropic drugs in the context of the European tradition, and English, Irish, and Scandinavian folk music.
E-mail: <info@arcanaeuropamedia.com>

Collin Cleary is an independent scholar living in Sandpoint, Idaho. He is a Fellow in the Rune-Gild and a contributor to *Rûna*. His long term project is to effect a synthesis of all Indo-European mythological systems in the form of an epic poem, and to codify the fundamental aspects of the Indo-European *Weltanschauung* in a series of philosophical essays. Email care of Joshua Buckley: < info@arcanaeuropamedia.com>

Michael Moynihan was born in 1969 in New England. He is a musician, author, artist, and publisher. He has recorded and performed music in the U.S., Europe, and Japan. The latest release of his and Annabel Lee's music project Blood Axis is *Absinthe: La Folie Verte*, a collaboration with the French group Les Joyaux de la Princesse. His book *Lords of Chaos* (in collaboration with Didrik Søderlind; published by Feral House) was recently translated into German. He has contributed to the anthology *Apocalypse Culture II* (Feral House) and recently edited *Introduction to Magic* and *Men among the Ruins* by Julius Evola (both published by Inner Traditions), as well as a volume of K. M. Wiligut's writings entitled *The Secret King* (translated by S. E. Flowers). He is the North American Editor of *Rûna*, published by Ian Read in London. Email: <himilkraft@comcast.net>

About the Contributors

Alain de Benoist was born on December 11, 1943. He is married and has two children. He has studied law, philosophy, sociology, and the history of religions in Paris, France. A journalist and a writer, he is the editor of two journals: *Nouvelle Ecole* (since 1968) and *Krisis* (since 1988). His main fields of interest include the history of ideas, political philosophy, classical philosophy, and archaeology. He has published more than 50 books and 3000 articles. He is also a regular contributor to many French and European publications, journals, and papers (including *Valeurs actuelles*, *Le Spectacle du monde*, *Magazine-Hebdo*, *Le Figaro-Magazine* in France, *Telos* in the United States, and *Junge Freiheit* in Germany). In 1978 he received the Grand Prix de l'Essai from the Académie Française for his book *Vu de droite: Anthologie critique des idées contemporaines* (Copernic, Paris 1977). He has also been a regular contributor to the radio program France-Culture and has appeared in numerous television debates.

Stephen Edred Flowers is the world's leading expert on esoteric, or "radical," Runology. He has published over 20 books on this and related subjects. In 1980 he founded the Rune-Gild, the world's largest and most influential initiatory organization dedicated to Rune-Work on the Odian path. His work in Runology extends into academic pursuits and in 1984 he received a Ph.D. from the University of Texas at Austin with a dissertation entitled *Runes and Magic*. He is presently working on three books of general cultural interest: *The Northern Dawn: A History of the Reawakening of the Germanic Spirit*, *Wave of the Future: The European New Right and its Meaning for America*, and *The Pagan Right*. He has just founded the Woodharrow Institute for general studies in the culture and arts of the Germanic and Indo-European peoples. Edred is also the owner of Rûna-Raven Press and lives with his wife, Crystal, at Woodharrow near Austin, Texas. His work is devoted to seeking the principle of *RUNA*—the Mystery—as understood in the mythic idiom of the Germanic peoples.

Joscelyn Godwin's books on esotericism have been translated into French, German, Spanish, Italian, Greek, and Japanese.

They include *Robert Fludd, Athanasius Kircher, Mystery Religions in the Ancient World, Harmonies of Heaven and Earth, Music and the Occult, Arktos, The Theosophical Enlightenment*, and many editions and translations, notably of the *Hypnerotomachia Poliphili* of 1499. His latest book, *The Pagan Dream of the Renaissance*, will appear in 2002 from Phanes Press. He was born in England and has taught since 1971 in the Music Department of Colgate University, Hamilton, NY 13346.

Annabel Lee is a musician, writer, and amateur mountain climber (the highest peak attained so far is 18,192 ft. / 5,545 m.). She holds an M.A. in German and an M.F.A. Born in Manhattan and raised in the industrial landscape of Germany, she now spends most of her time in the northern woods. Her most recent work includes translating *Shamanism and Tantra in the Himalayas* by Christian Rätsch and Claudia Müller-Ebeling (Inner Traditions, 2002) as well as translations for the revised edition of *Plants of the Gods* by Drs. Hofmann and Schultes (Inner Traditions, 2001). She is the co-director of the independent publishing company Dominion Press. In addition, her violin and compositions can be heard on more than fifteen recordings including those of Alraune and Blood Axis.

Nigel Pennick was born in Guildford, Surrey in southern England in 1946. Trained in biology, for 15 years he was a researcher in algal taxonomy for a government institute. During this time, he published 29 scientific research papers including descriptions of 8 new species of marine algae and protozoa before moving on to become a writer and illustrator. He is the author of over 40 books on European folk arts, landscape, customs, games, magical alphabets, and spiritual traditions.

Steve Pollington is a freelance researcher and teacher in the field of Old English studies. His recent works include a treatment of military themes in Old English literature and Anglo-Saxon archaeology; fresh translations of three Old English medical texts with detailed examination of their magico-medical background; and a unique *Old English–Modern English Dictionary and Thesaurus*. He is a contributor to the prestigious *Oxford Companion to Military History* and has appeared on radio and television. He is currently researching the social aspects of the warband in pre-Christian Europe.

Alby Stone was born near Southend-on-Sea, Essex, UK, in 1954, and obtained a B.Ed. (Hons) at Thames Polytechnic in 1986 (specialist subjects: historical and sociological studies and language acquisition). He works as a civil servant in London, where he has lived since 1982. Mr. Stone is interested in ancient European and Asian myth, religion, cosmology, language, and archaeology. Publications include: *A Splendid Pillar: Images of the Axis Mundi in the Grail Romances* (1992), *The Bleeding Lance: Myth, Ritual, and the Grail Legend* (1992), *The Questing Beast and Other Cosmic Dismemberments* (1993), *Ymir's Flesh: North European Creation Mythologies* (1997), and *Straight Track, Crooked Road: Leys, Spirit-Paths and Shamanism* (1998). He is also a regular contributor to several journals, including *3rd Stone*.

Markus Wolff is an artist, musician, and lay historian residing in Portland, Oregon. He was born in Germany and has also lived in Austria and Australia. His current interests include the history of *Jugendstil* and German Symbolist art. Wolff's articles have appeared in such magazines as *Hagal*, *Zinnober*, *Sigill*, *Irminsul* (Australia), *Esoterra*, and *Vor Tru*.

Also Available from Arcana Europa Media:

The Northern Dawn: A History of the Reawakening of the Germanic Spirit

Stephen Edred Flowers

ISBN 978-0-9720292-8-5, 188 pages, paperback, $20.00

Throughout the United States and Europe, a revival of interest in all things Germanic is taking place. But as Stephen Flowers argues in the pages of his far-reaching book, this is only the latest phase in a larger reawakening with a rich, if troubled, history. He defines what constitutes the Germanic Tradition, and explains how this tradition was fragmented and submerged with the coming of Christianity to the Goths, the Franks, the Anglo-Saxons, and the Scandinavians. More importantly, he shows how the northern spirit survived in myriad and sometimes surprising places: from literary works such as *Beowulf* and the *Nibelungenlied*, to the teachings of Christian mystics like Meister Eckhart, and in the religious, political, and legal institutions of medieval England, Iceland, and Scandinavia.

History of the Rune-Gild

Edred Thorsson

ISBN 978-0999724545, 270 pages, paperback, $24.00

In this fascinating and informative volume, Edred Thorsson describes his childhood as a "monster kid" in the late 1950s and early 1960s, and documents the first stirrings of *Rûna*—or "the Mystery"—in his life. He describes his formative (and often humorous) experiences with various occult organizations and the strange and eccentric personalities whom they attract. He chronicles his distinguished academic career and his relationship with scholarly mentors like Prof. Dr. Edgar Polomé and Prof. Dr. Klaus Düwel. He provides the background for his connections to the world of occult publishing and his involvement with neopagan (or heathen) organizations like the Asatru Free Assembly and the Ring of Troth (now known simply as The Troth—the name Thorsson originally gave it). Throughout it all, Thorsson has relied on the hidden hand of the "Old Man" (Odin or Woden) to guide his life's mission of (re-)establishing a traditional Rune-Gild in North America and Europe.

Remnants of a Season: The Collected Poems of Robert N. Taylor

Robert N. Taylor

ISBN 978-0972029278, 173 pages, hardcover, $25.00

Issued on the occasion of Robert N. Taylor's seventieth birthday, *Remnants of a Season* is the first major retrospective of Taylor's poetry. Published as a handsome clothbound volume featuring a stamped cover, black endsheets, and archival-quality paper, the book also includes a new introduction by *TYR* editor Joshua Buckley, illustrations, a select bibliography of Taylor's published work, and a discography of his music. Now available in a limited edition of 500 hand-numbered copies, *Remnants of a Season* is sure to become a sought-after collector's item, and is a fitting tribute to a fascinating, if little-known, figure on the outer fringes of American culture.

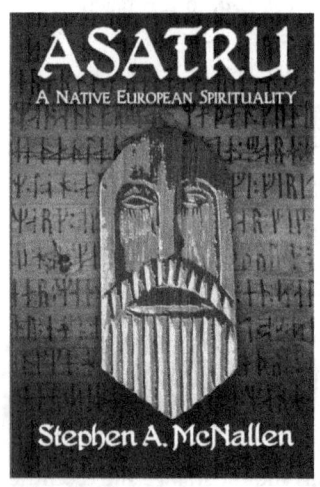

Asatru: A Native European Spirituality

Stephen A. McNallen

ISBN 978-0972029254, 212 pages, paperback, $20.00

When Steve McNallen pledged his loyalty to the Gods and Goddesses of Northern Europe in the late 1960s, he could have hardly imagined the far-reaching implications of this personal act of devotion. Now, over forty years later, Asatru (an Icelandic word that means "true to the Gods") is one of the fastest growing new religious movements in America. In *Asatru: A Native European Spirituality*, McNallen describes the origins and development of Asatru, its kinship with other tribal and ethnic religions, and the cosmological and philosophical underpinnings of this dynamic and inspiring faith. More importantly, McNallen explains his vision of what Asatru can and must become. Asatru is more than just another empty offering on the spiritual smorgasbord of post-religious America. For men and women of European descent, Asatru is a key to unlocking our vibrant spiritual heritage.

The Nine Doors of Midgard: A Curriculum of Rune-work

Edred Thorsson

ISBN 978-0971204485, 272 pages, paperback, $24.00

The Nine Doors of Midgard are the gateways to self-transformation and mastery through the Runes. This complete course of study and practice has been used by the initiates of the Rune-Gild since 1980. Long out-of-print to the wider public and difficult to obtain, it is now being made available in a completely revised and updated fifth edition. The Runic Tradition represents a whole school of inner work as ancient as any other and with the added importance that it is the ancestral, or natural, path for folks of Germanic background. Through nine "lessons" the book takes the Rune-worker from a stage in which no previous knowledge of Runes or esoteric work is assumed to a high level of initiation.

A Book of Troth

Edred Thorsson

ISBN 978-0972029261, 149 pages, paperback, $20.00

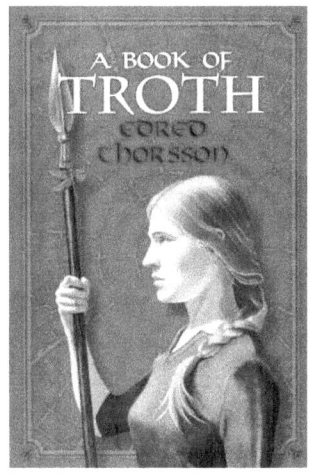

Originally written in 1988 as the foundational document for the Ring of Troth (now known simply as The Troth), *A Book of Troth* is Edred Thorsson's vision of how Germanic paganism, or Ásatrú, can be practiced in the modern world. While The Troth itself failed to live up to his expectations, today there are thousands of individuals performing the rites and rituals of Ásatrú, and Edred's ideas have been embraced by a whole new generation of readers. *A Book of Troth* contains a complete liturgy of rituals for celebrating both personal turning points in the life of the individual and the Great Blessings of the Year. This wholly revised third edition includes a new introduction by Asatru Folk Assembly founder Stephen A. McNallen, and also includes Edred's seminal essay "The Idea of Integral Culture: A Model for a Revolt Against the Modern World."

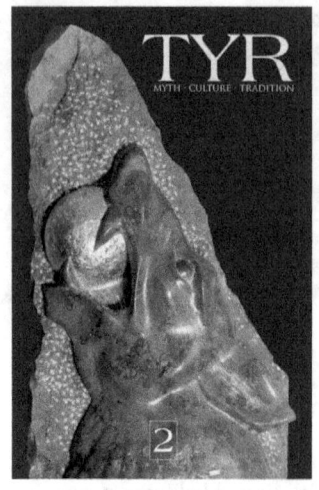

TYR: Myth, Culture, Tradition 2

Edited by Joshua Buckley and Michael Moynihan

ISBN 978-0999724576, 430 pages, paperback, $25.00

Julius Evola on "The Doctrine of Battle and Victory," Charles Champetier's interview with Alain de Benoist, Alain de Benoist on "Thoughts on God," Collin Cleary on "Summoning the Gods," Stephen McNallen on the "Ásatrú Revival," Nigel Pennick on "Heathen Holy Places," John Matthews on "The Guardians of Albion," Steve Pollington on "The Germanic Warband," Michael Moynihan on "Disparate Myths of Divine Sacrifice," Christian Rätsch on "The Sacred Plants of our Ancestors," Joscelyn Godwin on Herman Wirth, Peter Bahn on "The Friedrich Hielscher Legend," Markus Wolff on Ludwig Fahrenkrog, Stephen Flowers on "The Northern Renaissance," Joshua Buckley's interview with "technosophical" musicians Allerseelen, and an extensive book and music review section, featuring sidebar interviews with Coil and P. D. Brown.

TYR: Myth, Culture, Tradition 3

Edited by Joshua Buckley and Michael Moynihan

ISBN 978-0999724552, 538 pages, paperback, $25.00.

Thomas Naylor on "Cipherspace," Annie Le Brun on "Catastrophe Pending," Pentti Linkola on "Survival Theory," Michael O'Meara on "The Primordial and the Perennial," Alain de Benoist on "Spiritual Authority and Temporal Power," Nigel Pennick on "The Web of Wyrd," Thierry Jolif on "The Abode of the Gods and the Great Beyond," Stephen Flowers on "The Spear of Destiny," Joscelyn Godwin on Philip Pullman's "Dark Materials" trilogy, Ian Read on "Humour in the Icelandic Sagas," Geza von Neményi on the "Hávamál," Gordon Kennedy on the "Children of the Sonne," Michael Moynihan on "Carl Larsson's Greatest Sacrifice," Christopher McIntosh on "Iceland's Pagan Renaissance," Jónína Berg on Sveinbjörn Beinteinsson, "Selected Poems" by Sveinbjörn Beinteinsson, Vilius Rudra Dundzila on "Baltic Lithuanian Religion," James Reagan on "The End Times," interviews with the stalwart folk singer Andrew King and the modern minnesinger Roland Kroell, Collin Cleary on "Paganism Without Gods," Róbert Hórvath on Mark Sedgwick's "Against the Modern World," and extensive book and music review sections.

TYR: Myth, Culture, Tradition 4

Edited by Joshua Buckley and Michael Moynihan

ISBN 978-0972029247, 430 pages, paperback, $25.00

Alain de Benoist on "What is Religion?", Collin Cleary on "What is Odinism?", Nigel Pennick on "Traditional Time-Telling in Old England," Claude Lecouteux on "Garden Dwarves" and "Geiler von Kaiserberg and the Furious Army," Steve Harris on "Barbarian Suffering," Stephen Pollington on "Germanic Art in the First Millennium," Michael Moynihan on "Rockwell Kent's Northern Compass," and Christian Rätsch on "The Mead of Inspiration," interviews with pioneering psychedelic explorer Ralph Metzner, Sequentia's Benjamin Bagby, and Cult of Youth's Sean Ragon, and much more.

TYR: Myth, Culture, Tradition 5

Edited by Joshua Buckley and Michael Moynihan

ISBN 978-0999724521, 394 pages, paperback, $25.00

Collin Cleary's "On Being and Waking," Jack Donovan on "Starting the Sacred World," Bradley Taylor-Hicks on "Reclaiming Sacred Space," Joscelyn Godwin on "Alain Daniélou in the Age of Conflicts," Steven Posch on "The Last Pagans of the Hindu Kush," Nigel Pennick on "Northern Cosmology: The World Tree and Irminsul," Richard Rudgley on "Pagan Palingenesis," Stephen Edred Flowers on "Germanic and Iranian Culture and Myth," Wolf-Dieter Storl on "Indo-European Healing Lore," Michael Moynihan on the cult film *Koyaanisqatsi*; interviews with traditional bladesmith J. Arthur Loose and avant-garde composer Dylan Sheets; and much more.

On Being a Pagan
Alain de Benoist

ISBN 978-0999724507, 262 pages, paperback, $20.00

What is paganism? In this penetrating and tightly argued manifesto, French philosopher Alain de Benoist seeks to answer this question with passionate intellectual vigor and a tremendous erudition. Arising out of the "monotheism vs. polytheism" debate that reverberated through Parisian intellectual circles in the late 1970s, this is neither a survey of ancient pre-Christian religions, nor is it an argument on behalf of any modern neopagan sect. *On Being a Pagan* draws on Nietzsche, Heidegger, ancient philosophy and mythology, and biblical hermeneutics to articulate a pagan theology based on a common Indo-European foundation.

In keeping with the critical tradition which hearkens back to the Greek philosopher Celsus, Benoist contrasts the heroic pagan worldview with Christianity's attempts to hobble everything that is beautiful and strong. He compares the cyclical pagan conception of time to the de-mythologizing, linear understanding of history favored by the prophets. Most disturbingly, he traces the roots of modern totalitarianism and intolerance—of both the left and the right—to the leveling ideology of ancient Judeo-Christian monotheism, with its underlying rejection of diversity and *différence*.

Originally published to wide critical acclaim in 1981, Benoist's text is as relevant today as it was when it first appeared—and perhaps even more so for the English-speaking world. This newly revised translation now features a new Foreword, an extensive interview with the author, and includes his reflections (both positive and negative) on the various groups and individuals that have attempted to resurrect the pagan spirit. Rather than simply dissecting the 2,000-year Christian interregnum, Benoist's greater purpose is to point the way forward to a world that *could have been*, and which may only now be in the first stages of being reborn.

Alain de Benoist was born on December 11, 1943 and studied Law, Philosophy, Sociology, and the History of Religions in Paris. The author of more than 100 books, 2,000 articles, and 700 interviews published over the last half-century, his work has also been translated into fifteen languages. He is the editor of three journals: *Nouvelle École* (since 1968), *Éléments* (since 1973), and *Krisis* (since 1988). In 1978, he received the Grand Prix de l'Essai from the Académie Française for his book *Vu de droite: Anthologie critique des idées contemporaines* (Copernic, 1977). His two most recent books, both published in 2017, are *Le moment populiste: Droite-gauche, c'est fini!* (Pierre-Guillaume de Roux) and *Ce que penser veut dire* (Le Rocher).

Coming Soon from Arcana Europa Media:

The Eldritch World

Nigel Pennick

Deluxe Hardcover Edition

"We shall follow the footsteps of Orpheus, Thomas the Rhymer, Tannhäuser, Flannery, MacCrimmon, and the Pied Piper of Hamelin. We shall visit the Weïrd Lady of the Woods, hide with King Charles in the Royal Oak, and frequent the forest crossroads under the raven wings of night on a mission with the Freischütz. *Do you dare take the first step on a journey from which there can be no return?*"

For most of us, life is a largely monotonous affair—an endless round of school, work, and social and family commitments, punctuated by idle chatter. But beyond this drab and uninspiring reality, there is another world altogether, a world where the contours are sharper and the colors are brighter. This is the domain described by mystics and Surrealists, esoteric poets and psychedelic voyagers. For Nigel Pennick, who has spent much of his life mapping out this hidden terrain, there is a name for it: the Eldritch World.

The way that we experience the eldritch is invariably tied to the circumstances of our birth, or to what philosophers might call our *being-in-the-world*. The eldritch has a history and its roots run deep in the land. In Nigel Pennick's case, it manifests through the myths, folklore, and customs of his native Britain. A gentleman scholar in the Victorian style, Pennick has made a career out of documenting these fast-disappearing traditions and of working toward their revival. He is a mummer and a magician, a Pagan, and a practitioner of the traditional arts and crafts.

Yet unlike many of Pennick's other writings, *The Eldritch World* is not about runes, or geomancy, or the ancient customs of pre-Christian Europe. *The Eldritch World* is a meditation on what these things mean and why Pennick has devoted his life to them. It is also a manifesto: against the soulless mediocrity of the modern world, and for a reinvigorated Spirit of Place.

Nigel Pennick is the author of over fifty books, and his work has been translated into ten languages. He is an artist and a musician and is a member of the Traditional Music of Cambridgeshire Collective. His recent titles include: *The Toad Man* (2012) and *The Ideal Tower* (2018), both published by the Society of Esoteric Endeavour; and *Runic Lore & Legend: Wyrdstaves of Old Northumbria* and *Witchcraft & Secret Societies of Rural England: The Magic of Toadmen, Plough Witches, Mummers, and Bonesmen*, both forthcoming from Inner Traditions in 2019.

www.arcanaeuropamedia.com

www.ingramcontent.com/pod-product-compliance
Lightning Source LLC
Chambersburg PA
CBHW070536010526
44118CB00012B/1146